FOUR LIONS

COLIN SHINDLER is a social and cultural historian, lecturing at Cambridge University. He is also a television drama producer and screenwriter. Among the dozen books he has written are the bestselling childhood memoir *Manchester United Ruined My Life* and *National Service*, a social history of conscription 1946–62.

FOUR LIONS

The Lives and Times of Four Captains of England

COLIN SHINDLER

HEAD
*of*ZEUS

First published in the UK in 2016 by Head of Zeus Ltd

1 3 5 7 9 8 6 4 2

A catalogue record for this book is available from the British Library.

ISBN (HB) 9781784082734
ISBN (E) 9781784082727

Designed and typeset by e-type, Aintree, Liverpool

Printed and bound in Germany by
GGP Media GmbH, Pössneck

Head of Zeus Ltd
Clerkenwell House
45–47 Clerkenwell Green
London EC1R 0HT

WWW.HEADOFZEUS.COM

CONTENTS

This book is dedicated, with love, to the partners of my children: Susan Subbiondo Shindler and Joel Reid

ACKNOWLEDGEMENTS

Most of the opinions expressed in this book were shaped by conversations with friends from many walks of life – fellow historians, journalists, television executives, agents, football administrators and former players – all of them people who have been as obsessed with the game as I have been for more than sixty years. I have quoted many of them directly and at length because in so many cases what they had to say was interesting and rearranging their words into reported speech could only diminish their impact.

In particular, I would like to place on record my thanks to Jimmy Armfield, Patrick Barclay, David Bernstein, Matt Dickinson, Trevor East, Paul Fox, Brian Glanville, Michael Grade, Peter Hennessy, Jon Holmes, David Kynaston, Gary Lineker, Gary Newbon, Dominic Sandbrook and Bob Willis for their insights and the generous measure of time they spent with me. They are all men whose work I admire tremendously. Jon Holmes gave me bed and breakfast; Gary Lineker shut out the rest of the world for two hours in the Groucho Club, which takes some doing when you're as in demand as he is. The conclusions drawn from them and any mistakes which might have resulted from those conclusions are entirely mine.

The idea for this book came from my partner Katherine Fisher whose creative input into much of my work I willingly acknowledge. My thanks to Geoff Watts and Stan Hey who both diligently read all the early drafts, to Amanda Ridout, Richard Milbank and everyone at the publishing house Head of Zeus who helped to bring the book into the daylight, and to my agent and friend Luigi Bonomi whose sage advice has sustained and fortified me for nearly twenty years.

OF CAPTAINS AND CAPTAINCY

OF CAPTAINS AND CAPTAINCY

At the last count there have been 109 captains of the England football team since Cuthbert Ottaway led out his men to play Scotland on 30 November 1872 in the first ever international match. Not all of them became legends of the game. Who now recalls Arthur Grimsdell? Or Basil Patchitt? Or Charles Wreford-Brown? Who even remembers that the honour once devolved to Trevor Cherry and Colin Bell apart from the players concerned and their close family? If you think about England captains, two names come instantly to mind, provided you were watching football before the start of the Premier League. Billy Wright and Bobby Moore each captained the side on ninety occasions over a ten-year period. A book about the captains of England has to start with those two. Arguably more contentious is my choice of the other two – Gary Lineker and David Beckham. Third on the list of longest-serving England captains is Bryan Robson who skippered England on sixty-five occasions, more than any other player apart from Moore and Wright. He was an inspiration to both Lineker and Beckham and would, on the face of it, be a more logical candidate for inclusion than Lineker, having captained the side in fifty more matches than his erstwhile team-mate. It isn't just an aversion on the part of this author to spend more time than is strictly necessary in the environment of Manchester United that consigns Bryan Robson to the Outer Darkness. The criterion for selection to this Inner Conclave is based on the captains being somehow representative of their age. Robson was a fist-pumping captain of the old school and does not satisfy the strict entry requirements.

Even Kevin Keegan would appear to have a better claim for inclusion than the former Leicester City, Everton and Spurs striker. Keegan stands eighth in the list of England captains with thirty-one matches as skipper out of a total of sixty-three games played. Uniquely, he is the only captain who has also managed his country, apart from Alf Ramsey who filled in as captain for three matches during the reign of Billy Wright. It is certainly possible to argue Keegan's cause as an innovator. In fact, it could be said that Keegan did all the things that Lineker did but he did them ten years earlier. He moved from an unfashionable club, in his case Scunthorpe United, to the heights of international football; he moved abroad to play in Germany in the late 1970s at a time when the most recent precedents who had gone in search of European glory had been Jimmy Greaves and Denis Law a decade and a half previously, both of whom had returned home as fast as they possibly could. In contrast, Keegan became European Footballer of the Year twice. Unlike George Best, he took a thoughtful stance on commercial endorsements and on the direction of his career off the pitch. However, he ended up as a manager, just as so many players had done before him. Lineker on the other hand carefully planned an entirely new career after retirement and he planned it in the media with the help of his agent, whose significant influence on the lives of footballers beyond his own client list will be fully demonstrated in subsequent pages. That's why Lineker makes the cut and Keegan doesn't.

David Beckham needs little justification to be asked to sit at this table. If Lineker was known nationally and in parts of Spain and Japan during his playing career, Beckham was known globally. There has never been a captain of England like David Beckham. Having survived the dark days of 1998 and the public opprobrium that followed his dismissal in the defeat by Argentina in that year's World Cup, Beckham was made captain of England in 2000 by Peter Taylor and confirmed in office the following year by Sven-Göran Eriksson. Clever manipulation of the media and shrewd commercial moves by his management team in conjunction with his own fierce resolution combined to change his personal circumstances to an astonishing degree. Beckham's celebrity (fame is not a strong enough word to describe his position in contemporary culture) is so powerful that it is impossible to imagine a situation occurring in which he would be targeted in the way that Bobby Moore was before the start of the World Cup finals in 1970 when he was falsely accused of stealing a bracelet from a gift shop in a Bogotá hotel.

Beckham is not English in the way that Wright, Moore and Lineker were as captains. He belongs to the world and the affection for him is as intense, possibly even more so, in those countries where he is visible only as an image on a television set, computer screen, tablet or mobile phone. Beckham does not represent the England of Churchill as Wright did, or the England of Harold Wilson as Moore arguably did. His gold leaf-covered statue has been placed at the altar of a revered Buddhist temple in Bangkok. It would be absurd to imagine Billy Wright, or indeed any other English footballer, being accorded such deification. It is hard to think of a country in the world that doesn't know of David Beckham or of a country that wouldn't welcome him in the extravagant way in which the world's Roman Catholic communities greet the Pope.

Research commissioned by the Foreign and Commonwealth Office and major international institutions based in Britain indicates that David Beckham appears on every list of the three most recognised British names. He may not be selling too many shirts and associated tat in the so-called Islamic State but that's about the only place on earth where he might be accused of stealing a bracelet. From the stop press of the *Wolverhampton Express & Star* where Billy Wright first saw his name as captain of the England football team to an altar in a Buddhist temple in Thailand is a journey only sport can provide. Through the lives of these four men we can trace the contours of the cultural landscape of their country over the past seventy years.

The four captains evoke almost instantly an image that defines them. For Billy Wright it might be the photograph of him exchanging pennants with Ferenc Puskás; for Moore it is almost certainly one of him holding the Jules Rimet trophy; Lineker is seen almost every week during the football season in the studio of *Match of the Day* and then of course there is Beckham whose image is ubiquitous from wearing sunglasses to the notorious photograph of him in his underpants exhibiting his tattoos. Mention of this last poster might give the impression that this book is simply the statement of a prejudiced, old-fashioned, myopic traditionalist that the world is going to hell in a handcart. That might still be the impression that is conveyed at the conclusion of this story but that is certainly not the reason the book was written, although the author's prejudices no doubt shine through.

In his G. M. Trevelyan Lectures delivered in Cambridge in the Lent term of 1961, which later became the basis of a popular and briefly highly influential work of historiography called *What is History?*, the Marxist historian E. H. Carr mused on the relationship between the historian and his subject:

Study the historian before you begin to study the facts. This is, after all, not very abstruse. It is what is already done by the intelligent undergraduate who, when recommended to read a work by that great scholar, Jones of St. Jude's, goes round to a friend at St. Jude's to ask what sort of chap Jones is, and what bees he has in his bonnet. When you read a work of history, always listen out for the buzzing. If you can detect none, either you are tone deaf or your historian is a dull dog. The facts are really not at all like fish on the fishmonger's slab. They are like fish swimming about in a vast and sometimes inaccessible ocean; and what the historian catches will depend partly on chance, but mainly on what part of the ocean he chooses to fish in and what tackle he chooses to use – these two factors being, of course, determined by the kind of fish he wants to catch. By and large, the historian will get the kind of facts he wants. History means interpretation.

In other words, by referencing different images from the ones quoted above, different captains or even different facts from the lives of the same four players, it would be possible to construct an entirely different narrative of the pattern of post-war English social history. Possible – but pointless.

I first became aware of football around the age of five or six, during the time of the Suez crisis – a not entirely coincidental collision of facts of which E. H. Carr would no doubt quickly approve. It was, as subsequent pages will detail, a time that demonstrated to the world that Britain was no longer the Great Power she had been before the outbreak of war in 1939. My generation of baby boomers was taught in primary school that national pride was extremely important and was to be found in the British triumph in the Second World War with particular reference to the dark days of 1940 when We Stood

Alone. We could also point to the profusion of pink on the maps of the world which decorated our classrooms and which boasted still of the extent of the British Empire, now slowly dissolving into the more politically acceptable concept of the British Commonwealth.

We had conquered Hitler's Germany and we had conquered the world's tallest summit, Mount Everest. Despite the fact that the two men who reached it were a New Zealander and a Nepalese sherpa, it was, after all, Sir John Hunt's expedition and he was a jolly fine example of British pluck, spirit and entrepreneurial organisation. Almost as importantly, we had recently conquered Lindsay Hassett's Australians, regaining the Ashes for the first time in nineteen years. The first England football match I became dimly aware of was the 7–2 crushing of Scotland at Wembley in 1955 and the following year's 4–2 victory over the rising stars of Brazil. At the end of that 1954–5 season, England went on tour and won 5–1 in Helsinki and 3–1 in Berlin against West Germany who were, at the time, the world champions, having won the 1954 World Cup by defeating the popular favourites, Hungary. The Germans called it 'The Miracle of Bern'. We remembered who had won the century's two world wars. The victory in Berlin seemed an appropriate reminder to the Germans not to get above themselves.

Those of us fortunate enough to be born in the years after 1945, who grew up after the end of rationing, who received non-repayable grants to fund our time at university, who started looking for work when full employment was not a historical or possibly mythical concept and who bought our houses before the house-price inflation of the 1980s and 1990s, have a particular view of life, history and sport shaped by exactly those experiences. For all the scepticism I now feel for the English Premier League and its soap-opera excesses, I know perfectly well that a ten-year-old boy today, who is as in love with football as my generation was in 1960 will, in forty or fifty years' time, pine nostalgically for the days of 2016 when real footballers played for the love of the game or some such mystical nonsense. It is the consequence of history and the consequence of the natural process of ageing.

I am of the generation that lived through 1966 and 1970. I was seventeen when England won the World Cup and nineteen when Manchester City won the First Division League Championship. Both events seemed to me to be entirely logical if not predictable. I had lived through dark times and had emerged triumphant to bask in the sunshine of victory. If I had learned anything from the story of the Second World War, it was that this was how the narrative went. A similar feeling arose when I first read Herbert Butterfield's book *The Whig Interpretation of History*. Butterfield's general theory was that nineteenth-century historians were inclined to present the past as the inexorable march of progress towards enlightenment, citing in particular the growth of constitutional government, democratic freedoms, progress in science and widespread economic prosperity. The Industrial Revolution gave the British economy a head start and the astonishing acquisition of other people's lands and natural resources gave the country an empire that stretched around the globe, ruled by a handful of men who had been educated at English public schools.

Yes, there were problems caused, it was generally agreed, mostly by the ambitions of the Kaiser and Hitler, although some were also caused by the feckless Irish and other unreliable foreigners. Then there was the ingratitude of the working classes and of the colonial peoples who mysteriously did not seem to appreciate the manner in which Britain had so nobly shouldered the White Man's Burden. However, that burden, like the Whig interpretation of history, always held out the promise of a Happy Ending, as in a Hollywood film. When

Bobby Moore held aloft the Jules Rimet trophy and when the whistle blew at St James's Park (as it was called then) on the last day of the 1967–8 season to proclaim Manchester City's ascendancy it was not only a joyous experience for me but in some way it felt to me as if it had been divinely so ordered.

Of course, nothing lasts in sport and it is the change that is the real problem not the absurd belief in some kind of Golden Age, as people in the inter-war years harked back to a non-existent Elysium before the outbreak of war in 1914. The eras of Billy Wright and Bobby Moore might not have been a Golden Age, but the 1950s and 1960s were decades in which football was played in a different spirit from the relentlessly hysterical and frequently unsavoury atmosphere on the pitch and in the stands that exists today, for all the so-called 'gentri-fication' of football and the specious nonsense talked about the football 'family'.

Football in the 1960s probably contained just as many insalubrious characters as it does today. Those who knew football men like Alan Hardaker do not recall them with any fondness. Hardaker ran the Football League as a personal fiefdom and ordered Chelsea to pull out of the new-fangled European Cup in 1955 because he believed that they shouldn't get mixed up in some fancy foreign competition when their job was to play English football with English players for English spectators. We might wonder at the ineptitude of the current FA but nobody could seriously want to return to the days of Bert Millichip or Harold Thompson. Burnley supporters of a certain age might pine for their wonderful championship side of 1960 but would they welcome back their neighbourhood butcher and petty dictator Bob Lord, who was their chairman for twenty-five difficult years? Those of us who have little time for the over-mighty rulers of Abu Dhabi certainly have no wish to return to the days of Peter Swales, and even those

Manchester United supporters who love United but hate the Glazers probably wouldn't be that thrilled to have Louis Edwards – what is it about the meat trade? – reinstated in the Old Trafford boardroom. The choice is a stark one: the trivial ambitions of local tyrants weighed against the geopolitical and financial ambitions of multi-national corporations, Russian oligarchs and Middle Eastern dictators.

In the years between 1966 and 1970 when, as indicated above, I was more in love with football than at any other time in my life, England were world champions and were developing a team to play in the 1970 World Cup in Mexico that looked as though it might be even better than the team of 1966. The era of rationing and austerity into which I had been born but of which I had little memory was long gone. Abortion and homosexuality were tolerated for the first time by parliamentary legislation. The laws on obscenity were relaxed and the Lord Chamberlain's Office no longer acted as the censor of stage plays, thereby – as Kenneth Tynan remarked – dragging British theatre kicking and screaming into the second half of the eighteenth century. The early 1960s appears in retrospect to have been a golden time for the British theatre and British television. British films, too, were benefiting from the terminal decline of the old Hollywood studio system and for all the boom-and-bust nature of the British economy, people were far more prosperous and generally better off than they had been at any time in the 1950s. Despite the fact we all recognised we were living 'under the shadow of the Bomb', it seemed to my teenage self to be an era of boundless optimism. The strength of the England football team was a significant factor in that heady feeling.

It would be absurd to claim that the eras of Billy Wright and Bobby Moore were 'better' or more important than the era of David Beckham and Wayne Rooney. The eras were separated by decades of rapid social change so they were just different from each other. There are any number of ways in which this can be illustrated. One might be a comparison of the 'autobiographies' of famous sportsmen. *The World's My Football Pitch* by Billy Wright, published by Stanley Paul in November 1953, is unlikely ever to join the ranks of the literary classics. Possibly November 1953 was an unfortunate month to choose to launch a book 'written' by the captain of the England football team, as his side were notoriously beaten at Wembley 6–3 by the superb Hungary team on the last Wednesday afternoon of the month. The defeat, England's first by a foreign team on home soil, provoked a national trauma that was not healed until Bobby Moore lifted the World Cup in July 1966. A work of no distinguishable literary merit written at a time of sporting humiliation is perhaps best consigned to oblivion, but what makes the book so interesting more than sixty years after its publication is the manner in which it is written and in particular its genuine reverence for the hierarchy of the Football Association.

On the first page Wright tells the story of the 'splendid banquet' given in his honour by the FA at the end of the 1951–2 season to mark Wright's breaking of Bob Crompton's record of forty-one England caps which had come to an end when Archduke Franz Ferdinand was assassinated in Sarajevo.

The banquet was conducted in that kind manner which has become their trademark... Mr Amos Brook Hirst, the FA Chairman... shook hands, congratulated me, and then revealed a grand human touch by announcing that Mr Arthur Drewry, for so long chairman of England selectors, had been invited to make the presentation...

Mr Drewry rose and handed out a pat on the back which made me blush. I looked beyond the handsome figure of Mr Drewry to the many tables packed tight with friends and acquaintances...

We should perhaps at this point withdraw into the ante-chamber at Lancaster Gate, where BBC radio reporters used to lurk in the days when the wooden balls were slipped into the velvet bag and given a good shake before the draw for the next round of the FA Cup. We could then leave Billy and his all-male dinner-jacketed acquaintances to their misty-eyed reminiscences of an international career which had begun in a war-weary country six years earlier.

Sporting biographies, and that pernicious innovation the sporting autobiography, which the subject has neither written nor, in some cases, even read, tend to follow slavish lines of fashion. Currently, the books that sell the best are those which reveal to a gawping public the tensions of the dressing room. It appears that cricket fans who used to flock to the ground to admire the virtuosity of Kevin Pietersen at the crease want to read about their hero's apparent contempt for his team-mates and management staff rather than his duels with the best bowlers of his time. Similarly, fans who have admired Roy Keane as a footballer are fascinated by his loathing of the man who had been his manager during his successful years at Manchester United.

Books that contain such controversial opinions and lurid revelations are seized upon eagerly by newspapers for seriali-sation in an attempt to boost circulation. Editors of radio and television programmes can't get enough of them because they are quite sure that this is what their listeners and viewers want and that their programme's ratings will benefit accordingly. It is all a long way from Billy Wright's reverent gratitude for the beneficence bestowed in kindly paternal benevolence by the Football Association in May 1952.

Wright discovered that he had been appointed captain of England for the match against Northern Ireland in October 1948 while sitting on the bus that took him from the Wolves training ground to his digs in Tettenhall. On the seat next to him was a large ham he was taking home for his landlady, Mrs Colley. In rationed Britain, this present from the grateful people of Denmark, against whose national side Wright had recently appeared in an international match played in Copenhagen, was of considerable value. Alan Bennett's film *A Private Function*, set at the time of Princess Elizabeth's wedding to Prince Philip in November 1947, makes clear the lengths to which British people might go in search of a loin of pork or a shoulder of ham.

I made myself comfortable and feeling rather drowsy settled down to a smooth uneventful journey. 'Congratulations,' said a cheery voice from somewhere behind my left shoulder. 'It's a great honour to be chosen to captain England.' I turned to see the clippie, Miss Helen Mearden, thrusting a copy of the *Wolverhampton Express & Star* at me. 'Look in the Stop Press,' she added quickly, obviously noting my look of blank disbelief. But she was right. The Stop Press informed me in an impersonal inky manner:

England team to meet Ireland in Belfast: Swift (Manchester City); Scott (Arsenal) Howe (Derby); Wright (Wolves) capt. Franklin (Stoke) Cockburn (Manchester Utd); Matthews (Blackpool) Mortensen (Blackpool) Milburn (Newcastle United) Pearson (Manchester Utd) Finney (Preston).

My hands were shaking quite literally with excitement as I re-read the paragraph time and time again. They were still shaking when we reached Tettenhall and, after a desperate scramble back into the bus to snatch up the forgotten ham, I ran every yard of the way home. 'What's all the excitement and hurry about?' asked Mrs Colley. 'Have you come into a fortune?' 'Better than that,' I replied, 'I'm captain of England.'

Allowing some licence for the somewhat breathless prose of the ghost writer, the picture painted is nevertheless that of an overgrown child almost speechless with excitement. It chimed with the readers because that childlike enthusiasm combined with a deep-seated patriotism is presumably how they too saw the captaincy of the England football team in 1948. Such emotion leaves other nations mystified.

In 2008, Fabio Capello arrived as manager of the England football team puzzling over the English obsession with their football captain and left after making a stand on retaining John Terry as his captain when his employers removed the armband from the Chelsea defender. At his first press conference, Capello was asked repeatedly which player he had in mind to lead England out at the start of his first match in charge. He dismissed the enquiry as an irrelevance to his wider task, which was to ensure that England qualified for the 2010 World Cup and then to make sure they were competitive when they got to South Africa. The assembled journalists, however, were not to be so casually dismissed. More questions on the topic followed: 'Can you give us a hint, Fabio?' 'Can you tell us his initials, Fabio?' It was partly mischievous, of course, but the mischief disguised a more profound anxiety. The journalists knew that Capello's decision really mattered to their readers because for them the England football captain is anointed, not merely appointed.

Gary Lineker, despite having been an England captain, understood Capello's befuddlement after his own experience of playing in Spain:

In England we probably overvalue the importance of the England football captaincy. In Barcelona, the players vote for who they want to be the captain. They vote for three or even four choices so if the captain who is the first choice is injured or dropped he remains as the squad captain but the guy the players voted as No. 2 will assume the armband and so it goes on. I'd never seen that till I went to Barcelona but when I saw that I started to think, 'Why should the manager pick the captain anyway?' The captain is the representative of the players and therefore should be chosen by the players. Eight times out of ten the manager would probably pick the same person. I thought that was a much better idea.

That was not dissimilar to Capello's stated position on arrival in 2008 because the Italian understood from his own experience of captaincy that it was given to the player on the side with the most caps. It was a reward for seniority, a label only, of no real consequence. By the time he resigned in 2012, ironically over the issue of captaincy, Capello understood very well that the captaincy of the England football team was like the captaincy of no other country.

Where does this idiosyncratic feature of English sport originate? The captain of the England cricket team, whether the Test or the one-day captain, wields considerably more influence on the field of play because the game is longer and more fluid than football and the options available – and therefore the decisions that he must make – are so much more numerous. He might lead the team on to the field after discussions with the coach about who would be the best bowlers to exploit the prevailing conditions, but once the opposition's innings has started, the pitch – which appeared to be green when he won the toss and put the other side in to bat – might have turned out to be as flat as a pancake. Even more worrying, Anderson and Broad are both pitching the ball in their own half of the pitch and are being cut and pulled at will by Warner and Finch. All the carefully conceived plans to keep the Australians under control at the start of their innings have gone out of the window by the end of the sixth over. It is entirely up to the captain how to get England out of the mess they now find themselves in.

The history of the England cricket team captains in the twentieth century is a useful comparative tool as we seek to examine the social or cultural origins of the mystique of the England football captain. Until the abolition of amateur status by MCC in November 1962 (not insignificantly, a date situated between the end of English football's maximum wage in 1961 and the landmark decision in the George Eastham High Court case which was finally decided in July 1963) all England cricket captains (apart from the anomaly of Len Hutton) were amateurs and almost invariably they had some if only minimal contact with one of the two ancient universities. Even after the abolition, the captaincy was held by the former amateurs M. C. Cowdrey (Tonbridge and Brasenose College, Oxford), then E. R. Dexter (Radley and Jesus College, Cambridge), followed by M. J. K. Smith (Stamford School and St Edmund Hall, Oxford) before Ray Illingworth (Pudsey and Yorkshire) was reluctantly given the job and complicated matters by proving to be an outstanding captain and winning the Ashes in Australia in 1971.

It is arguable that the qualities inculcated in the public schools in the Victorian era and in the ancient universities between 1850 and 1950 are fundamental to the English conception of sporting captaincy. Academic excellence was of little importance. If you could make a stab at translating Julius Caesar's commentaries on the Gallic Wars from Latin to English that pretty much fitted you to run some part of the British Empire or change the bowling and set a new field at Lord's. Being 'clubbable' was clearly important and the ability to shout 'follow me, lads' was as vital at the Sydney Cricket Ground as it was in the trenches on the first day of the Battle of the Somme. The slaughter of 'the flower of a nation' during the Great War, with death making no distinction between officers and other ranks, calls to mind some aspect of captaincy. Whether you spoke fluent Latin and Greek or you could scarcely articulate an English sentence, what was required from an officer in the heat of battle was a quality of character and integrity sufficient to inspire others in what might well be a doomed cause.

The ideals of muscular Christianity developed in the High Victorian Age rather weirdly persist in the realm of contemporary English sport and particularly sporting captaincy, as they do not appear to survive in other areas of national life. Victorians placed considerable emphasis on integrity, courage and honour because those qualities built character. Sport was encouraged precisely because the playing of football, cricket and rugby pre-eminently led directly to the display of those virtues. Of course, a gentleman like the good Dr W. G. Grace was the most blatant cheat, but the money-making activities of this 'shamateur' and his determination to win by any means never affected the public perception of his heroic status. Is the difference in response to Grace then and John Terry now simply one of class snobbery?

Even in the meritocratic twenty-first century it is interesting that England cricket captains such as Andrew Strauss (Radley College) and Alastair Cook (Bedford School) retain something of the social class of the old Oxbridge-dominated days. The captain of the England football team, however, requires qualities different from his cricketing counterpart. It is perhaps easier to define what an England football captain should *not* be than to define precisely the attributes he must possess. David Bernstein was the FA chairman when John Terry was dismissed as England's captain and in a revealing interview he gave at the time to Matt Dickinson of *The Times* he made plain the qualities he thought the captain of the England football team should display.

> There's something particular about an England football captain and actually I believe rather different to the way captains are perceived on the continent. And when you look at the statue outside Wembley of Bobby Moore, you can hardly say more than that because the history of Bobby and Billy Wright and so on is the stature that one is looking for from England captains. This particular accusation [of racially abusing the Queens Park Rangers defender Anton Ferdinand] – which of course is totally unproven, I must keep saying that – the FA board, 14 people who had a uniformed view on this, felt that going into a European Championship with all the connotations that are involved and a long period to go between now and the championships, that it was an overhanging issue that was not appropriate and not in the best interests of England for that to be allowed to continue.

It is not surprising that John Terry was defended by Capello as well as Chelsea supporters. He was, for a long time, the best central defender in the country, unstinting in his effort, thoughtful in his positioning and over the course of his career he won more than a dozen trophies. He was, however, a constantly controversial figure and his misbehaviour provoked widespread condemnation long before the Anton Ferdinand incident which lost him the England captaincy. Previous to that he had been one of the Chelsea players who had abused

American tourists after 9/11, he had urinated on the floor of a nightclub and had to deny allegations that he had taken an undercover journalist on a tour of the Chelsea training ground in return for cash. There were also the widely reported infidelities, including an affair with the former girlfriend of his team-mate Wayne Bridge. It could be argued that it was less surprising that he lost the captaincy than that he had hung on to it for so long. As a central defender and as an inspiring captain he had many virtues. As a role model for the rest of society, especially as far as impressionable youngsters were concerned, he had none apart from those playing qualities already mentioned.

One reason why it was not appropriate for Terry to continue in the role clearly was to do with the impending court case arising from the Anton Ferdinand incident, which would not be heard until after the 2012 European Championships had concluded. A second was the seriousness of the charge, but much more interesting is Bernstein's instinctive evoking of the image of Terry's two main predecessors, Bobby Moore and Billy Wright, two men cursed by a fondness for more alcohol than was good for them or indeed for the image of the England football captain. Happily for his clean-cut image, Wright's alcoholism did not take hold of him until after he had finished playing; while Moore never allowed the effects of heavy drinking to impair the majesty of his performances on the field. He was fortunate nonetheless that his alcoholic excesses did not become known to the general public during his playing career. Nowadays, players are at the mercy of anyone with a mobile phone and a thirst for malice and personal publicity.

Both Wright and Moore played in a post-war era in which the captaincy of England automatically conferred on the holder of the office the odour of instant sanctity. To an extent it still does so – just as long as the captain is not the subject of negative comment for actions committed either on or off the field of play. It is arguably only England that demands such a high price of its football captains. Matt Dickinson makes the point that

> You can have a lengthy ethical debate as to whether what Ryan Giggs was alleged to have done is worse than what John Terry was alleged to have done. But when Diego Maradona is appointed the captain of Argentina nobody sits there for a second worrying about his history of drug addiction. When he deliberately punches the ball past Shilton with his fist none of the papers headline an article that criticises him for not representing the kind of Argentina we want people to see.

The two 'untouchables', Wright and Moore, both captained their country for ninety matches and made over 100 appearances in an England shirt, but the reason their stars shone so brightly for so long was because in the 1950s and 1960s supporters of the England football team had no appetite for the demystification of their heroes in any walk of life they admired. There were plenty of seemingly untainted heroes around in those early post-war days: Hutton and Compton, Matthews and Finney, Winston Churchill, Field Marshal Montgomery, John Mills, Laurence Olivier, Edmund Hillary and Sherpa Tensing – the news of whose successful conquest of Mount Everest reached Britain on 2 June 1953, the day of the coronation of the radiant young Queen Elizabeth II. A month previously, Stanley Matthews had finally won his FA Cup winner's medal to national rejoicing; Gordon Richards – knighted in the Queen's Honours List – finally won his first Derby at the end of his career four days after the coronation; and at the end of August, Denis Compton swept a four down to the gas holders at The Oval to regain the Ashes for England. At the dawn of the New Elizabethan Age, Great Britain appeared to have a surfeit of heroes in many fields of sporting endeavour. Even though the Hungarians scored thirteen times in two matches against the England football team, in the national consciousness the 7–1 defeat in Budapest in May 1954 was quickly obliterated by the triumph of Dr Roger Bannister who ran the first sub-four-minute mile that same month.

How heroic can a hero be if his behaviour away from his principal field of activity does not arouse the same universal acclaim that it attracts on the field? Compton held what people now would certainly regard as unappealingly supportive opinions about the South African government during the period of apartheid; Montgomery's egotistical behaviour provoked one of Churchill's great bons mots – 'In war unbeatable: in peace unbearable'. Recent research suggests Montgomery was a sufferer from Asperger's syndrome. Churchill himself, with his gargantuan appetite for alcohol, would not have escaped condemnation in our more censorious age. A BBC television programme about the 1945 general election, transmitted in May 2015, included at least one contributor who passionately argued that Churchill had been drunk during the great wartime speeches that had united a nation engaged in a life or death struggle against fascism.

What these men achieved in public life nevertheless remains unsullied. The chances of it being revealed that Hillary and Tensing were actually helicoptered to the summit of Everest and that they faked their heroic climb to the top are non-existent. The British people in 1953 wanted to believe in the essential goodness of their heroes. They had recently fought a victorious war against a regime that was a byword for evil. The triumph of 1945, which left the nation mired in debt and mentally exhausted, stimulated in them a need for war heroes like Douglas Bader and Violette Szabo, and on the sports field the likes of Denis Compton and Stanley Matthews were similarly admired and loved. Tall-poppy syndrome was an illness that had not been diagnosed, for few manifestations of it had yet presented themselves.

Of course, there were no camera phones around to provide visual evidence of player misbehaviour (although Matt Busby in the 1960s was kept remarkably well supplied with details of George Best's nocturnal antics by an army of informants) and there were no twenty-four-hour rolling news channels and radio stations to be kept supplied with scandal masquerading as news. In those days, journalists maintained relationships with players which the media managers of the twenty-first century now prevent because they are so paranoid about the possibility of bad news stories involving the players for whom they are responsible. In a different age, journalists frequently placed personal loyalty to a player above professional loyalty to their editor who was hungry for a good story.

The ubiquitous and shadowy media managers who now hide the players from public view behind electronic gates and tinted car windows do a severe disservice to the players and to the game, as well as to the integrity of the English language. People tend to assume that these players have something to hide and reporters therefore dedicate themselves to the noble task of discovering exactly what it is that the clubs and their employees are so desperate to keep hidden. Who among us could withstand that level of scrutiny of our private lives? Surely, at some point, someone will gasp 'too much information' and the cameras and sound equipment will thankfully be packed away. At the time of writing, however, that happy day appears some way distant. Steven Gerrard, an admirable player in so many ways, retired from English football in 2015 accompanied by hosannas of gratitude – but he will not go down in history as one of England's great captains. Since Beckham resigned the captaincy in tears after the 2006 World Cup in Germany, England has not possessed a captain who has inspired the nation and his team-mates in the way that Moore and Wright were popularly supposed to have done.

Wayne Rooney, the current England captain, knows from previous encounters with the tabloid press that every personal indiscretion he commits off the field of play while he is England captain will simply provide more fodder for the ravenous appetite of a slavering media. Whether such revelations are in the public interest or simply what the public is interested in is a moral dilemma which is unlikely to find a resolution any time soon. There appears to be no diminution in the fascination of the British public for evidence of the moral fallibility of their 'heroes'.

England football captains are the mirror of the culture of their times. If what we wanted in the slow tortuous haul back to economic stability during the 1950s was a shock-haired, smiling, cheerful Billy Wright, in the cool stylish 1960s our leader was the coolest man in the country, the graceful, unruffled and stylish Bobby Moore. Likewise, Gary Lineker's England career tells us something about the social changes wrought under Thatcherism while David Beckham's life reveals a Britain that would be unrecognisable to anyone who saw Billy Wright's first match as England captain on 9 October 1948. It is likely that when he exchanged pennants with Johnny Carey, the captain of the Northern Ireland team, that highly prized ham which Wright had carried with him from Copenhagen was still being parsimoniously shared out and carefully replaced in his landlady's fridge – in the event that she actually possessed a fridge. The likelihood is that the ham would have been kept in her larder under a tea towel. It was hard for footballers to become conceited when they were sub-jected to the same petty privations as everyone else. In Billy Wright, England found the perfect captain for the resumption of football in the post-war era.

CHAPTER ONE

THE AGE OF BILLY WRIGHT

THE AGE OF BILLY WRIGHT

I n Michael Powell and Emeric Pressburger's film *A Matter of Life and Death*, David Niven plays an RAF pilot trying to fly back to base a badly damaged and burning Lancaster bomber after a mission over Germany on 2 May 1945. He manages to make contact with an American radio operator played by Kim Hunter and gives her the bare details of his life before bailing out without a parachute. 'Age – 27; education – interrupted, violently interrupted; religion – Church of England; politics – Conservative by nature, Labour by experience.' It's rather an odd message to leave in the circumstances but then it's rather an odd film.

Nevertheless, as the results of the general election two months later were to confirm, Niven's summary of his life would have been recognisable to millions of Britons after nearly six years of total war. Britain had changed out of all recognition from the country that had tried its best to appease Hitler in the late 1930s to the country which, as soon as Churchill became prime minister in May 1940, had had no choice other than to fight on until unconditional surrender had been achieved. It was generally believed that Churchill's personal popularity, supported by a famous victory, would be enough to win his Conservative party a healthy majority.

On 5 July 1945, less than two months after Germany had surrendered unconditionally and more than a month before Japan was to do so, the country went to the polls. The ballot boxes remained sealed for three weeks to permit the collection of those overseas votes which had been cast by men and women still in the armed forces. Although Labour won a landslide victory with an overall majority of 146, the result, in those days free of today's ubiquitous if frequently wrong opinion polls, came as a surprise, particularly to Winston Churchill. Clementine Churchill, worried about the strain of continued high office on the health of her husband, called the result 'a blessing in disguise'. Churchill growled that as far as he was concerned it was a blessing that was very well disguised indeed.

On the evening of 26 July, having tendered his resignation as prime minister to the king, Churchill left Buckingham Palace in a chauffeur-driven Rolls-Royce. Almost as if it had been scripted by a Labour spin doctor in order to emphasise that things were going to be different from now on, fifteen minutes after the Rolls-Royce had purred away Mrs Attlee drove her husband in the family Standard Ten into Palace Yard. As revolutions go, it lacked the iconic symbolism of the storming of the Bastille in July 1789 but it said much about the Attlees' marriage and provided an endearing view of the lack of importance they attached to the principle of ostentation in ritual. Theirs was a devoted marriage and nobody seemed to think it strange that the wife of the Labour prime minister was widely believed to have had distinctly conservative instincts. It is perhaps as well, however, that there were no spin doctors around at the time.

During the election campaign, Mrs Attlee had sat patiently in the Standard Ten knitting the time away as her husband made his speeches from the hustings. Now she was driving

Clem in his best formal clothes to kiss hands with the mystified monarch who had admitted that the result 'had come as a
great surprise to one and all'. The crowd of Labour supporters
who lined The Mall cheered and shouted, 'We want Attlee', as
the Standard Ten clanked its way towards Buckingham Palace.
The new prime minister waved politely from the passenger
seat. David Niven's brief summary of his new political inclina-
tions illustrated how Labour simply chimed with the zeitgeist
of a post-war world in a way that the Tory party did not.

There were two things that almost everyone who voted for
Labour was agreed upon, male or female, middle class or
working class: there must be no more war and there must be
no return to the economic and social conditions that existed in
Britain in 1939. For all their genuine admiration of Churchill
as the man who had won the war, there was an ingrained belief
in most of the electorate that he was more interested in foreign
affairs than domestic concerns and that his party was still the
party of inherited wealth, privilege and the dole. Those with
memories which started before Dunkirk remembered Churchill
as the man who, as home secretary in 1910, had sent the
British Army to Tonypandy to help police crush the civil unrest
of discontented Welsh miners. If there was some dispute as to
how responsible Churchill was for the brutality that ensued,
his role in it was never forgotten in that part of Wales. He had
been the main architect of the disaster of Gallipoli in 1915, he
had been the chancellor of the exchequer who had wrongly
returned Britain to the gold standard in 1924; he had been
appallingly rude to Gandhi, implacably opposed to Indian
independence, and had chosen the wrong side in the Abdication
Crisis. His warnings about Nazi Germany in 1938 were what
everyone remembered, but placed in the context of his previously chequered political career, the rejection of Churchill at
the polls in 1945 becomes more credible.

There had been much grumbling about the controls imposed by his coalition government during the war but it was grudgingly admitted that they had succeeded in creating a fairer society. The Conservatives in office alone, without Labour as a wartime coalition partner, would, judging by their past record, be only too keen to return to the laissez-faire economics that had, it was widely believed, been responsible for their failure to deal with the coruscating effects of the Great Depression. The new Britain that everyone wanted to see rise from the ashes caused by the German bombs had therefore to include significant government intervention and legislation. Churchill, one of whose election radio broadcasts included the unfortunate combination of the words 'Socialist' and 'Gestapo', was not the man for this kind of job. Attlee was.

The problem was that the nation was virtually bankrupt and what Attlee believed the Labour party had been elected to do was drastically to reform society at all levels. The railways and the mines were to be nationalised into new organisations called respectively British Railways and the National Coal Board; a National Health Service was to be formed; the recommendations of the Beveridge Report which had been published in 1942 had to be implemented to create a more just system of welfare in a society that would now care for its citizens from the cradle to the grave. Two years later, the Education Minister R. A. ('Rab') Butler announced that the secondary school system was to be subjected to the provisions of a new act that would transform the future social landscape.

The 1944 Education Act started out with the most admirable remit. In place of the sprawling mess that included non-fee-paying elementary schools, church schools, public schools and direct grant grammar schools, there was going to be a system of state education that was uniform and entirely free to all children. Primary schools would run from the age of five till eleven. Secondary schools would take children from eleven to sixteen, two years beyond the current school-leaving age of fourteen. The secondary system would be a tripartite arrangement consisting of grammar schools for those children of an academic bent, secondary moderns for those less inclined to want to proceed to the sixth form and university, and technical schools for those with an interest in technology which was to be highly valued in the new technocratic Britain.

This remaking of the British school system was a fundamental part of the new progressive egalitarianism that dominated public thinking during and immediately after the war. Children would now have opportunities based entirely on their abilities, not on where they were born or how much money their parents had. The Eleven Plus examination, and the allocation of school that followed the result of it, was to be the means that would reorganise Great Britain and make it fit for purpose in succeeding generations. Twenty years later, the division of children in this manner at the age of eleven was deemed to be unfair to an extent that bordered on child exploitation, but that should not disguise the admirable intention at the White Paper stage of the Butler Act.

All this proposed government legislation had to be paid for with money the country didn't have, particularly now that Lend-Lease had ended with the Allied victory. John Maynard Keynes was sent off to Washington to negotiate a loan from the only developed country with any money, but he found America unexpectedly unwilling to reward with cash the gallant sacrifices Britain had made in 1940 and 1941 and he returned home without the grant or gift that had been hoped for. Instead Britain had to make do with a loan of $4.33 billion at 2 per cent; that at least permitted Attlee to begin his revolutionary legislative programme, although many critics regarded the interest to be paid as punitive. Only Marshall Aid, which arrived to save Europe from Communism a few years later as part of the US-funded post-war recovery programme, kept the British economy afloat in these desperate years.

People might have felt at the end of six long years of war, with all the sacrifices that hard-earned victory had entailed, that they were entitled to some of the fruits of that victory. Instead, the welcome arrival of peace did not diminish the queues, fill the shops with goods or end the rationing. In our age of obesity it is salutary to examine briefly what men and women in England were allowed to eat in a week in the year that football restarted after the war:

1s 2d (6p) worth of meat
3 oz bacon and ham
8 oz sugar
2.5 oz of tea
2.5 pints of milk
2 oz butter
2 oz cheese
4 oz margarine
1 oz cooking fat
1 egg (per fortnight)
12 oz of sweets (per month)

This food could only be bought after seemingly endless queuing. In newsreels of the time it is rare to find fat young people, which is perhaps the only positive note to strike as the full implications of rationing sink into our overfed and over-privileged minds.

In 1950, when Jimmy Hill, future Coventry City manager and *Match of the Day* presenter, was playing for Brentford against a representative Dutch FA XI in Holland, he was confronted by an array of food whose amount and variety astonished a man used to the rigours of post-war British rationing. Hill and his hungry team-mates inevitably over-indulged – to the extent that, at the start of the game, many of them could scarcely run. They managed a 1–1 draw but all they could remember about the trip was the food. They had never even seen so much food in their lives, let alone eaten it.

Homes that had been destroyed by the Luftwaffe were not replaced, although the prefabs and the planned new towns offered hope to a small number of fortunate families. Houses were in desperately short supply and couples who wished to marry frequently had to continue to live with one set of parents throughout the 1950s. The impact of this difficult state of affairs on the marriage is displayed in Stan Barstow's 1960 novel *A Kind of Loving* although it is one moment in John Schlesinger's 1962 film version that stays in the memory, when Vic Brown (Alan Bates) has returned to the house after drinking to forget the strains being placed on his new marriage. Inevitably, he throws up over the back of the sofa, watched in horror by his house-proud and unforgiving mother-in-law (Thora Hird). 'Disgusting!' she says contemptuously. Britain was, and continued to be for the first six years after Victory in Europe and Japan, a country of exhaustion and drabness, its towns pock-marked by ubiquitous bomb sites, its population grateful for the gift of life and the cessation of hostilities, but it was still an unremittingly hard time for most of them.

The war against Japan might have been finished by the slaughter caused by the atomic bombs dropped at Hiroshima and Nagasaki in August 1945 but the rest of the world now lived permanently in the shadow of the hydrogen bomb as the nuclear capability of combatant nations proliferated in the 1950s. The Cold War made the possibility of world annihilation by mutually assured destruction a constant presence. Great Britain might have contributed a significant amount to the development of the Manhattan Project but she emerged from the Potsdam conference, at which Truman had told Attlee and Stalin of its success, as the least important of the three Allies who were henceforward replaced by the Two Superpowers. 'I did not become the King's First Minister to preside over the liquidation of the British Empire,' Churchill had gruffly informed Roosevelt when the latter wanted to know Churchill's plans for the colonies after the war. Indeed he did not, but his immediate successor did.

British people in the 1950s watched, frequently in tight-lipped disappointment, as their troops were evacuated from their former colonial territories. It was a changed world but not one our parents rushed to acknowledge. They had made sacrifices. It was important to them that their children knew how much they had sacrificed and that those children should themselves grow up in a spirit of similar selflessness.

The working-class footballer of the post-war era played in a deferential society in which, like his parents before him, he 'knew his place'. In this rigid social hierarchy, women were subordinate to men and children to their parents. The national anthem was still played in theatres and cinemas before or after each night's entertainment, although the bolder sections of the movie audience in the late 1950s might walk out as soon as it started, which would never have happened before 1939. The anthem, like the union flag – before it was appropriated by football hooligans and the makers of kitsch underwear – was an object of veneration. Politicians, the church and the royal family were all afforded the greatest respect by a country that knew neither Jeremy Paxman nor Jeremy Clarkson. Doctors could pontificate in hospitals and surgeries without fear of physical violence. It was a world in which teachers rather than their pupils held the weapons of mass destruction even if they were usually a cane or a worn-out plimsoll. A flick knife was the most potent of teenage weapons and these tended to be used to slash the seats on the upper decks of double-decker buses, out of sight of the conductor. There was an almost unquestioning respect for family, education, government, the law and religion. In short, it was a long time ago.

The world of football was also stratified along social lines. Nobody wanted to run a football club for the money that could be made out of it. Money wasn't important but prestige and power were. Football was still the glory game that bred heroes, not the arena for conspicuous consumption that feeds on its own media hype. The only large car in the car park belonged to the chairman. Players still knew what the inside of a bus looked like even when they were the captain of the England football team. It was the era of the maximum wage and contractual serfdom. The talented youths who chose football over cricket or other sports did not do so because the financial rewards were so disproportionately large and indeed football clubs and county cricket clubs encouraged players who were good enough to play both sports professionally to do so.

Managers were former players who invariably hadn't been able to save anything from their careers and still lived from one weekly pay packet in a sticky brown envelope to the next, usually in a small terrace house owned by the club. They, like their trainers, were just grateful to be allowed to continue to earn a wage from the game they loved. Trainers, those track-suited men who sprinted on to the field when summoned by the referee to attend an injured player, were most unlikely to have any medical knowledge. The players themselves were on a lower level and the juniors or apprentices led an existence that most managers thought scarcely worth acknowledging except for that brief moment when their signature as a school-boy might be sought by a rival club.

The Football League did not resume its traditional fixture list until the 1946–7 season but such was the clamour for an immediate return to normal sporting life that the summer of 1945 featured a series of five 'Victory Tests' played between a combined Australian Services XI and an English national side. These cricket matches were significant not so much for the crowds which predictably poured in to see the five three-day games (Lord's claimed that 93,000 entered through the turnstiles at one of the matches, the highest recorded attendance at any three-day game) but for the manner in which they were played. England and Australia had fought out some grim Test matches in the 1930s. The 'Bodyline' series of 1932–3 gave added credence to Orwell's dictum about the high seriousness in which professional sport was played, but these Victory Tests were played in a spirit of sportsmanship that nobody who witnessed them could recall seeing in Test matches of previous years. Denis Compton was still on overseas service, but England were able to select Hutton, Washbrook, Edrich, Ames and Hammond. For Australia, the skipper Lindsay Hassett was the only player with Test match experience. Appropriately, perhaps, the series ended with honours even, with two wins apiece for England and Australia and one match drawn.

It is the essential contention of this book that sport holds up a mirror to the society in which it is played and nothing could better illustrate the new world landscape than the visit of Moscow Dynamo to Britain in the autumn of 1945. They played four matches against Chelsea (3–3), Rangers (2–2), Third Division Cardiff City (which finished 10–1 to the visitors), and to their great joy they beat Arsenal 4–3 in farcical conditions when fog drastically reduced visibility. It was a bad-tempered tour, full of the diplomatic manoeuvrings which were shortly to become a hallmark of the Cold War, and it led

George Orwell to write his famous essay in *Tribune* in which he described sport as 'war minus the shooting'.

Despite the onset of the Cold War, Attlee was determined that Britain's broken economy would not stop him attempting to create the New Jerusalem. It was believed that the past six years of death and deprivation had been to no purpose if, at the end of it all, the country returned meekly to the status quo as it had existed in 1939. For a few years after the end of the war, even in the midst of food rationing, housing shortages and widespread bereavement, there was a high moral seriousness about life in Britain that was not to endure. The BBC, whose Light Programme and Home Service had played their part in uniting the nation during the war years, now established the Third Programme, 'the envy of the world' and its successor, the estimable Radio 3. It was also the time of the Workers' Education Association which opened up new vistas for soldiers whom life in Depression Britain would have consigned to the scrapheap. Other institutions to make a similar impact included the Army Bureau of Current Affairs (ABCA) and the Arts Council, which grew out of the wartime Committee for the Encouragement of Music and the Arts. Did this seriousness have its roots in the lack of alternative forms of entertainment? Certainly cinema attendances and football and cricket crowds were never as large as they were in the immediate post-war years. In the mid-1950s, with the end of rationing, the beginnings of commercial television and the start of the 'affluent society', this high moral seriousness faded, but in the years after 1945 there was a curiosity in the country as to how they could create something new and worthwhile. It might have been a drab and deprived time yet it produced some of the greatest British films ever made. These were the years that saw the making of *Brief Encounter*, *Great Expectations*, *Oliver*

Twist, Odd Man Out, Fallen Idol, The Third Man, Black Narcissus, Henry V, Hamlet, The Red Shoes and the best of the Ealing comedies.

Ealing's *Hue and Cry*, starring Harry Fowler, Jack Warner and Alastair Sim, was filmed on the streets of London in 1946 and can be seen today as an almost documentary record of what the centre of the British Empire looked like after the war. The film is an enchanting story of a group of East End kids who foil a gang of robbers who are using a children's comic to communicate their plans. Looking at it today, its most distinctive feature is its use of bombed-out locations in London's East End and Docklands whose rubble-strewn sites become the background for an adventure story. The children include only one girl – who is just about tolerated by the others in the manner endlessly repeated in boys' stories before creeping feminism enforced a change. If the film is known today at all, it is probably for its climax, which depicts hundreds of boys from all over London converging on a handful of unfortunate petty criminals. In keeping with Ealing's tendency in the last years of the war to foster inclusive images of British society, the children are mostly working-class, and include, in the interests of the unity of the British Isles, a young Scottish boy. Scottish stories and characters regularly appear in Ealing comedies – one only has to think of *Whisky Galore* and *The Maggie*, although one can safely ignore *Scott of the Antarctic*. The social demographic of *Hue and Cry* was fundamental to the ethic of Ealing Studios and the success of their films indicates that the philosophy was shared by their audiences. Nevertheless, what one retains after a viewing of *Hue and Cry*, apart from the pleasure of a rattling good yarn, is an appreciation of the physical devastation unleashed on London and other major cities by the Luftwaffe.

Christopher Isherwood was visiting from his home in

America at the time and his comments, as quoted by David Kynaston in *Austerity Britain*, paint a similar portrait:

> Plaster was peeling from even the most fashionable squares and crescents... In the Reform Club, the wallpaper was hanging down in tatters. The walls of the National Gallery showed big, unfaded rectangles, where pictures had been removed and not yet re-hung. Many once stylish restaurants were now reduced to squalor... London remembered its past and was ashamed of its current appearance.

It wasn't just the cities that were so badly affected. The entire country might not have been bombed but the impact of drabness and greyness was ubiquitous. Fay Weldon arrived in Britain as a fifteen-year-old from New Zealand in 1946 and wrote poignantly over half a century later of her bitter disappointment at the first sighting of the Mother Country which was not the iconic white cliffs of Dover but the somewhat less iconic grey docks of Tilbury at dawn:

> Where were the green fields, rippling brooks and church towers? Could this be the land of Strawberry Fair and sweet nightingales? Here was a grey harbour and a grey hillside, shrouded in a kind of murky badly woven cloth which, as the day grew brighter, proved to be a mass of tiny, dirty houses pressed up against one another, with holes gaping where bombs had fallen, as ragged as holes in the heels of lisle stockings. I could not believe that people actually chose to live like this. The greyness was so vast, as far as the eye could reach.

There is no doubt that it was widely believed that the sooner football and cricket resumed a full programme of

competitive action the better it would be for the country.
That general belief notwithstanding, the Football League
decided to postpone restarting its competition until the
autumn of 1946 but the FA agreed to reintroduce the FA
Cup in 1945–6, although for this one season it was played
in an unfamiliar format of two-legged ties throughout the
competition. It was won by Derby County and, as in 1933
and 1934, the losing side, this time Charlton Athletic,
returned to Wembley the following year and won. That following season of 1946–7 saw not only the start of a proper
full Football League fixture list but also the resumption of
international matches, and in the first one, which was played
at Windsor Park, Belfast, Billy Wright made his England
debut at right-half. Apart from Tommy Lawton and Raich
Carter, everyone on that England team was making his full
international debut, although some of them, including Frank
Swift and Laurie Scott, had made appearances in wartime
internationals.

Unlike established players like Scott, Wilf Mannion and
Stan Cullis who lost six years of their international careers to
the war, Wright was just fifteen and had only been on the
Wolves ground staff for a year when war had broken out. It
was later discovered that, possibly because of the rationing
which tried hard to dole out 'fair shares for all', the health of
the nation actually improved during the war and certainly
Wright's future career benefited from his time as a physical
training instructor. He was initially assigned to work in a tyre
factory but preferred to be 'lost at sea' than stay there so he
applied to the Royal Navy but, as was the way with so many
young men who preferred the navy to the hard slog of the
army, he was sent to the army's Infantry Training Centre at
Aldershot. He emerged as Sergeant W. A. Wright of the
Shropshire Light Infantry in the peak of physical fitness, which

left him well placed to begin his full-time professional football career with some advantages.

Men who knew Billy Wright in the early part of his career tended to say the same things about him – that he was a shy boy, initially underweight, cheerful, polite and respectful, but above all he conveyed a bubbling enthusiasm for the game and never gave less than his best. He was well behaved, a good listener and eager to learn. There are elements of the young David Beckham in this description of Wright, although it is entirely possible that every young apprentice, desperate to make good in the game, would exhibit those qualities and not all of them would go on to captain England. He was never regarded as an outstandingly skilful player but his wholehearted commitment was noted by other players. It was this quality that persuaded both Stan Cullis and Walter Winterbottom to mark him out as a future captain for Wolves and England.

It wasn't just the outbreak of war that nearly aborted Wright's embryonic playing career. Within a few months of his joining the ground staff at the start of pre-season training in July 1938, the Wolves manager, Major Frank Buckley, had told him that he was simply too short and slight ever to make it as a professional in such a physical game. Fortunately, the Major was convinced by the trainer, Jack Davies, that Wright was big where it mattered – in the heart. He rescinded the decision and set him up in digs 'in a real home at Tettenhall and with a real family'. 'Mr and Mrs Arthur Colley became like a second mum and dad to me,' wrote Wright in one of his many autobiographies. He remained in these lodgings until he met Joy Beverley when he was in his early thirties and his term as captain of England was nearly at an end. The influence of the landlady was all-pervasive in a country short of housing and in a society which did not permit young people much domestic autonomy prior to marriage.

One advantage of his wartime posting as a PT instructor was that Wright could continue to play for Wolves in the rudimentary ad hoc football programme that was set up to give a deprived population some sense of sporting pleasure. However, in a 1942 League Cup semi-final against West Bromwich Albion, Wright hobbled off the field with a painful ankle injury. An X-ray the following day revealed a bad fracture and the diagnosis was that Wright's career as a professional footballer was over at the age of eighteen. Fortunately, surgeons had recently developed the technique of inserting a pin into the broken bone to hold it together and Wright was the recipient of an innovative piece of surgery that allowed him to continue to play. It is likely that this incident, which so nearly ended his career before it had properly begun, was sufficiently traumatic to convince Wright that he needed to give the game his total and undivided attention.

He went dancing in the evenings as many young men did because that was the obvious way to meet girls. Billy had been told that he needed to improve his balance as a player and that dancing would be a good way to do it so he went to the Palais de Danse less for romantic reasons than to take part in a late-night training session. Even so he would stick to orange juice and be back home and tucked up in bed – alone – by 10.30 p.m. Billy's behaviour may sound almost priggish to twenty-first-century ears, but it was not uncommon in young people in the early post-war era. Marriage was the only socially respectable context for sex. During the war years, when nobody knew what the next day might bring, moral strictures had eased: young people were not prepared to die in battle – or in the rubble caused by a German bomb – without having experienced the mysteries and ecstasies of sex. With the advent of peace, however, pre-war social norms soon reimposed themselves.

It was not uncommon for Billy to go out with Mrs Colley for an evening together at the pictures, rumours of which today would send tabloid hacks and photographers crazy with excitement. But Mrs Colley, particularly after Billy's own mother died of cancer when she was still in her early forties, maintained a strongly maternal watch over her young lodger. Girls might have come calling but few got past the doorstep of the Colley house in Tettenhall. Mrs Colley would certainly have approved when Wright decided to follow the advice of a Wolves director, Arthur Oakley (who was also a vice-president of the Football League), and study English and engineering (a rather eccentric combination, one can't help observing) at a daytime educational institute after morning training. Wright was conscious that he had left school at fourteen and was anxious to catch up on the education he had missed. It chimed

well with the sense, common to so many men at the conclusion
of the war, that they had to make the best of whatever opportunities came their way. Without wishing to impugn Wright's
motives in any way, it cannot but have helped his desire to be
noticed by the England selectors. In the weird, amateurish way
in which England teams were selected before Alf Ramsey
assumed complete control on taking over the manager's job at
the end of 1962, having a man like Arthur Oakley mention to
the people who mattered that this young chap Wright seemed
to be made of the right stuff couldn't possibly have harmed his
cause. By this time of course his football had improved rapidly,
partly due to the fitness which came as a consequence of his
wartime duties as a physical training instructor.

Just as cricket had eased itself back into its stride in the
summer of 1945 with those Victory Tests against the Australian
Service XI, so football did something similar during that rather
odd first winter of peace. Billy Wright was first picked to play
for England as an inside-left, partnering his club-mate Jimmy
Mullen in a Victory international against Belgium in January
1946 but Frank Soo failed a late fitness test and Billy took his
place as right-half, the position he then retained for the next
eight years or so. The Arsenal left-half Joe Mercer was the
England captain that day and the manner in which his half-back
partner calmed the nerves of the debutant made a big impression on the future England captain. Over the eleven years of his
own captaincy Wright was to replicate those words and the
concern many times. England won the match 2–0. When full
internationals resumed with a match against Northern Ireland
in front of an enthusiastic crowd of 57,000 at Windsor Park on
30 September 1946, Wright was in a new half-back line which
also included Neil Franklin of Stoke City and Henry Cockburn
of Manchester United. There was also a new captain, George
Hardwick, Ronald Colman lookalike and Middlesbrough

left-back, who was to remain as captain for the next twelve matches until a knee injury caused his retirement from international football. Hardwick had the interesting record of playing all of his thirteen international matches as captain.

The match against Northern Ireland ended in a thumping 7–2 win, a highly satisfactory start for the Football Association and their new 'manager' Walter Winterbottom. The partnership between Wright and Winterbottom, like the subsequent one between Bobby Moore and Alf Ramsey, was to be the fulcrum of the England team for more than ten years. Moore and Ramsey worked well together without doubt and there was considerable professional respect between them, but it would be fair to say that there was also a certain amount of personal disengagement. Ramsey had been a professional footballer who retired just before Moore made his debut for West Ham United so the two men knew enough about each other for a certain amount of familiarity to breed a little contempt. Winterbottom had played briefly as a half-back for a not very good Manchester United side in 1936–7, but in the following season he made only four first-team appearances and his playing career was ended by a spinal disease. Fortunately for his future career prospects, Winterbottom had also been training as a teacher. After graduating from Carnegie College of Physical Education in Leeds, he became a lecturer there.

Billy Wright was immediately impressed by the new man charged with the destiny of the England football team. He later 'wrote': 'It is difficult at first glance to imagine Mr Walter Winterbottom as chief FA coach and manager of England's International team. Walter has the look of a schoolmaster – as indeed he used to be – but as he sucks his beloved pipe he could easily be mistaken for a deep-thinking atom scientist.'

It is reading claptrap like this, even if the claptrap is understandable in the context of the time, that makes entirely credible Brian Glanville's story of overhearing Arthur Rowe, the manager of Tottenham's 'push-and-run' Championship side of 1951, remarking, 'Billy Wright? Right nana.' In fact, as a judgement on Wright as a player or captain that would be unfair and inaccurate. Rowe was almost certainly referring to Wright's brief but calamitous spell as manager of Arsenal. Nevertheless, Rowe's words also evince a contempt for Wright's instinctive deference to authority. There is no doubt that the pipe-clenching, cerebral Winterbottom would have been regarded by Wright when he was a player and a captain as a man to whom he would be expected to listen most attentively and with appropriate respect. After saluting. Winterbottom had 'a good war', reaching the rank of wing commander in the RAF and working at the Air Ministry with overall responsibility for training PE instructors at home and overseas. He also ran coaching courses for the FA at grammar schools in London. In 1946, Stanley Rous, who was the secretary of the Football Association, persuaded the FA council to appoint Winterbottom as the FA's first Director of Coaching and suggested he take on the additional responsibility of being the first England team manager. They were of course two distinctly separate jobs, but in the FA's convoluted way of thinking it was assumed that because Winterbottom might be good at one he was also the right man for the other. He was a serious, rather scholarly, bespectacled man who might have played Barnes Wallis in *The Dam Busters* if the producers hadn't cast Michael Redgrave, but it was as a thoughtful Director of Coaching that Winterbottom made his biggest contribution, mostly because he didn't have an ignorant, self-important, self-interested selection committee looking over his shoulder all the time. Winterbottom set up the network of coaching schools which eventually gave coaching opportunities and inspiration to, among others, Ron Greenwood, Dave Sexton, Don Howe, Bobby Robson and Malcolm Allison.

Winterbottom had first met Stanley Rous on an experimental coaching course in 1937 and the two men had warmed to each other immediately. Rous was the third member of the triumvirate that ran the England football team in the Wright era but he was the man who wielded the real power. It was rather like the famous *Frost Report* sketch in which John Cleese, Ronnie Barker and Ronnie Corbett, standing in descending order of height, delineated the British class structure. Winterbottom looked up to Rous because he had 'innate breeding' and Rous was his employer, but looked down on Wright because – although he was popular – he was only a player and had no education. Wright looked up to both of them, giving him a crick in his neck. Rous, meanwhile, looked down on both Winterbottom and Wright. He had fought in the First World War, had been a games master at Watford Grammar School and then become a referee, taking charge of the 1934 Cup Final. Brian Glanville, doyen of British football writers and accomplished novelist, knew him well.

> Stanley Rous was a magnificent administrator, very honest, highly ambitious and a dreadful snob. He wasn't even remotely interested in the troops on the ground. He ignored me for years, pretended he didn't know who I was, but as soon as I wrote *Along the Arno* which was published in 1956 and got rave reviews he completely changed and he started buying copies and giving them to all his friends. Suddenly it was, 'God bless you, dear boy'. You had to do something significant outside football before Stanley gave you any credit.

Billy Wright's face fitted perfectly in the hierarchy of Rous, Winterbottom and the captain. Paul Fox, the BBC executive who introduced Wright to the world of television,

noted the instinctively deferential attitude Wright displayed to them:

> Billy represented the best of football – he was good-looking and modest, a good honest decent footballer who respected his elders and who said yes sir, no sir and three bags full, sir. Billy knew that Walter was the boss and that he had a boss, Stanley Rous or the chairman of the FA so he knew his place in the pecking order.

If Winterbottom was the uncomplaining, put-upon civil servant and Wright the eternal schoolboy enthusiast and hero, then Rous was happy for them to become the public face of the England football team. He knew where the real power lay, because he himself wielded it – and for thirty years he never relinquished his firm grip on it.

England's results in that 1946–7 season seemed to bear all the comforting hallmarks of pre-war, self-congratulatory dominance. Wales were defeated 3–0, Holland went to Leeds Road, Huddersfield, and were overwhelmed 8–2 and at the end of the season France were well beaten 3–0 in a match played at Highbury. The post-season tour in May 1947 started off badly with a 1–0 defeat in Switzerland but it had the merit of persuading the myopic selection committee that it might be a good idea if they played both Stanley Matthews and Tom Finney, two of the best players in the world, in the same side in the same match. A week later in Lisbon, a rampant England with a mouth-watering forward line of Matthews, Mortensen, Lawton, Mannion and Finney humiliated Portugal by ten goals to nil, Mortensen and Lawton scoring four goals each. England's demolition of Portugal came at the start of what was to be a blissful summer: on the cricket field Denis Compton and Bill Edrich each scored over 3,000 runs, it seemed as if the sun was always shining and, briefly, the travails of the economy and the recent passing of the coldest winter in living memory, exacerbated by the lack of fuel for heating, were laid to rest. There was no television to beam England's outstanding display in Lisbon back into British living rooms; the best that supporters could hope for was a few minutes on a newsreel that might be seen at the start of the following month in the cinema, but there was no disguising the pride that the country took from the 10–0 scoreline. Whatever the social and economic problems that afflicted the nation, it appeared that there was still an England football team of which to be proud.

Two weeks before the triumph in Lisbon, an ostensibly even more symbolic victory took place at Hampden Park in Glasgow, when a Great Britain XI overwhelmed the Rest of Europe by six goals to one. In 1946, the first post-war FIFA Congress welcomed back the four UK football associations after an absence of almost twenty years, following negotiations between the FIFA president Jules Rimet and his future successors, Arthur Drewry and Sir Stanley Rous. To help celebrate this momentous occasion, a match between a British team and one from the rest of Europe was arranged for the following year. Hard as it might be to appreciate with our jaundiced 2016 knowledge, one of the reasons that FIFA was so keen on the idea was that the organisation was financially embarrassed owing to the lack of competitive action during the Second World War. It was thought that the match might generate some desperately needed revenue. As a gesture of goodwill it was decided that the gate receipts from the game would be donated to FIFA. There is some dispute as to the official attendance which, though large, was not as large as the 135,000 who regularly crammed the terraces of Hampden for the far more serious clash with England. However, FIFA pronounced itself delighted with the £35,000 it pocketed from the match.

If Winterbottom was powerless to prevent the regular selec-
tion of the England team from turning into a political contest,
on this occasion he clearly had no choice but to let the four
associations get on with the job of choosing his team for him.
It seemed inevitable that the team would include the two
Derby County inside-forwards who had helped to win the FA
Cup in 1946 – the Englishman Raich Carter and the incompa-
rable Irishman Peter Doherty. In the event, neither was chosen.
The final selection contained five Englishmen, Swift, Hardwick,
Matthews, Lawton and Mannion, all of whom were to feature
in Lisbon a fortnight later; three Scotsmen in Billy Liddell,
Archie Macaulay and the uncapped Billy Steel from Greenock
Morton; two Welshmen, Tottenham's fierce left-half Ron
Burgess and the Wales captain Billy Hughes; and finally, in
what must have been a political compromise, the Belfast-born
Irish centre-half Jackie Vernon who was playing for West
Bromwich Albion. Wright could not have complained about
being left out of such a team but Neil Franklin, the skilful and
widely admired Stoke and England centre-half, would have
had reasonable cause to curse the political manoeuvrings.

The continentals had held a practice game, beating Holland
2–0 in front of 70,000 spectators in Rotterdam, before their
Austrian coach Karl Rappan selected his squad and retreated
to a training camp in Troon on the Ayrshire coast. Rappan's
team eventually comprised nine different nationalities, including the Republic of Ireland's Johnny Carey, but although a big
crowd turned up at Hampden on the day, the atmosphere
reflected the game's exhibition status and bore little resemblance to the cauldron of vitriol in which Scotland v. England
matches were usually contested. It must have been strange and
somewhat disconcerting for the Scots to look down on to their
home pitch and find themselves expected to cheer for Stanley
Matthews and Tommy Lawton whom they had traditionally

abused. At least Great Britain were playing in dark blue, a hue
not too distant from Scotland's traditional shirt colour.

The Rest of Europe, who played in light blue (no doubt as
a tribute to FIFA's long-standing interest in the Boat Race)
contained some fine players but very few of the names would
have made an impact on the home spectators. They came from
abroad and their names sounded funny. They weren't visible
on satellite television and none of them, of course, played for
British clubs but, despite being handicapped by the fact that
they were both foreign and unknown, the Rest of Europe side
started the stronger and dominated the opening stages. An
opening goal by Wilf Mannion, who was the star player on the
day, was quickly equalised by the Swede Gunnar Nordahl. The
game was eventually won and lost, however, during a remarkable four-minute period in the first half when Britain scored
three times, including one from the penalty spot following a
bizarre handball from Josef Ludl, the Sparta Prague striker,
who dived full-length into the box, hand outstretched, to stop
a Matthews pass. Now this, the crowd must have nodded
sagely, was the sort of thing foreigners did or at least the sort
of thing they did when they had been mesmerised by the
Matthews magic. With the match effectively won by half-time,
the British side eased off in the second half, although eight
minutes from time the crowd was treated to a final goal by
Tommy Lawton who rose in his inimitable style to head a
Matthews cross powerfully past the France goalkeeper, Julien
Da Rui, and give Great Britain a crushing 6–1 victory.

The *Daily Telegraph* patriotically declared that Great
Britain had given their opponents a 'lesson in football' and
'outplayed the cream of Europe', while Pathé News loudly
proclaimed the well-known fact that 'British soccer is still the
world's best'. The football correspondent of the *Glasgow
Herald*, however, offered a more cautious tone and felt the

hosts had been flattered by the result, which owed much to the enterprise of Mannion and Steel up front rather than to any tactical or skilful superiority. Indeed, it was the quality of the finishing that was the real difference between the two sides, with Gunnar Nordahl in particular guilty of wasting three good early opportunities to put the visitors ahead with only Frank Swift to beat.

If FIFA took £35,000 from the match, the British public took something much more significant and possibly dangerous – a reinforced conviction that British was best. The overwhelming scoreline certainly suggested that British football had effortlessly reinforced its natural superiority, given the fact that much of that superiority was based on the idea that what happened when England travelled abroad did not count. They had to deal with foreign weather and foreign food and if Johnny Foreigner did by some underhand means manage to win the match it would all be reversed when the foreigners saw the white cliffs of Dover and tasted six inches of British steel – or alternatively tasted a full English breakfast in the era of rationing which would have left them gasping, feeling both full and hungry at the same time as wanting to revisit whatever had been mistaken for bacon and eggs which had known neither pig nor fowl.

At the end of the 1947–8 season, following regulation victories over Scotland, Sweden, Belgium and Wales, came what was long regarded as the most impressive result of England's post-war renaissance – 4–0 against Italy in Turin in May 1948. It was a scoreline that slightly flattered England because it required some heroic goalkeeping from Frank Swift to keep a clean sheet against wave after wave of attacks from the Italians, who had won the last World Cup to be played, in 1938. Their team included six of the gifted Torino side which was to be decimated in the Superga air disaster the following year. The

Italian captain, Valentino Mazzola, was one of those to die and in a tragic coincidence the England captain on the day, Frank Swift, was to suffer an identical fate nine years later when a plane carrying the Manchester United team crashed at Munich.

Perhaps the England players felt that the fates owed them something because all of them were disconcerted by the visible economic prosperity which they could not help but contrast with what they had just left behind in England. Wright's recollections of the match begin with yet another ritual grovelling before the omniscient FA:

> With typical Football Association thoroughness it had been decided that the players should prepare for the match against Italy at the delightful resort of Stresa, which nestles on the shores of Lake Maggiore, and a motor coach was waiting to take us from the airport through the Italian countryside to what would be our headquarters for 'Operation Victory'. Italy was certainly an eye-opener for us! After years of austerity at home we were struck by the atmosphere of prosperity as we slowly drove through the streets of Milan. The men and women appeared well dressed and the shops looked better stocked than those we had left behind in England... at first sight Italy appeared to be a land of plenty. With a charm so typical of the man, Vittorio Pozzo, the grey-haired Italian journalist and still sole selector and team manager of the Italian national side, had a small sack of rice for every member of the England party. It may sound an odd gift, but at the time rice was as precious as gold dust at home.

By 1948 it was reported that Hiroshima, utterly devastated by the atomic bomb which had been dropped in August 1945, was already 85 per cent rebuilt. The British people had demonstrated clearly enough their willingness to make do and mend if the government was doling out the rations on a 'fair shares for all' basis, but it disturbed them mightily to see that the countries that had lost the war and killed many British soldiers while doing so, appeared to be enjoying the fruits of peace much more quickly than the British, for whom rationing was now more stringent than it had been in wartime. The national mood of grumbling that was to overturn the big Labour majority that had been acquired in the 1945 election was clearly already entrenched. Wright's observation, although phrased in the positive, good-humoured spirit that the captain of England was supposed to convey in public at all times, nevertheless indicated some of the disillusion that had already set in back home.

Of course, Wright couldn't help observing that the Italians' obsession with style probably hadn't done them any favours on the field. He noted their skin-tight shirts, and shorts so short 'they would have raised eyebrows at Wembley', but more self-defeating was the fact that none of them were wearing any shin-pads. England players might have been wearing baggy shirts and shorts that would have raised eyebrows for different reasons on the New Look catwalk at Christian Dior's showroom but to an English defender like Henry Cockburn the sight of those unprotected Italian shins and calves was an open invitation to restage the Battle of Anzio. In this light the eventual 4–0 scoreline becomes a little more explicable.

The British public seemed to have good reason to exult in what appeared to be a golden era for English football. The quality of players such as Matthews, Finney, Lawton, Swift, Mortensen, Mannion, Wright and Franklin, and the consistency of their results – particularly those victories against Portugal and Italy (and not forgetting their contribution to the

triumph over the Rest of Europe) – all suggested that the following decade would be a good one for English sport and that
England would be at the centre of the international game.

In 1948, the British public welcomed, in keeping with the
age of austerity, the games of the Fourteenth Olympiad
to London. The 1944 summer Olympics had been allocated to
London but sadly most of the athletes were fighting on the
beaches and fields of Normandy at the time. In October 1945,
the chairman of the British Olympic Council, Lord Burghley
(immortalised in *Chariots of Fire* by Nigel Havers leaping over
hurdles topped with glasses filled with champagne), went to
Stockholm and saw the president of the International Olympic
Committee to discuss the question of London being chosen for
the first post-war Games. As a result, an investigating committee was set up by the British Olympic Council to work out in
some detail the possibility of holding the Games. After several
meetings it was agreed that London should apply for the allocation of the Games in 1948. In March 1946, the IOC, through
a postal vote, gave the summer Games to London ahead of its
rivals Baltimore, Minneapolis, Lausanne, Los Angeles and
Philadelphia.

After the initial pleasure of being awarded the Games had
worn off, the realities of hosting such a competition in the
social and economic conditions that prevailed in 1948 almost
caused Britain to hand them over to the USA but it appears
that King George was keen for the country to continue to act
as host. Certainly the official report of the London Olympics
shows that there was no case of London being forced to run
the Games against its will, so despite the shortages and restrictions London pressed on. In stark contrast to the Games of
2012, the Austerity Olympics was budgeted at £743,000 but
only cost £732,268. In 2016, that sum would pay Yaya Touré's
wages for less than three weeks.

No new venues were erected for the 1948 Games. An old, weed-infested velodrome in Herne Hill in south London was spruced up and made fit for the cycling competitions; basketball was found a home at the Harringay Arena; the shooting went to Bisley, the rowing to Henley, as expected, and the yachting was sent off to Torbay in Devon. No money was spent on an Olympic village to house the athletes. Male competitors stayed in military camps in Uxbridge, West Drayton and Richmond, while female competitors were housed in London colleges. Local athletes stayed at home and many commuted to the Games via public transport. As food and clothing rationing were still in force, competitors were encouraged to buy or make their own uniforms. Athletes were, however, provided with increased food rations, which amounted to around 5,500 calories a day instead of the normal 2,600. They were also provided with free (presumably clean at the outset) bed linen. Towels, however, were not provided and all athletes had to bring their own or borrow someone else's wet one. In the true spirit of the Games, which sadly has long since slipped away, many countries contributed to help increase provisions, with Denmark providing 160,000 eggs and the Dutch sending over a hundred tonnes of fruit.

The Games opened on Thursday 29 July, a hot and brilliantly sunny day. Army bands began playing at 2 p.m. for the 85,000 spectators in Wembley Stadium with their heads covered if not by hats then by what passed in those days for conventional beach headgear – handkerchiefs knotted at the four corners or carefully folded copies of the *Daily Mirror*. At 4 p.m., the time shown on Big Ben on the London Games symbol, King George VI, wearing naval uniform, declared the Games open. He was not parachuted into the stadium, as his daughter was to be sixty-four years later, and Aneurin Bevan's National Health Service, which had come into being just twenty-four days previously, remained unreferenced in an opening ceremony during which 2,500 pigeons were set free and the Olympic flag was raised to the top of its 35-foot (11m) flagpole at the end of the stadium.

To everyone's relief, the king managed to get through the briefest of opening remarks without a stammer before gratefully handing over to the Archbishop of York to give the dedication address. In those days nobody seems to have wondered if that might offend the Catholics, the Jews, the Muslims, the Hindus or the Buddhists in attendance. Indeed, the Games took place during Ramadan, but not one of the 228 Muslim athletes voiced an objection. Most people only saw what happened at Wembley Stadium that day on a newsreel in their local cinemas. What they tend to remember of the event is the entry into the stadium of the handsome, blond twenty-two-year-old John Mark from Surbiton, bearing the Olympic torch. Mark had recently competed in the quarter-mile event for Cambridge in the Varsity match. It had been rumoured in the days leading up to the opening ceremony that the torch might be carried by the Duke of Edinburgh on the grounds that he was both handsome and of Greek extraction. Fortunately, considering the language that might have been heard had the flame not lit on command, the honour went to the 6 foot 3 inch Mark who was training to become a doctor at St Mary's Hospital in Paddington.

What the crowd didn't know was that the previous runner with the torch, inspired by the densely packed cheering crowds, had run so quickly that he had arrived at the stadium five minutes too early. He and Mark had to sit in the dressing room with the torch while the order of ceremonies proceeded along its pre-arranged schedule. Four o'clock was the King's Speech, at 4.01 p.m. the flag would be raised, at 4.05 the pigeons would be released (presumably some way distant from the royal party) and at 4.07 Mark would enter the stadium with the flaming torch aloft – which is exactly what happened. Mark entered the stadium to the sound of rolling guns and excited acclaim from the sweltering spectators, held aloft the flaming torch, climbed the steps towards the cauldron, saluted the crowd and then turned and lit the Olympic flame. Any uncomfortable thoughts that might have flickered across people's minds that this was Britain's version of a celebration of Aryan supremacy were immediately extinguished when the massed bands of the Brigade of Guards struck up 'God Save the King', the national anthem was sung and all the athletes turned and marched out of the stadium, led by Greece and tailed by the hosts. The hot weather was a talking point for the first-time visitors to Britain who had been expecting rather cooler temperatures. Just south of Wembley, the heat created a crack in an aqueduct carrying the Grand Union Canal over the North Circular Road. Water cascaded over the edge, causing a major flood on the road below. On Monday 2 August, the heavens opened and the athletics heats had to be delayed as men with pitchforks went round the track pricking the ground to allow the water that had collected in large puddles to run away, but the competition soon restarted.

The hundred tonnes of fruit was not the only contribution made to the Games by the people of Holland. It was the Dutch athlete Fanny Blankers-Koen who proved to be the star of the competition. The thirty-year-old 'Flying Housewife' and mother, who had survived the traumas of Nazi occupation, won four gold medals in the 100m and 200m, 80m high hurdles and the 4x100m relay. Her extremely narrow victory over twenty-one-year-old Dorothy Manley, a shorthand typist for the Suez Canal Company from Woodford Green, in the 100m, was greeted most sportingly by the home crowd whose desire for a British gold medal was not clouded by jingoistic

myopia. Manley cried on the podium, not out of the frustration of defeat but out of the exhilaration and emotion of the
moment. When the winner returned home to a delighted
Netherlands, the people of her country honoured her with a
bottle of advocaat and a bicycle. History does not record
whether or not she attached a shopping basket to the front,
but either way it is a comforting reminder that the purpose of
competing and the reward for winning Olympic glory were
not always commercial contracts and endorsements worth
millions of dollars.

Although Leni Riefenstahl had provided the enduring
images of the 1936 Berlin Games with her remarkable film
Olympia, the London Olympics of 1948 were the first to be
transmitted on British television, as the BBC paid 1,000
guineas (£1,050) for the broadcasting rights. Television was
still regarded by the BBC as a very junior service compared
to BBC Radio, which had emerged with great distinction
from the war. When the television service reopened after the
war it was with a smaller budget than it had been awarded
in 1939. As a consequence, one of its 'major new series on the
BBC!' for the 1946–7 season, *How to Furnish a Flat*, had to
be cancelled – according to a programme planning committee report – 'owing to the unavailability of the furniture'.
Nevertheless, one of the dominant cultural strands of the
second half of the twentieth century was the increasing power
and influence of television. It will be seen in future chapters
how it was television which crucially affected both the way
sport has grown and the way in which it has been consumed
in this country.

Back in 1948, the Olympics certainly promised those who
would have been bitterly disappointed at the cancellation of
such a 'ground-breaking, BAFTA award-winning, iconic series'
(copyright BBC Publicity) as *How to Furnish a Flat* some form

of compensation in the shape of the Games of the XIV Olympiad. Of course, only those fortunate enough to afford a television and live within a twenty-five-mile radius of the transmission station at Alexandra Palace in north London could actually enjoy the spectacle. Nonetheless, this new medium helped to promote the Games in a way never seen before by the British public, as the spirit of the event captured the nation. It was just a different spirit and a different nation in 1948 from what it had become by 2012.

A total of 4,104 athletes were to take part from a record number of fifty-nine nations although only 385 of the competitors were women. This was in keeping with the tenor of the times. Even during the war, when women were everywhere encouraged to contribute to the war effort, their male employers were exhibiting some reservations. One official piece of advice to the latter included: 'Give every girl an adequate number of rest periods during the day. You have to make some allowance for feminine psychology. A girl has more confidence and is more efficient if she can keep her hair tidied, apply fresh lipstick and wash her hands several times a day.'

Possibly even in the middle of the 100m dash.

Even in the brave new world brought forth by the 1944 Education Act which theoretically provided equal facilities for boys and girls, many schools for girls rejected athletics, which it was thought might damage female internal organs. Women were therefore permitted to take part in only nine events which, oddly, included the shot putt but excluded the possibility of swimming further than four hundred metres. All equestrian, shooting and rowing events were also forbidden to potential women entrants.

The athletes of Germany and Japan were not invited for fairly obvious reasons, although German prisoners of war were involved in the make-do-and-mend activities that prepared the facilities. Indeed, photographs of the time show them putting the finishing touches to the old Empire Way leading from Wembley Park Tube station to the stadium. The road was later renamed Olympic Way even when the stadium was still called the Empire Stadium. The Soviet Union was invited but declined to send any athletes to compete, which was perhaps as well because the Allied Berlin airlift of much-needed supplies had started at the end of June in a response to the Russian attempt to blockade West Berlin. The first of what would become familiar Cold War standoffs was underway and the Olympic Games in particular and sport in general were integrally involved.

The Games ended on Saturday 14 August, the same day that the final Test match against Australia at The Oval started – and almost finished after England were bowled out just after lunch for fifty-two. The first innings only lasted that long because play had begun half an hour late. In the end, after the Australian opener Arthur Morris had made 196, a higher total than either of England's innings in the match, the final Test finished twenty minutes into the morning of the fourth day. Bradman's memorable two-ball duck and John Arlott's famous commentary on his last brief appearance at the crease were probably what most people remembered from this match, but the series as a whole had been a triumphant success.

English cricket benefited from the crowds and the financial returns, cricket supporters benefited from some superb cricket played by a very talented Australian side that included Lindwall, Miller, Johnston, Morris, Barnes and young Neil Harvey as well as the incomparable Bradman. Unfortunately, Bradman had won his battle of wills with Miller and, despite the widespread joy with which the Australians were greeted by crowds who were thrilled to watch cricket in the sun, Bradman's attitude ensured that in future the Ashes Tests reverted to the grim, attritional character that would scar them for years to come. There was just a chance in those post-war years that sport could become a torchbearer for the sort of society that visionaries like Miller dreamed about. It seems unfair to blame Don Bradman for the fact that that never happened: indeed, when he sailed away from the shores of Great Britain at the end of the 1948 tour, it was with loud hosannas ringing in his ears.

The distinguished lawyer Sir Norman Birkett, a much-admired after-dinner speaker in addition to his many other accomplishments, wrote later of the tour:

> The great crowds... gave utterance to their deep-seated satisfaction, after years of darkness and danger, that cricket had once more come into its kingdom in these great and historic encounters. For not the least of the deprivations of war is that the glory and grace of cricket depart... To see the Australian team emerging once more from the pavilion after the years of war was to be filled with thankfulness and pride and happiness, and not a little emotion.

The wider revision of that 1948 tour was still some years distant and, much as England yearned to regain the Ashes, when the Australian cricketers sailed home at the end of their nearly six-month-long tour they took with them the thanks of a grateful nation and left behind the warmest of memories as well as a sober realisation that English sport was essentially in the doldrums. Their cricketers had been predictably walloped down under in 1946–7, but a team containing Hutton, Washbrook, Edrich, Compton, Evans, Bedser and Laker had been no match for the Australians in home conditions and until a new generation of players emerged (as it would with May, Cowdrey, Tyson, Statham, Trueman, Wardle and Lock) there was little prospect of the Ashes coming home – although, of course, by tradition the Ashes never leave the hallowed precincts of Lord's.

The football team which we had left at a seeming peak of glory after demolishing Italy in Turin was starting to show disturbing signs of fallibility. On the occasion of the receipt of Billy Wright's infamous ham, England had only managed a scoreless draw with Denmark and even that result seemed in danger in the eighty-ninth minute when the Danish outside-right Johan Ploeger appeared to have scored the winning goal, only to see his effort ruled (somewhat dubiously) offside. The Danes were all amateurs who had finished third in the Olympic Games in London six weeks previously. Indeed, this was their first match against professional opposition. It was as if England had been held to a draw by the Isthmian League amateurs of Walthamstow Avenue. Goalkeeper Frank Swift, after captaining his country for the second time, admitted that standing on the goal line was no position from which to do the job properly and he duly resigned. Billy Wright, who had already been the captain of Wolverhampton Wanderers for over twelve months, was appointed in his stead in the haphazard but endearingly bumbling manner described at the start of the book.

Wright saw his job as captain quite clearly:

The captain of a football team is first and foremost the 'foreman' of the side on the field. His team-mates may often turn to him for guidance and the captain should always be ready to give it. In fact, one needs to be father, mother, friend and team-mate all rolled into one. There has been considerable criticism of my captaincy because I do not make a habit of shouting at players on the field... I appreciate that if there is one thing a player dislikes more than anything else it is to be shown up in front of thousands of spectators... My decision was to encourage my players quietly and above all else to try and set them an example. I have never regretted it... I feel the best way a skipper can inspire his team is to roll up his sleeves and by personal effort set an example the rest of the side can follow.

Wright surprisingly indicated that he did much more than exchange pennants and spin the coin at the start of the match when he revealed two dramatic substitutions he made on the field without reference to Walter Winterbottom. During the match against Scotland at Wembley in 1951, Wilf Mannion was carried off with a fractured cheekbone after only eleven minutes. Indeed, so badly was he injured that he had to be taken to hospital, accompanied by Winterbottom. Rather oddly, it appears from Wright's account that the manager left no instructions for how England should play with the ten men remaining. Left to his own devices as captain, Wright transferred Tom Finney from the left wing to play at inside-right in order to continue the supply of passes to the potential match-winner Stanley Matthews at outside-right, leaving debutant Harold Hassall of Huddersfield Town to look after the left-hand side of the forward line by himself. It did little good as Scotland ran out 3–2 winners and Wright himself gave, by his own estimation, his worst ever performance in an England shirt.

Initially, however, it appeared as if Wright's captaincy methods would be effective. Although Wolverhampton didn't win either the league or the Cup in 1946–7, his first season as captain, they competed successfully and it was clear that Wolves would be a force in post-war domestic football. In international terms, his captaincy could not have started more promisingly. Normal public service was resumed in October 1948 when, in Wright's first match as captain, England beat Ireland at Windsor Park 6–2 with a hat-trick by Mortensen and a rare goal by Matthews from a centre which curled against the far post and cannoned into the net off the head of the surprised Irish goalkeeper. Wales were then beaten 1–0 and Switzerland were demolished at Highbury 6–0 before Scotland came to Wembley in November and won 3–1 to clinch the 1948–9 Home Championship. It looked like the traditional England – Swift and Wright, Franklin and Cockburn, Matthews and Finney, Mortensen and Milburn – but the Scots were rampant and, of course, as noted previously, they won at Wembley on their next visit in 1951 after Wright's attempt to repair the damage to the team caused by Wilf Mannion's fractured cheekbone.

Scotland would make a habit of spoiling an England party, but losing to Scotland in the Home Championship was not to be compared with losing to a genuinely foreign side on home soil and so far England had never suffered that indignity. Sweden, who had left Highbury with their tails between their legs after a 4–2 defeat at the start of the 1947–8 season, took their revenge eighteen months later in a 3–1 win in Stockholm and looked much more like the side that had won the gold medal at the London Olympics. Their innovative coach was the Englishman George Raynor whose mercurial career saw him coach Sweden to the 1958 World Cup Final but, bizarrely, start the following domestic season as the manager of Skegness Town. He returned to manage Sweden for the third time in 1961 and finished his managerial career being sacked by Doncaster Rovers. It was Raynor who, having secured a 2–2 draw with his Sweden side against the rampant Hungarians in November 1953, just days before Hungary were due to play England at Wembley, told someone at the English FA that the way to deal with the deep-lying Hungarian centre-forward Nándor Hidegkuti was to depute a man to mark him all over the pitch. The advice was, of course, ignored as if it had also come with the suggestion that Stanley Matthews should be the player to do it.

By the end of the 1940s England's football was starting to stagnate. The great pre-war players – Swift, Lawton, Mercer, Carter and Cullis – had either retired or were on the verge of doing so. Matthews, Finney, Milburn and Mortensen certainly had some of their best days ahead of them but, had the FA been able to see it, European countries who were also struggling to recover from the effects of the war were making significant progress because their administration was not as hidebound as it was in England. Disillusion with bureaucracy was ubiquitous in the Britain of the late 1940s. The persistence of rationing long after the war had finished made the Labour government of Clement Attlee extremely unpopular. The infiltration of government into every area of public life had negative as well as positive consequences.

The social and political conditions that prevailed in Britain at the end of the 1940s were satirised to memorable effect in 1949 in perhaps the finest of the classic comedies produced by Ealing Studios in the immediate post-war period. *Passport to Pimlico*, although undoubtedly making reference to the contemporary Berlin blockade, was essentially a very English story about a district in London which discovers that it is actually not part of the area governed by the LCC but belongs to the medieval state of Burgundy. When children inadvertently set off a bomb left over from the war, the explosion reveals a buried cellar containing artwork, coins, jewellery and an ancient document written on parchment. Margaret Rutherford plays the expert historian Professor Hatton-Jones who authenticates it as a genuine document, a royal charter from the time of Edward IV that ceded the house and its estates to the last Duke of Burgundy when he sought refuge there during the time of the Wars of the Roses. The new Burgundians realise, to their delight, that the British government no longer has any legal jurisdiction over them and that Pimlico is therefore not subject to rationing and other bureaucratic restrictions.

Their delight, however, is quickly tempered as the district is instantly flooded with entrepreneurs, crooks and eager shoppers. A noisy free-for-all ensues, which the old-fashioned neighbourhood PC – now the Chief Constable of Burgundy – finds himself unable to handle. Then the British authorities close the 'border' with barbed wire. Having left England without their passports, the bargain hunters have trouble returning home – as one policeman replies to an indignant woman, 'Don't blame *me*, Madam, if you choose to go abroad to do your shopping', a line that would have sounded comically absurd in 1949, before the era of the booze-cruise and cross-Channel shopping trip.

The Burgundians decide that two can play at this game and stop an underground train dead in its tracks. 'The train is now at the Burgundy frontier,' explains the oleaginous Raymond Huntley, an agent of the newly formed Customs and Excise department who asks the bewildered passengers on the District and Circle Line if they have anything to declare. The infuriated British government retaliates by blockading Burgundy (just as the Soviets were doing to the Western sectors of Berlin in 1948) and the residents are invited to 'emigrate' to England. But the Burgundians are 'a fighting people' and, though the children are evacuated, the adults stand fast. In one of screenwriter T. E. B. Clarke's most felicitous speeches, Mrs Pemberton (Betty Warren), married to Arthur (Stanley Holloway), sticks her head out of the window to berate a neighbour who is thinking of giving up the fight, 'Don't you come that stuff, Jim

Garland. We've always *been* English and we'll always *be* English; and it's precisely because we *are* English that we're sticking up for our right to be Burgundians!'

Pimlico is now deprived of electricity, food and water, which, for film-goers, would have carried an uncomfortable whiff of the real-life austerity of the government of Clement Attlee. Inevitably, the common sense and 'Dunkirk spirit' of the British comes to the rescue and ordinary, kind-hearted people begin throwing food parcels across the barrier in an improvised 'airlift', echoing the one that ended the Berlin blockade. A helicopter drops a hose to deliver milk and pigs are parachuted in. The government comes under public pressure to resolve the problem and, in the end, Pimlico returns to British rule, having loaned the British government the proceeds of the buried treasure unearthed by the bomb. All ends happily but with the street party, arranged to celebrate the end of Burgundian rule in Pimlico, spoiled by a torrential downpour.

Passport to Pimlico is a delightful film, still fresh and funny today, painting a bold portrait of a vanished London, much as *Hue and Cry* did. Underlying the comedy, however, is a sense of boiling frustration at the petty restrictions of life in Britain in 1949. These restrictions were as much a feature of the lives of footballers as they were of the rest of the population. The maximum wage had its merits – no player would leave a small-town club for a big-city club for an extra pound note in the wage packet. It kept Finney at Preston and Matthews at Stoke and Blackpool for the duration of their careers. Such democratic niceties proved insufficiently robust for Charlie Mitten at Manchester United and Neil Franklin at Stoke City when Bogotá came calling. The Colombia Football Association had been expelled from FIFA for doing exactly what Chelsea, Manchester City and the rest of the Premier

League have been doing for years – crawling the kerbs of
the football world and waving large wads of cash out of the
driver's window.

In 1950, the maximum wage would have been £12 a week
during the season for a professional footballer in England.
Neil Franklin, England's skilful ball-playing centre-half, was
offered by the Santa Fe club a £2,000 signing-on fee and £60
a week in wages along with a 'villa' (rarely a house) and a
motor car. During his last match for England in front of the
traditional 135,000 at Hampden Park, he was heard to observe
bitterly in reference to the marching band that left the pitch as
the players entered the arena, 'Look at that lot. They're all on
bigger money than us.' No wonder the financial incentives
dangled by Bogotá were so inviting. It was money Franklin
could never have expected to earn had he continued his career
in England so he seized it eagerly, as did the Manchester United
outside-left Charlie Mitten, who was on just £10 a week. But
perhaps neither Franklin nor Mitten appreciated the extent of
the vindictiveness they would face from their clubs and the
football authorities.

Franklin had applied for a transfer from Stoke City and
had been kept waiting for three hours by the club's directors
before they would even allow him into the boardroom to
discuss it. Around the same time Danny Blanchflower was
transferred from Barnsley to Aston Villa for £15,000. He was
told to sit in the kitchen of a Barnsley hotel with a cup of tea
as the chairmen of the two clubs haggled over his price as if he
were a piece of meat. His sole demand was that the training
during the week at Villa included the use of a football because
he never saw one at Barnsley until Saturday afternoon. Nobody
in football was therefore surprised that Neil Franklin felt
attracted by the bait held out to him from Bogotá. They were
just surprised when he decided to take it.

Inevitably perhaps, in neither case did their time in South America pan out in quite the way the players had anticipated. The life, even in the sunshine, was so foreign that neither family settled and within months they decided to return – like the Burgundians of *Passport to Pimlico* – to the whips and scorn of life in Austerity Britain. In South America, Franklin and his homesick wife lasted just six games; Mitten made it through the season but eventually they both had to face the wrath of the men who felt they had betrayed their birthright. There was no mercy shown, even by their managers Bob McGrory and Matt Busby, who had been impoverished players in Scotland and England and knew precisely what a life of financial hardship professional football could entail. Franklin was suspended indefinitely by Stoke, but after six months he was sold to Second Division Hull City. He never regained his England place and faded into obscurity via spells at Crewe Alexandra, Stockport County and Macclesfield Town. As for Mitten, he was banned for six months by the FA, who also fined him six months' wages. As soon as he was available for selection for Manchester United again, Busby, who had ostracised him after his return, sold him to Fulham.

Franklin had fled Britain for the lotus land of Bogotá in a mysterious midnight flit that seemed to be the model for the flight to Moscow the following year of Burgess and Maclean. He announced that he would not be available to play in the World Cup in Brazil that summer because his wife was due to give birth. This was a surprising reason in an era when men were rarely present at the birth of their children, that sort of thing being regarded as 'women's business'. All became clear, of course, when Franklin emerged blinking in the sunlight of Bogotá. Without him, the England football team struggled to find a replacement centre-half for four years until a chapter of accidents led Billy Wright to move to that position himself.

With Franklin still in it, the national team won all its fixtures in the 1949–50 season, including a 9–2 thumping of a
hapless Northern Ireland, and England travelled to Brazil in
1950 for their World Cup debut in good spirits. Walter
Winterbottom, however, was not best pleased that his star
player, Stanley Matthews, was being sent by the FA on a goodwill tour of Canada just before the most important tournament
in world football was due to start on the other side of the
globe. The Blackpool winger arrived in Rio de Janeiro after
England had won their opening match against Chile 2–0, but
in time to play in their second group match against the United
States in Belo Horizonte on 29 June. The chairman of the
England selectors, the very same handsome Mr Arthur Drewry
who was so fulsomely praised by Billy Wright in the Prologue,
was in sole charge of selection for England in the 1950 World
Cup. By trade, he was a Grimsby fish merchant and, armed
with all the football knowledge that is traditionally associated with the fish business, he told both Winterbottom and the
agitated Stanley Rous that he never changed a winning team
and that Matthews would have to wait his turn. Mr Drewry
was to become president of FIFA from 1955 until his death in
1961. He served concurrently as the chairman of the Football
Association. He was a scrupulously honest man.

The general level of professionalism at the Football
Association can best be illustrated by the fact that nobody had
bothered to check the nature of the food that would be served
to players who were used to conventional English cuisine.
They were staying in the Luxor Hotel overlooking Copacabana
Beach and were expecting food in keeping with the Luxor's
luxurious reputation. Nobody in the England party would
clearly be particularly inconvenienced by badly cooked food
served in very small portions as that was basically what they
were used to back home, but what they were served up in

Brazil defeated the hardiest of English stomachs. The captain later wrote gulpingly:

> Breakfast for the continental, of course, is little more than coffee and rolls. But we all preferred our customary eggs and bacon, toast and marmalade and it was arranged on arrival in Rio that we should all have this meal in bed. The Brazilian notion of bacon and eggs, alas, didn't exactly tally with ours. I sat up eagerly in bed the next morning – to be faced with one of the most unappetising sights I've ever set eyes on. The eggs had been cooked in black oil (still clinging to the edges) and the bacon looked like ham of doubtful quality. Jimmy Dickinson was sharing a room with me and I'm afraid neither of us could even look at the meal, let alone eat it, without shuddering.

Legend has it that Mr Winterbottom endeared himself to his players by marching into the hotel kitchens and attempting to do the cooking for the team. In the unlikely event that this story is true, sadly it did nothing to offset the humiliation awaiting them in Belo Horizonte. Alf Ramsey was one of the players concerned and it must have significantly affected his decision in 1970 to be meticulous about food preparation when he was in charge of England's World Cup preparations for Mexico.

While the laziness and amateurishness of the FA's preparation was unforgivable, there were problems beyond even the FA's ability to control. The game against the United States was scheduled to be played in Belo Horizonte, three hundred miles inland from Rio. The coach ride from the airport to the team's base sixteen miles from Belo Horizonte involved negotiating 167 hairpin bends on a road that was barely clinging to the mountainside out of which it had been carved. The players were housed in a series of wooden huts in a miners' camp. The match itself was played on a cramped, narrow pitch pitted with tiny stones which negated England's strength down the wings. The stadium was still being built and the dressing rooms were so dirty that Winterbottom ordered his players back on the coach and the team changed in a sports club a ten-minute drive away. It was unsettling, undoubtedly, but no more so than when a First Division team was drawn to play a non-league side in the third round of the FA Cup.

That fount of footballing wisdom Mr Arthur Drewry may be excused a certain amount of overconfidence in his selection for the match against the United States. After all, England – who still believed they had the best team in the world, even if recent events had caused this judgement to be called into question occasionally – were playing a bunch of part-timers, boosted by three immigrants in Joe Maca from Belgium, the captain Ed McIlveney from Scotland (and former right-half for Wrexham) and the man who scored the goal heard around the world, Joe Gaetjens from Haiti. Gaetjens later returned to his native country and joined the resistance to the Haitian dictator François 'Papa Doc' Duvalier but was arrested and allegedly murdered by the 'Tonton Macoutes' – Duvalier's feared secret police – in prison; an unhappy end to a life that contained at least this one glorious moment. A hard cross was heading straight for the arms of the Wolves goalkeeper Bert Williams when Gaetjens tried to duck out of the way but the ball flicked off the top of his head and deflected into the net just inside the near post.

The Haitian's goal came eight minutes before half-time. It seemed highly unlikely to most observers that a forward line of Tom Finney, Wilf Mannion, Roy Bentley, Stan Mortensen and Jimmy Mullen would not, in the second half, simply change up into third gear, cruise past the inexperienced

defenders, equalise immediately and then help themselves to a hatful of goals. A relieved Stan Mortensen thought he had done exactly that when he turned a low cross into the net and trotted back towards the centre circle, only to see an American defender back-heel the ball out of the net, kick it clear and the referee wave both arms to indicate 'Play on!' This wasn't the end of Mortensen's interesting afternoon, as his captain later recalled:

Mortie raced on to a through-pass from Wilf Mannion. He evaded Charlie Colombo, America's centre half and was left only with the goalkeeper standing between him and glory. Mortensen, however, had not given a thought to the defenders behind him; come to that neither would I in similar circumstances. The Americans obviously did not relish the possibility of Stanley getting the equaliser. Racing up from behind, one of the American defenders threw himself full length to bring down Mortie with the

finest flying tackle ever seen outside Twickenham. The free
kick – as is so often the case – brought no reward.

Later, a Mortensen header from a Ramsey free-kick
appeared to have crossed the line but the referee disallowed
the goal. The American goalkeeper, Frank Borghi, had started
his sports career as a baseball catcher but abandoned it to
drive the hearse for his uncle's funeral parlour. In that second
half he was hit in the face three times by hard shots that
seemed destined for the back of the net. It defied belief when,
two minutes from the final whistle, he made a miraculous save
from an Alf Ramsey free-kick that seemed certain to bring
England a face-saving draw. Even that stoic, phlegmatic
Tottenham full-back permitted himself an expression of
despair in this moment. England had spent almost the entire
game camped in the American half of the field.

Of course the Americans had played bravely and far better
than anyone, including themselves, had expected. The England
forward line had created the dozens of chances that it was
expected to do – it was just that none of them were converted.
The match finished England 0 United States of America 1.
Over forty years later the *Sun* would headline another England
defeat by the same opponents YANKS 2 PLANKS 0, but that
was to be somewhat unfair to a country that was, by then,
making serious strides towards being a competitive international football team. In 1950, the press was hardly kind to
either the underachieving players or the manager but the cas-
tigation was better deserved. The only conceivable response to
this freakish result was the one constantly given by *Spitting
Image*'s Jimmy Greaves puppet – a bewildered look followed
by the platitude 'Funny old game!'

Despite the unfortunate events in Belo Horizonte,
England's defeat of Chile meant they could therefore still

progress from the group stages if they could defeat Spain in the last of their group matches. The last time they had played Spain had been in 1931, when England had won 7–1, but that pre-war thrashing was hardly a guide to current form. Despite a widely shared belief that the freak result of Belo Horizonte would never be repeated, in fact England once again lost 1–0 in a game in which they largely dominated. This time both Matthews and Finney were selected. Mortensen and Milburn, who had been expected to fill their boots in the Brazilian sunshine, failed to score, and the England football team went home at the end of the group stage to face headlines with which their supporters were to become increasingly familiar over the years. Wright's captaincy and Winterbottom's management, inevitably, came under particular scrutiny. While the headlines did not compare for savagery with those that would greet later England managers, both Walter Winterbottom and the Wolves skipper knew perfectly well that they were not among the most popular men in the country at the start of July 1950. Still, Brazil was a long way from England and most newspapers allocated this foreign competition only a limited amount of space. It wasn't as if England had been beaten at home by Scotland, after all.

Four days before the calamity at Belo Horizonte, on 25 June, Communist North Korean troops had crossed the 38th Parallel, surprised the South Korean army (and the small US force stationed in the country), and captured Seoul within three days. The United States believed that the only political response to Communist aggression wherever it occurred in the world was an instant military reaction. It responded by pushing a resolution through the United Nations Security Council calling for military assistance to South Korea. The Soviet Union was not present to veto the resolution as it was boycotting the Security Council at the time. So, with the resolution confirmed, President Truman rapidly dispatched US land, air and sea forces to Korea to engage in what he termed a 'police action' on behalf of the United Nations.

Britain was inevitably drawn into the conflict as a permanent member of the UN Security Council and in its new position as the junior partner in the military coalition with the United States. Young British men who had been conscripted into the armed forces as part of their National Service, and had been anxious to avoid a dangerous posting to British-ruled Malaya, where a Communist insurgency had broken out in 1948, were now faced with the prospect of having to fight in an even more terrifying war in Korea. Despite assurances to President Truman from the UN Supreme Commander, General Douglas MacArthur, that China would not enter the war, they did so, to Truman's intense fury. To widespread astonishment Truman sacked the seemingly untouchable MacArthur. He could afford to. He wasn't running for re-election in 1952.

The USSR might have accepted that the Allied airlift had broken its blockade of Berlin in 1949 but that same year the Soviets had detonated their first atomic bomb and the American and Western belief that the world was safe because only the United States had a nuclear capability was revealed as a false hope. Men who had gladly laid down their arms in 1945 were forced to pick them up again or watch their sons go off to fight and possibly die when the Korean War started five years later. The world was unsafe, there were spies everywhere and, as far as England was concerned, nothing was sacrosanct.

On the same day that England's football team was defeated by the United States of America, 29 June, its cricket team was defeated at Lord's, the home of cricket, by West Indies. This comprehensive victory for the Caribbean islanders by 326 runs was largely the result of the eighteen relatively inexpensive wickets taken by two quiet, unassuming – and until this moment entirely unknown – young spin bowlers called Sonny Ramadhin and Alf Valentine. By the end of the summer they were very well known indeed. Their heroic feats, immortalised in the 'Cricket, Lovely Cricket!' calypso composed by the Trinidadian Lord Kitchener ('those two little pals of mine, Ramadhin and Valentine') made the host country sit up and take notice. By the end of the summer they had helped the West Indies to clinch a famous 3–1 victory in the four-match Test series. A war-weary England might lose to a rampant, well-fed Australia without arousing too much internal criticism, but defeat at home to an upstart like West Indies suggested that the world was about to be turned upside down.

Two years before this triumph for West Indies, the *Empire Windrush* had docked at Tilbury and disgorged the first significant boatload of Caribbean immigrants. Many of them no doubt thoroughly enjoyed the discomfiture of their hosts in the Test series of 1950 when they realised the true nature of the 'welcome' that awaited them in cold, grey, drab Austerity Britain. The social disturbances that accompanied this first wave of Caribbean arrivals were confined to the few cities with growing numbers of black immigrants but, in the later summer of 1958, disaffected white youths began attacking black people in London's Notting Hill. The riots continued for five nights with the police seemingly incapable or unwilling to impose themselves on the rapidly growing violence. As was revealed by government papers, the home secretary of the time, R. A. Butler, was assured by the police that the disturbances were not racially motivated. He chose to believe that the violence, as intimated by the police, was the result of both white and black Teddy boys indulging in their favourite sport of hooliganism. It was safer and easier to accept that recommendation than to examine the causes of racial unrest and do something about them.

The Notting Hill riots were a problem for a future Conservative government. In 1951, the unpopular post-war Labour government lost seats and confidence as its time started to run out. However, in the general election of February 1950 it still managed to gain over 50 per cent of the votes cast and widen its popular vote margin over the Conservatives to more than three million but, partly owing to boundary revisions, it lost seventy-eight seats, the Conservatives gained ninety and restricted Labour to an overall majority of only five seats – a poor return for the governing party given the nature of their 1945 victory and the reforming zeal of the Attlee government. However, there was no public appetite for more sacrifice and the outbreak of the Korean War placed a strain on the slowly recovering but still deeply fragile economy. With taxes bound to rise and depress the population still further it is perhaps surprising that in the circumstances Labour performed as well as it did.

The wafer-thin Labour majority of five seats inevitably affected the government's ability to pass legislation in the House of Commons and eighteen months later Attlee was forced to go to the country again in the vain hope of acquiring a stronger mandate. His cause had not been helped by the resignation of Aneurin Bevan who in the 1950–51 Labour government had been moved from the Ministry of Health to the Ministry of Labour. When Hugh Gaitskell introduced charges for NHS dental work and spectacles in order to raise money for the new war effort, Bevan could not accept what he regarded as the wanton damage wrought upon his creation, the National Health Service, and retired to the backbenches. He was followed by Harold Wilson, the former president of the Board of Trade whose time in the sun was still to come, and by John Freeman, later to become a BBC television interviewer on the *Face to Face* programme. Wilson repaid this demonstration of solidarity by appointing him High Commissioner to India and successively British Ambassador to the United States.

In the general election of 1951, the Conservatives, still led by the seventy-seven-year-old and increasingly frail Churchill, were returned to office with an overall majority of sixteen. Labour, despite once again winning a majority of the popular vote, retreated into an opposition that was to last for thirteen years. Before it faded into history, however, the post-war Labour government produced one last hurrah – the Festival of Britain. After Britain began withdrawing troops from India in 1947 and from Palestine the following year, it seemed as if a country that had been struggling to prosper in the post-war world had started to wear its history like a burden to be shouldered rather than a garland to be proudly displayed. The Festival revealed to a surprised but largely enthusiastic Britain that the country was actually innovating. Its imperial glories might be fading in the rear-view mirror, but the prospect through the windscreen was one of optimism. This came as a revelation to nearly everyone, although not necessarily a pleasant one.

Particularly, it came as an unwelcome surprise to Evelyn Waugh (and most of the rest of his class) who denigrated the Festival as 'monstrous' in his novel *Unconditional Surrender*. They thought that there was little to celebrate in Britain although what was being celebrated was not their vanishing Britain and it came just as they thought that the country was returning to its senses, having taken leave of them in July 1945. The Festival wasn't the Britain of the working classes who, as Michael Frayn wrote perceptively some ten years later, were nothing 'more than the lovably human but essentially inert objects of benevolent administration'. The Festival of Britain in 1951, he went on to demonstrate, was the Festival of 'the radical middle classes – the do-gooders; the readers of the *News Chronicle*, *The Guardian* and *The Observer*; the signers of petitions; the backbone of the BBC'.

Nothing became Attlee's Labour government quite like its leaving of office. After six years of monochrome austerity, legislative worthiness and social bleakness, its farewell performance took place on the South Bank as the Festival of Britain crowned the summer of 1951 in a blaze of triumph. The Labour government of 1997 tried hard to copy its success with the ill-fated Millennium Dome but failed miserably. The 1951 Festival was conceived initially as a centenary celebration of the 1851 Great Exhibition but its real purpose was to release the creativity of British architecture and design and at the same time to give the long-suffering population a glimpse into the lifestyles of the future. It succeeded triumphantly. The eight million people who visited the site on the South Bank and the Pleasure Gardens in Battersea never forgot the experience. The press, which had been sceptical in the years leading up to the unveiling by the king on 3 May 1951, as it would be again in the weeks leading up to the opening of the Millennium Dome in 1999, changed its tune and hailed the explosion of British talent that was on display. The BBC promoted the Festival untiringly. Everyone had been understandably worried lest the war in Korea become a third world war with the potential for nuclear holocaust. Somewhere in the triumphant Dome of Discovery or gazing in wonder at the Skylon or marvelling at the water mobile, the crowds which, against expectation, had continued to pour on to the South Bank of the Thames rediscovered their faith in the future of the country. The police were struck by the absence of both crime and hooliganism.

At the end of September, after a midnight cabaret from Gracie Fields, the Festival of Britain was closed to the sound of booing from Londoners and visitors who had so enjoyed its many delights. One of the first acts of the new Conservative government when it took office in late October was to tear down the buildings on the South Bank, erected especially for it, apart from the Royal Festival Hall, which had always been intended as a permanent legacy. The Conservatives had a different vision of Britain and most of the public took to it rapidly because prosperity was on its way, government controls were to be lifted, the shops were slowly being stocked with goods that people wanted and could now afford to buy. The Festival had been 'a rainbow', Frayn concluded – 'a brilliant sign riding the tail of the storm and promising fairer weather. It marked the end of the hungry forties and the beginning of an altogether easier decade.'

After the humiliation of their exit at the group stage from the World Cup in Brazil in 1950 the England football team resumed what it believed to be normal public service. In the 1950–51 season, only that 3–2 loss to Scotland marred an otherwise undefeated year and in 1951–2, despite a few draws, England remained unbeaten throughout. Although the friendly against Italy in Florence in May 1952 resulted in a 1–1 draw, only Wright and Finney remained from the eleven who had conquered their hosts in Turin in 1948. If the England team was therefore perceived to be weaker than it had been, its performance in the match in Vienna the following week resolved those doubts as they won with a famous goal by Nat Lofthouse eight minutes from time. Billy Wright remembered the game with great affection:

A proud gathering of British servicemen were present, enthusiasts and patriots who had converged on Vienna from stations all over Austria. 'A win for us today could do more good for us than a thousand victories round a conference table.' Having failed to beat us by science, the Austrians fell back on tactics better suited to a saloon-bar rough house. Ankle tapping, shirt pulling, elbow digging, late tackling... they used them all.

It was the nature of the winning goal that remained in the minds of all those who saw it and plenty of those who only heard about it. For Billy Wright it remained one of his favourite moments in an England shirt.

From an Austrian corner, Merrick caught the ball and threw it to Finney near the centre circle, who controlled and slipped it sideways to Lofthouse. He galloped from the half way line pursued by the fleet footed Austrians. As the goalkeeper advanced, Lofthouse hammered it past him as the pursuing pack enveloped him and Musil the keeper crashed into him and he was carried off. The ten men held out and at the final whistle a jubilant mass of British soldiers flooded onto the pitch and carried us on their shoulders to the dressing room.

'We ain't half pleased, mate,' said one Cockney. We were so pleased to have given the British army boys something to cheer them up. We were carried back to our dressing room on the shoulders of cheering Tommies, who had come from their posts in Germany in their thousands.

Nat Lofthouse, who became known as the 'Lion of Vienna' after this performance, was the archetype of the heroic, unselfish English centre-forward who believed the primary purpose of his job was to give the goalkeeper and the centre-half who was marking him a hard, physical game. In fact, the ten men of Vienna didn't remain so for long because the shaken Lofthouse soon re-entered the field of play and nearly scored a fourth England goal when he hit the post in the last minute.

Lofthouse was not a particularly skilful player but he was not a thug, at least not by the accepted standards of the 1950s. As far as he was concerned he played the game fairly and the real villains, predictably, came from abroad. In his book *Lion of Vienna*, published in 1989, Lofthouse recalled the utterly appalling behaviour of the Spanish football team during the 1–1 draw England secured in Spain in 1955.

Quite how tough they were we couldn't begin to guess. I've never known anything like it. We were kicked all over the field. And they singled out Stanley Matthews for special treatment. I don't think their left-back made one genuine attempt to go for the ball all afternoon. It's a wonder Stanley didn't break both legs. [It] was the first and only time the great Sir Stanley ever lost his cool on a football pitch.

People often ask me how we coped with tactics like that. We simply had to turn the other cheek. It was no good getting involved in a kicking match. And for me there was always national pride at stake. As we went out onto the pitch, our manager Walter Winterbottom would touch the white shirt and say quietly, 'Don't disgrace it, lads. Play hard but play fair.' And we tried to live up to that. Yes, we had trouble with Latin sides over the years. They could all play the game but there was always something going on. I never relished playing against them... South Americans would never resort to anything like that. Even the centre-halves were comfortable on the ball and quite happy to play their way out of trouble. Even in their own penalty area. It was something completely new to me.

The problem with foreign players – if they weren't lying down and appreciating the honour of being defeated by the country that had invented the game – was that they were either very filthy or very skilful. The combination of the two was impossible to deal with. Looking at the England football team of the early 1950s, one is inescapably reminded of Captain Blackadder in the trenches reminiscing about the military glories of the heyday of the British empire: 'Back in the old days... the prerequisite of a British battle was that the enemy should, under no circumstances, carry guns... The kind of people we liked to fight were two foot tall and armed with dry grass.'

But then came Hungary.

England's proud record of never having lost to a foreign team on home soil had been in jeopardy for a while. Scotland had been winning at Wembley on an occasional basis for many years. The Republic of Ireland had beaten England 2–0 at Goodison Park in 1949 but somehow that didn't count. The Rest of Europe – who had been crushed 6–1 in 1947 in the match held as a benefit for the cash-strapped FIFA – returned to Wembley in October 1953 in an exhibition match to mark the ninetieth anniversary of the foundation of the Football Association. This time the quality of the opposition – and the result – were very different from 1947. The only Hungarian on show was Kubala who had already transferred his allegiance to Spain but the presence of Hanappi and Ocwirk from Austria, Boniperti from Italy and the Swede Nordahl who had played in 1947 alerted England to the news that tactics on the Continent had moved on. Only a ninetieth-minute penalty, coolly converted by Alf Ramsey, gave England a scarcely deserved 4–4 draw. The following month the roof fell in.

If England didn't know much about the Hungarians before 25 November 1953 they should have done. Hungary had been losing finalists in the 1938 World Cup and had provided many of the coaches for Italy's Serie A. On top of that, they possessed three of the best club sides in Europe in MTK, Ferencvaros and the Hungarian army team Honved. Hungary had beaten Yugoslavia 2–0 in the final of the Olympic Games of 1952 in Helsinki, scoring twenty goals in five games. Stanley Rous had watched the Magyars in action in Finland and – once the idea had been approved by the Hungarian politburo – had set up an England v. Hungary game at Wembley.

Brian Glanville was expecting England to struggle against Hungary.

I knew they were in for it because I'd seen the Hungarians beat Italy 3–0 in Rome and I wrote in the old *Sport Express*, 'Look out, the Hungarians are coming'. There was an old sports editor of the *Daily Telegraph* called Frank Coles, a slob and a drunk, and he said, 'What will they do in the middle of winter against an English team playing for points? The English team would run straight through them.' A fat lot he knew.

Something of Captain Blackadder's attitude to foreigners is apparent in a story Billy Wright later told against himself. As the two teams made their way out to the pitch side by side, the England captain couldn't help noticing their opponents' strange footwear: 'I looked down and noticed that the Hungarians had on these strange lightweight boots, cut away like slippers under the ankle bone. I turned to big Stan Mortensen and said, "We should be alright here, Stan, they haven't got the proper kit."'

England's footwear was the traditional heavy leather clod-hoppers. In later years Tom Finney recalled the England kit with a shudder:

> They had one size of shirt for everyone in the England squad. So if you were six foot two it strangled you and if you were my size it came down below your knees. Same with the socks. When you put them on they reached the top of your thighs. Then those boots... stiff leather, up over the ankles, bulbous toe caps. Felt like diver's boots. When it rained and the shirt collected water and the socks were soaked we must have weighed a ton apiece. I don't know how we moved.

Yet at the time of the game against Hungary there was a profound mistrust of foreigners and their streamlining ways. Foreigners wore clothes and ate food that was different from ours. We preferred to stick to what we knew and felt comfortable with. And that applied also to the way in which we played football. Kenneth Wolstenholme, observing Puskás juggling the ball with his left foot just before the kick-off, wondered whether the Hungarians were going to deploy such

wizardry during the game itself, and, if that were to be the case, whether England might find these foreigners a tricky proposition. If there was any English superiority in the comment it took precisely sixty seconds for it to vanish without trace. Hidegkuti, the Hungarian number nine, puzzled the England centre-half Harry Johnston by hanging back in midfield from the kick-off. When he eventually received the ball on the edge of the England penalty area after England had clumsily lost the ball from their own throw-in, he was, of course, unmarked. He took three quick steps and blasted the ball past the stunned England goalkeeper, Gil Merrick. The photographers, who had gathered, as they traditionally did, round the goal of England's opponents because that was where they were expecting all the action to be, exchanged nervous glances. Could they have chosen the wrong end?

After twenty-seven minutes, England were already 4–1 down but it was the third goal which summed up England's play that afternoon. The outside-left Czibor found acres of space down the right wing. Alf Ramsey, who would have marked him had he come down the left wing as he was supposed to, had no idea whether to follow him or leave him. Czibor then picked out Puskás in the inside-right position. Billy Wright, as Geoffrey Green memorably described it in *The Times*, came over to challenge the Hungary captain but was left sprawling on his bottom 'like a fire engine heading to the wrong fire' as Puskás dragged the ball back easily with the sole of his left boot before thumping it into the roof of the net. It was so easy that it was a shock to everyone; even the Hungarians who could scarcely believe that the Old Masters of world football could be humiliated so easily. They played like champions and with the bearing of champions – so much so that they were sent off from Victoria station with the cheers of the fair-minded English public ringing in their ears. In Budapest, the entire Communist Party hierarchy assembled to greet the triumphant Magyars, alongside thousands of delighted Hungarians in and around Keleti station. The players were publicly honoured with the People's Order of Merit and secretly rewarded with cash. It was, the Hungarian Communist regime seemed determined to emphasise, a triumph not just for eleven players and for the nation of Hungary, but for an entire ideology.

Malcolm Allison, who had been present at Wembley that dank November afternoon, was profoundly impressed by what he had seen. Many of the young coaches who would begin to have an impact on English football in the 1960s felt similarly. Winterbottom, as a serious student of the game, soon recognised how far behind the English game was now lagging, but his anxieties had no impact on his employers at the Football Association. At the end of the decade Billy Wright wrote:

> I am quite sure that if managers and players of this country had allowed themselves to be influenced by Walter seven or eight years ago much of the heart searching now taking place at League level would not have been necessary. He has met with a great deal of resistance, both active and passive, and while I do not wish to apportion blame, it remains a fact that the march of tactics did pass us by.

When the rematch took place in Budapest in May 1954, Stanley Matthews was not selected. Instead his place went to the Portsmouth right-winger Peter Harris, whose only previous international game had been against the Republic of Ireland in the defeat at Goodison Park five years previously. At centre-forward was the ineffectual Fulham player Bedford Jezzard. England lost 7–1.

That same month saw the release of perhaps the most durable of the many British war films made in the 1950s. *The Dam Busters* re-created the RAF's 1943 'Operation Chastise' to destroy the Möhne, Eder and Sorpe dams using 'bouncing bombs', which flooded the Ruhr and Eder valleys. A paean to British – and imperial – courage (the crews of 617 Squadron including many men from Canada, Australia and New Zealand), the film attracted large numbers of cinema-goers, most of whom would have remembered the raid even if they didn't know the details. *The Dam Busters* makes no attempt to disguise the heavy losses sustained during the operation: when Guy Gibson meets the scientist Barnes Wallis who had invented the bouncing bomb on the morning after the raid, the two men are both aware that whatever they managed to destroy of the dams and the industrial infrastructure of the Ruhr, it came at a heavy cost in the lives of the air crews.

Barnes Wallis takes off his glasses and wipes them, muttering that the price was too high and if he had known at the start how many would perish he would never have begun his research. Gibson protests that all the men knew the risks and all the men who died would have done it all over again even knowing they would not return. His words are of some comfort to the scientist who suggests Gibson must be exhausted and that he should get some sleep. Gibson smiles wryly and says softly that he has some letters to write first. This poignantly understated admission that he now has to inform the families of the men who have lost their lives rather undercuts his previous assertion – which was intended to raise Wallis's spirits – but is a fitting ending to a film that celebrates rather than glorifies British and imperial heroism. Today we tend to associate the film with the stirring and upbeat qualities of the march composed by Eric Coates and used as its theme music, but in fact the film is much subtler than a jingoistic tale of British heroism and invention, which is how it is seen in retrospect by ignorant England fans waving their arms about like aeroplanes. *The Dam Busters*, *The Colditz Story* (1955), *The*

Cruel Sea (1953), *Angels One Five* (1952), *Reach for the Sky* (1956), *Ice Cold in Alex* (1958) and *Carve Her Name with Pride* (1958) were the best of a genre that proved consistently popular during that decade because by and large the portrayal of the British in these films as a self-sacrificing, dutiful and stoical people pretty much reflected how their audiences saw themselves.

The lingering impact of the war might have made British people more stoic than they are today in a time of comparative peace and absolute prosperity, but the war had been won and it was still popularly believed that England was supposed to win sporting as well as military battles. The second heavy defeat at football by Hungary, a Communist nation, caused some profound soul-searching. Hitler's Olympic Games in 1936 had demonstrated the propaganda effect of victory. Britain needed a win somewhere if only for the sake of parliamentary democracy. The winning back of the Ashes in 1953 gave some hope that the England cricket team was starting to recover after the ravages of war with the added benefit of Bradman's retirement, but that battle was traditional and only sporting with no Cold War overtones. The key ideological battles of the mid-1950s in this respect took place at Molineux in Wolverhampton, on the athletics track at Iffley Road in Oxford and at the White City stadium in west London. What gave them added significance is that they took place in the presence of television cameras.

On 6 May 1954, running for the Amateur Athletic Association against his old university, Roger Bannister won the mile race in a time of 3 minutes 59.4 seconds. Chris Brasher, who was to win Olympic gold at Melbourne in the 3,000m steeplechase, set a fast first lap before handing the pace-making job over to Christopher Chataway. The weather at Iffley Road was not ideal for record-breaking – a 15mph crosswind with gusts of up to 25mph meant that Bannister nearly called off the attempt but when he burst past Chataway and raced for the line he carried with him the hopes of the nation. When Norris McWhirter announced the winning time he could only get as far as 'Three minutes...' before the rest of the detail was drowned out by the cheering of 3,000 spectators who had gathered in the hope of watching history being made. The Australian John Landy set a new world record of 3.57.9 the next month but the young doctor from Oxford would always be associated with the supreme achievement of being the first to break the four-minute barrier.

In May 1954, Paul Fox was the editor of a new midweek sports programme on the BBC called *Sportsview*. Bannister's achievement was perfectly timed to help establish the show, as Fox recalls:

> We had a piece of luck with *Sportsview* because our third edition coincided with the Bannister four-minute mile. Norris McWhirter tipped us off that Roger was going for it that evening in Oxford so we had the Outside Broadcast camera there. I knew Roger well enough to have a car waiting for him to bring him back to the studio in London. He broke the four minute mile about six o'clock and by half past eight he was in the studio in London. It was a genuine scoop. I knew that gang – Bannister, Chataway, Brasher, the coach Franz Stampfl and so on. Chris Brasher became a *Panorama* reporter when I was editor of the programme.

Chataway became one of the first ITN 'newscasters' when Independent Television News went on the air and the reason that people knew him was that he had made his mark as an athlete first. The Soviet long-distance runner Vladimir Kuts had beaten both Chataway and the 'Czech locomotive' Emil Zátopek (triple Olympic gold medallist in Helsinki in 1952), to win the 5,000m at the European Championships in September 1954 but on home territory Chataway thought he could win. The *Evening Standard* arranged an athletics meeting between London and Moscow at the White City stadium for October 1954 which was effectively Great Britain v. the USSR. Kuts always tried to break the field by setting out at a terrific pace, but on this occasion Chataway managed to stay with him. However, on the last lap, Kuts was showing no signs of tiring and Chataway seemed unable to close the gap of two yards no matter how desperately he tried. With 200 metres to go Kuts was still leading as he was when the runners came round the bend and into the home straight for the last time.

The atmosphere was electric, for the race was being run not just under floodlights but under a travelling spotlight. All the anxieties of the atomic age, with its ever-present threat of nuclear annihilation, seemed to possess the full house of 60,000 spectators as they willed Chataway on. With eighty metres to go it seemed impossible but somehow, from somewhere, Chataway found a last reserve of energy. He kicked on and with less than ten metres to go he caught Kuts. Two metres from the finishing line he passed the Russian and broke the tape first as the crowd at the White City and the British public watching at home on television went wild with delight – not so much at Chataway's new world record of 13.51.6 – a full five seconds faster than Kuts's old record – but at the realisation that a major propaganda battle had been won. Unfortunately, just as Landy had soon broken Bannister's record, so Chataway soon surrendered his new world record back to Kuts who then went on to win both the 5,000 and the 10,000m at the Melbourne

Olympics in 1956. However, it was Chataway's performance at White City in October 1954, witnessed by millions of British television viewers, that lingered longest in the memory of British people. To them the Olympic gold medals were neither here nor there. An Englishman had triumphed over an intimidating foreigner – and a Commie to boot – through guts and determination. Paul Fox remembers that Chataway won more than the undying affection of the British sporting public that night:

> 1954 was the first year we ran the programme *Sportsview Personality of the Year* and it ensured that Chris won it and not Roger. It was done in conjunction with the *Daily Express* and Chataway was presented with the trophy at the Savoy Hotel by Field Marshal Montgomery. It didn't have the status that *Sports Personality of the Year* does now.

Prompted by Fox and the Head of Outside Broadcasts and *Sportsview* presenter Peter Dimmock, the Corporation was slowly learning that televised sport presented some distinct advantages. Fox recalled:

Sport was regarded at the BBC as 'below the salt' but it got audiences. News was top of course. However, Dimmock was well regarded at the BBC because he had made sure the Coronation had been a success. Churchill didn't want it televised, the archbishop of Canterbury didn't want it televised but in the end Peter did enough to persuade the duke of Norfolk, who was the Earl Marshal, that it was a good idea. He took him to the Abbey because what they were all really scared of was the lights would be too strong for a twenty-seven-year-old woman in an unbelievably stressful ceremony. And of course he left the lights off and turned them on when he needed them, took the close up and apologised. 'Oh sorry wasn't I supposed?'... etc. Too late. Dimmock also had direct access to Sir Ian Jacob, the Director-General, but Jacob didn't know a football from a rugby ball and didn't much care. Neither did Cecil McGivern [BBC Television Controller of Programmes] so they allowed Dimmock free rein.

A key moment in the history of sport on television was the 1953 Cup Final (immortalised as the 'Matthews Cup Final') which was broadcast on 2 May, a month before the Coronation. Many families who were planning to buy their first television set for the Coronation bought it early so that they could watch the Cup Final. Dimmock and Fox knew that sport was a growth area for television and *Sportsview*, an innovative sports magazine programme, quickly became a staple of midweek viewing.

Sportsview started because I wrote a memo to Peter
Dimmock saying what we need is a weekly sports news
programme. We started with a fortnightly programme.
Four weeks after I had written the memo it was on the air.
Dimmock was a driver and the best idea I had was that he
should present it. Peter was good at it and he knew the
football people which enabled him to bring all the contracts to the BBC. Peter was the key organiser for
Wimbledon and Ascot and all those places. That was
because people had seen him on the air introducing
Sportsview. Then we dreamed up *Grandstand* during the
Commonwealth games in Cardiff in July 1958. Three
months later it was on the air. Peter presented the first
three programmes when it went on air in October 1958
and then David Coleman took over.

The influence of television on sport and of sport on television became one of the main shaping factors in the cultural life
of Britain in the second half of the twentieth century. In the
twenty-first century it is perfectly apparent that television dic-
tates to sport because of the money it can provide or withhold.
In the 1950s and 1960s, as television slowly began to acquire
the broadcasting rights to big sporting events, frequently
granted with some reluctance and much suspicion, it was the
big dramatic sporting clashes that people remembered. The
BBC wanted television rights both to keep them out of the
hands of the ITV companies which were just starting up and
to increase the number of television licence fee-payers. ITV, in
turn, wanted them because this meant larger audiences and
allowed them to charge more for commercials.

In the autumn of 1954, Wolverhampton Wanderers, under
the captaincy of Billy Wright, played evening matches
under floodlights against three sides from Eastern Europe, but

it was the first two games, which took place around the time of the Kuts v. Chataway race, that captured the public imagination. This was partly because of the successful results but more importantly because they were seen on television. Wolves had won the First Division League Championship in May 1954 and their new floodlights were to be inaugurated with evening matches against the best of opposition from Europe. On 13 November, Spartak Moscow were crushed 4–0, which whetted the appetite for the match against Honved a month later. The army club included six of the Hungary national team which had beaten England so humiliatingly in London and Budapest and the way the Hungarians began the match at Molineux suggested that another hammering was on the way. After throwing flowers to the Black Country crowd who certainly had never witnessed such an entrance when the likes of neighbours West Bromwich Albion came to Molineux, Kocsis and Machos gave Honved a two-nil lead after fifteen minutes of a first half which they entirely dominated. Conditions deteriorated during the second half of what was a filthy December night, as a result of which the Hungarians' close-passing game broke down as the ball simply would not roll through the Wolverhampton mud.

Wolves themselves started sending long, high balls into the space behind the visitors' defence and profited accordingly. Johnny Hancocks pulled a goal back from a penalty early in the second half and constant Wolves pressure was rewarded when Roy Swinbourne equalised with fifteen minutes left. Like Vladimir Kuts, the Communist footballers could not withstand the pressure exerted by the forces of democracy and the crowd ecstatically acclaimed the winning goal thumped home by Swinbourne. It was a night that lived long in the memories of those who saw it live or on television, for it assuaged a great deal of the hurt that had been inflicted by the two overwhelming defeats for the national side. A headline in the *Daily Mail*, with traditional understatement, described Wolves as the Champions of the World, a statement that would have been greeted with some surprise at Real Madrid.

Billy Wright, whose captaincy of his country had attracted severe criticism, redeemed his reputation with an outstanding display. He was now playing at centre-half for both club and country, having switched from right-half where he had been ensconced since the restart of football after the war. Brian Glanville, who had been sceptical about Wright as he struggled in the early 1950s, enthusiastically welcomed the switch.

He was a far better player after 1954 when he switched to centre-half although he was not very tall. He was an incredible defender. Syd Owen and Laurie Hughes had played there but Hughes got injured in the Charity Shield in 1950 and we were always struggling after that until Billy Wright moved there.

Wright's change of position took place during the World Cup finals in Switzerland in 1954. Given that their last warm-up game before the tournament was the disaster in Budapest, England's fairly anonymous performance in the 1954 World Cup could be accounted a reasonable one. A 4–4 draw against Belgium was followed by a 2–0 win over the hosts but they were then well beaten by Uruguay 4–2 and returned home having reached the quarter-finals of the World Cup for the first time. Wright's move to centre-half was one of England's few bright spots of the tournament. His reputation as a player really rests on the consistently impressive performances he was to give in that position for the rest of his career.

Remembering the tussles he had with Nat Lofthouse, Wright recalls the personal duels that went on between wingers and full-backs and particularly centre-halves and centre-forwards: 'When I first started to establish myself as a centre half dear old Nat Lofthouse said with a straight face, "I'm not sure I can talk to you any longer, skipper. You've joined 'them'. I hate centre-halves." '

Lofthouse, however always rated Wright highly as a captain if not as a defender:

> I had great respect for Billy Wright who was captain of England in just about every game I played. Billy was a great player but above all he was a great captain, a true leader. He might be having a stinker but that didn't stop him shouting and encouraging all the other players around him. He never let his own performance affect his captaincy. Mind you, I always fancied my chances when I played against Billy. I could run and outjump him. So I looked forward to our meetings. Which couldn't be said of all the centre-halves I came up against… Manchester City's Dave Ewing was a big man, a pure stopper. And when you ran into Big Dave you stopped! Every time we played City I'd say, 'I've got to beat this devil today.' But I never did. I'd play like a real donkey. Dave always came out on top. With Billy Wright I was always confident but that doesn't mean he always had a bad game against me. Far from it. For Wolves and England he had the knack of getting the team to fit in around him. If he was struggling, someone else would cover up. He was a wholehearted player and a great skipper. He deserved every one of his 105 caps.

The praise for Wright's captaincy among his contemporaries is almost unanimous. It seems unlikely that Winterbottom would have asked him to lead out the England side on ninety occasions if he had thought there was a better alternative. Stan

Cullis, the manager of Wolverhampton Wanderers who had captained the club himself during his playing days and who did not tolerate anything less than total commitment from his players, made Billy captain of the club in 1947, a position he held until he retired twelve years later. Cullis never had a moment's anxiety that he might have chosen the wrong man: 'He was a born leader. Where Billy led, his team-mates followed. It's an old-fashioned word but his team-mates were loyal to him. Loyalty and Billy Wright went together like eggs and bacon.'

This ability to inspire loyalty in others was not related purely to football. The manner in which Wright went about his job as an executive at ATV Network in Birmingham was almost identical, as we shall see in a later chapter. Johnny Haynes, who was to lead England in twenty-two of his fifty-six appearances for his country, was always fulsome in his praise for the captaincy qualities of his predecessor, as he told Wright's biographer, Norman Giller:

> If there were any problems he would sort them out quietly. He did not flourish his fist like a Dave Mackay, or keep talking like a Danny Blanchflower. His way was to give quiet encouragement and he was always the first to shout 'Bad luck... keep going, lads' if things were going against us. Everybody who played with Billy learned a lot about humility. He was an outstanding man and such a good bloke that you wanted to play your heart out for him.

The last four years of Wright's captaincy saw England begin a promising recovery from the devastation of 1953 and 1954. The optimism sprang from the emergence of the youthful Manchester United side known familiarly as the 'Busby Babes', from its development under the tutelage of its formidable

Lanarkshire-born manager Matt Busby. In the emergence of three of those players in particular, England appeared to have the spine of a team that would be one of the favourites to win the 1958 World Cup in Sweden. The Manchester United of the late 1950s was, in stark contrast to the sides at the top of the Premier League in the early twenty-first century, almost exclusively made up of young Englishmen, with the exception of Billy Whelan, the Irish inside-right. As far as England were concerned, the three regular players were Roger Byrne, the accomplished left-back who was clearly destined to succeed Wright as captain of England as well as captain of the League Champions; Tommy Taylor, the spring-heeled centre-forward from Barnsley signed for £29,999 because Busby did not want the burden of being a £30,000 purchase hanging round the player's neck; and a left-half called Duncan Edwards.

Edwards occupies a unique position in English football history because his legendary status is based as much on what he did not achieve as on what he did accomplish. He made his debut in the First Division at the age of sixteen and two years later he made his first appearance for England in a 7–2 victory over Scotland. At the end of the 1955–6 season Edwards was the outstanding player in a fine 3–1 win in Berlin against West Germany, the current world champions. Edwards scored one goal, a pile-driver from outside the penalty area, and dominated the game in defence and attack, drawing extravagant praise from press, players and public alike. As in Vienna four years previously, the crowd contained a large contingent of British soldiers who were stationed in the British sector of Berlin. They duly invaded the pitch at the final whistle and carried off the heroic Edwards on their shoulders. Just as Nat Lofthouse's winning goal in the 3–2 victory over Austria had been greeted by a pitch invasion, so this reaffirmation that Britain was the world's footballing top dog was eagerly acclaimed by English football supporters, desperately anxious to forget those traumatic drubbings by Hungary.

Edwards's career and life were tragically short. In February 1958, at the age of twenty-one, he died in Munich fifteen days after the air crash that killed seven other United players (including Byrne, Taylor and David Pegg, another England international) and twenty-three passengers in total. It was heartbreaking for his family and friends, his club and, if such a word can be considered appropriate in the circumstances, for his country. Even if Byrne rather than Edwards would have been the England captain during the 1960s it seems very unlikely that Bobby Moore would have been able to have dislodged Edwards from the team in July 1966 when Edwards would have been only twenty-nine years old. The images of 1966, so clear in the mind's eye of every English person interested in football, might have been very different had that plane not tried to take off in the snow and ice at Munich.

In 1958 England were joined in Sweden to contest the World Cup finals by the three other countries of the United Kingdom, the last time all four countries qualified together for the same World Cup tournament. Wales and Northern Ireland exceeded expectations by qualifying for the knock-out stages but Scotland finished bottom of their group, gaining only one point and losing two of their three games. England fared slightly better, drawing all three group matches, including a goalless draw against the eventual winners Brazil. Finishing equal on points with the USSR, England played off against them but lost one-nil in a disappointing game.

Given the feeling at the start of February 1958 that England were strong candidates to win the Jules Rimet trophy – unlike many a tournament since this feeling was based on results and the strength of the squad rather than wish fulfilment and media hype – the 1958 World Cup was a damp squib for

England. Brian Glanville thought the squad selection was foolish.

> England lost Byrne, Edwards and Taylor who would have made a big difference but they left Nat Lofthouse at home. Nat Lofthouse! Vittorio Pozzo said that taking Derek Kevan instead of Lofthouse was giving way to brute force. 'He scores goals with the outside of his head.' Lofthouse scored twice as fast as Rooney – and he did it without the aid of penalties. They were entitled to take twenty-two players and they only took twenty.

He was equally dismissive about the new-look Hungary team which had been decimated by the after-effects of the 1956 Uprising, but was much more positive about Wales.

> By the time it came to the 1958 World Cup Puskás, Czibor and Kocsis had left for Spain, Hidegkuti and Boszik were too old and they were a team of kickers. If they hadn't kicked John Charles out of the play-off game against Wales I think Wales would have beaten Brazil. They were playing so well. Mel Charles was superb. Mel Hopkins played Garrincha out of the game and Pelé scored the scrappiest goal imaginable – it went in off the boot of Williams the full-back.

There was a pervading sadness about that 1958 England team, caused primarily, of course, by the absence of the Manchester United trio. Wright and Tom Finney were coming to the end of their careers; Stanley Matthews, who would play on until he reached the age of fifty, had already departed from the international stage after an unseemly public disagreement with Winterbottom; and Johnny Haynes, the bright new midfield star, suffered from a badly blistered foot and never demonstrated the form of which he was capable. The team which took the field for the vital play-off match against Russia included such footnotes to English football history as Peter Brabrook of Chelsea, Alan A'Court of Liverpool, Tommy Banks of Bolton and the heavily criticised Derek Kevan. They were decent enough players but not star names like Mannion, Lawton, Swift and Carter, who would have seriously worried the opposition. Bobby Charlton sat and watched from the sidelines. This side contained nothing like the quality of the England side that had managed to lose to the United States in 1950. Billy Wright did well to maintain his level of performance at the grand old age of thirty-four, but it was obvious by now that even the supremely fit Wolves centre-half was facing the final curtain.

England was changing as a country in the late 1950s but the country's football seemed stuck in the pre-Suez past, living, like Anthony Eden, off memories of past glories. In April 1955 the eighty-year-old Churchill had finally resigned as prime minister and was succeeded by Eden, his long-time deputy and foreign secretary. Eden was suave and sophisticated, handsome and well-liked. He could read Arab and Persian literature in the original and when he travelled to Cairo to persuade Egypt's new ruler, Colonel Nasser, to join the Baghdad Pact, which was designed as an anti-Communist alliance of Middle Eastern countries, he greeted his guest for dinner at the British Embassy in Arabic.

At home, Eden's arrival at 10 Downing Street was received with relief on both sides of the House and with great warmth by the electorate. It appeared as if the country that had finally abandoned all rationing two years before had now found a leader whose appeal to good manners and common sense was going to find a welcome reception in the country at large. An increase in the Conservative majority from sixteen in 1951 to sixty in the election held the month after Eden assumed power indicated that the British people were pleased at the prospect that lay ahead. Within eighteen months, however, it had all gone disastrously wrong.

On 26 July 1956, Nasser made a three-hour speech to a cheering crowd in Alexandria in which he announced the nationalisation of the Suez Canal. As much as the revelation of the Nazi–Soviet Pact on 23 August 1939 and Germany's invasion of Poland which began a week later, this was a stark test of Great Britain's power. Eden certainly saw it as a rerun of the fascist challenge to the Western democracies in the late 1930s. Having resigned in 1937 over the British government's policy of appeasement, he was in no mood to allow this flagrant breach of international protocol to pass without response. He embodied the post-war belief that had Britain stood up to Hitler in 1936, 1937 and 1938 war would not have broken out in 1939. Nasser was now posing, so he believed, the same question that Hitler asked. It was a familiar question. The United States had asked it in 1950 before President Truman committed American troops to fight the Communists in Korea. It was believed that unless the Western democracies showed they had the stomach to fight, as they had not in 1938, it would be an open invitation to the worldwide spread of international Communism.

In Eden's eyes, Nasser was an embryonic Hitler, testing his strength against the imperialist powers, seeing what he could get away with. More worryingly, his radical anti-imperialist philosophy was starting to have an impact in Jordan and Iraq and Britain's influence in the Middle East was being seriously undermined. Taking his cue from Nasser, in March 1956 the young King Hussein abruptly dismissed General Sir John

Glubb, the British commander of the Arab Legion in Jordan, another blow to British prestige.

The United States, however, did not see Nasser's actions as worthy of military intervention, so Eden had to resort to subterfuge and secret collusion with France and Israel. The three countries agreed that Israeli forces would invade Egypt and storm across Sinai towards the Canal as fast as possible. Britain and France, meanwhile, would drop paratroopers into the Canal Zone to establish peace, thereby seizing control of the disputed territory.

For Eden, the early promise of his premiership had dissipated all too rapidly. His health, which had been fragile since a failed gall bladder operation in 1953, continued to deteriorate. By-election losses, the inevitable consequence of apathy and traditional anti-government feelings between general elections, weakened his political position in Westminster. The rising tension in relations with Egypt made Eden feel as if he were caught up in an intensely personal battle with Nasser and in a radio broadcast of 8 August he echoed the familiar words of previous historical crises. 'Our quarrel is not with Egypt, still less with the Arab world. It is with Colonel Nasser.' Eden had set out on a path that would lead him to abject humiliation and inevitable resignation.

The prime minister misled the House of Commons about his intentions in Suez just as surely as Jack Profumo, the minister for war in a later Conservative government, was to do in 1963. Both men's political careers ended shortly after they had uttered their fateful untruths in parliament. The Israeli incursion began on 29 October 1956. The British government gave both sides twelve hours to pull back their troops from the Canal. Egypt, despite its anti-British posturing and aggressive intent, was surprised by the British response and unsure what to do. On 31 October, British troops were dropped into the

Canal Zone. The Americans were incensed at not having been informed about what Eden was up to and they began to apply economic pressure. The drain on Britain's gold and currency reserves increased rapidly with the Treasury losing approximately $100 million in the first week of November. President Eisenhower was running for re-election and was outraged that Britain had initiated military action without telling him at a time of such political sensitivity for him. In addition, he was made aware on 4 November, two days before his countrymen voted, that Russian tanks were rolling towards Budapest in an attempt to quell the Hungarian Uprising. Any lingering affection Eisenhower might have retained for Great Britain after his experience as Supreme Commander of the Allied Expeditionary Force was eradicated by Eden's misguided decisions at this time.

The Suez Canal was closed, shipping was stopped and the British economy lurched into crisis. Harold Macmillan, the chancellor of the exchequer, asked Washington for assistance and was brusquely informed that no funds would be forthcoming from the IMF unless British troops withdrew at once from the Canal Zone. Macmillan, having supported Eden's aggressive stance at the beginning of the Suez crisis now changed his tune. On 6 November Eden telephoned Eisenhower to tell him that British troops would immediately evacuate the Canal Zone. Eden had gambled and lost. The British public, whom he had imagined would instantly recognise the parallel with 1938 and support him, were in fact split down the middle. There was an instinctive British lion roar but there was no general acceptance of Eden's belief that Nasser was Hitler reborn. The British Empire effectively ended in the muddle and confusion of Suez. There were just too many dissenters and the country was torn between those who wanted to give the upstart Nasser a bloody nose and those who felt that such behaviour belonged to the days of nineteenth-century gunboat diplomacy rather than the mid-twentieth-century world.

John Osborne's play *The Entertainer*, which opened at London's Royal Court Theatre on 10 April 1957, caught this divided spirit of the times as Archie Rice's old dad wonders why 'People seem to be able to do what they like to us'. His daughter Jean attends the big anti-war rally in Trafalgar Square and his son Mick is captured in Suez and eventually murdered. 'Those bloody wogs, they've murdered him! The rotten bastards!' screams Mick's friend, Frank. Perhaps even more to the point, the previous year in Osborne's play *Look Back in Anger* which made his name and fortune, the anti-hero Jimmy Porter had declared:

> I suppose people of our generation aren't able to die for good causes any longer. We had all that done for us, in the thirties and the forties, when we were still kids. There aren't any good brave causes left. If the big bang does come and we all get killed off, it won't be in aid of the old-fashioned, grand designs. It'll just be for the Brave New-nothing-very-much-thank-you. About as pointless and inglorious as stepping in front of a bus.

It was a dramatisation of American Secretary of State Dean Acheson's later pointed comment that Great Britain had lost an empire and not yet found a role.

Eden was furious and humiliated over Suez. As is ever the way with politicians, he found fault wherever he could and television was an obvious target. When he made his major broadcast to the nation in the run-up to the Suez crisis on 8 August 1956 the lights in the television studio dazzled his eyes and he was very cross that he had to wear his glasses in order to read his speech. He blamed the BBC for thus deliberately humiliating him. He was to be incensed by the Corporation's refusal of a request from the Australian prime minister, Robert Menzies, to broadcast a message of support for his British counterpart. The relationship between television, particularly the BBC, and the government was ever thus fraught.

As the 1959 general election campaign got underway the Labour party asked for Alasdair Milne to be seconded to make their party political broadcasts as snappy as his *Tonight* programmes. Initially they were cheered by the utter incompetence of the Tories whose first broadcast came from Birch Grove, Macmillan's country house in Sussex. Milne recalled it with great glee.

> There sat Harold Macmillan, with his cabinet all gathered around him on sofas, all looking slightly shifty and uncomfortable. He explained to the viewers that he intended to give them an end of Parliament report and then called on each Minister in turn to speak. 'Derry,' he said turning to Chancellor Heathcoat Amory, 'a word about the economy. I think we're doing quite well, don't you?'

However, the Tories soon discovered the unfortunate consequences of such an approach, sorted themselves out, abandoned the BBC and enlisted the help of Norman Collins at ATV. Macmillan then pulled off a famous virtuoso performance, spinning a globe of the world and talking in masterly fashion about his involvement in world affairs. Forty-eight hours later the Conservatives won the election with an overall majority of a hundred seats.

For all its hauteur, the BBC was facing considerable pressure from a new commercial rival, Independent Television, which was launched in the London area on 22 September 1955. The BBC and its supporters reacted with predictable outrage as audiences abandoned the latest talk on hats or archaeology on BBC Television to absorb the hospital soap opera that was *Emergency – Ward 10*, the comedy of Alfie Bass and Bernard Bresslaw in *The Army Game* (a sitcom about National Service) and the seductive California sunshine that suffused the popular private eye series, *77 Sunset Strip*. The scriptwriters of BBC Radio's *The Archers*, hell-bent on destroying ITV's eagerly anticipated first night, had ignited a fire at Brookfield stables which killed the character of Grace Archer. Phil Archer's young wife died in vain, however, for the march of ITV was unstoppable. Audiences voted with the switch on the front of their new twelve-inch sets. The result was a landslide. In 1960, the advent of *Coronation Street* on Granada Television demonstrated that the complacency that had infected the BBC from its days as a monopoly was actually destroying the viability of the Corporation.

The ITV companies' only interests were ratings and a commercial profit for its shareholders. The BBC disdained to chase ratings, as a consequence of which the proportion of the viewing public that watched BBC Television slumped to 28 per cent by the end of 1957. On that basis the BBC simply could not justify the licence fee and so a battle began for the soul of the nation, a battle which continued to rage through the age of the video cassette recorder and time shifting, through the satellite and cable age and into the age of the podcast, streaming and the Internet. In 1953, when the BBC was forbidden by Buckingham Palace to show a close-up of the queen at the moment that the crown was placed on her head, the live broadcast on the American channel NBC cut to a commercial of the network's celebrity chimpanzee, J. Fred Muggs. For BBC loyalists, this disgraceful affront to the dignity of the sovereign was symbolic of the threat to traditional British values that the new commercial television would represent.

As the British economy stabilised in 1958 and the newly built transmitters carried *Gunsmoke* and *Huckleberry Hound* to all parts of the country, ITV's ratings soared and the advertising revenue poured in. The BBC was helpless to resist the rapid ebbing away of its audiences. It didn't know how to compete against an organisation that valued innovation and commercial success. It remained steadfastly British, scorning the easy path to audiences by buying American series or making programmes like the Americans'.

ITV, particularly ATV Network led by Val Parnell and Lew Grade, knew perfectly well what audiences didn't want. They didn't want those BBC lectures that were supposed to be 'good for them'. They didn't want Rediffusion's programmes with Sir John Barbirolli conducting the Hallé Orchestra or even ATV's own live production of *Hamlet* which played to less than 10 per cent of the audience and was mercifully terminated in the final scene when it overran. Master Control went to a pre-arranged commercial break and never returned to see if *Hamlet* had a happy ending. Nobody complained.

Grade knew exactly what it was that audiences did want – *Rawhide* and *Cheyenne*, *Maverick* and *The Untouchables*. If the programme had to be British, nothing beat *Sunday Night at the London Palladium* but preferably with a big American star at the top of the bill. The BBC had fought and lost. ITV was here to stay. One of the few battlegrounds where the BBC could exert some form of superiority was sport. The people who ran the big sporting institutions were 'BBC people' and they regarded ITV as rude, crude and unwelcome interlopers. This was where Peter Dimmock and BBC Sport came into their own, as Paul Fox recalls:

Stanley Rous at the FA was a gentleman and Dimmock got on with Stanley so we had the FA Cup final live from 1953 onwards. Dan Maskell knew everyone at the All England Club so we got the Wimbledon tennis and Dimmock and Peter O'Sullevan knew everyone in the racing world so that was available and rugby became available because the RFU welcomed us as did the AAA for athletics. The Grand National was difficult and it wasn't televised until 1960 because Aintree was run by a lunatic woman called Mrs Mirabel Topham, a former Gaiety Girl, and her mad nephew. Dimmock laid siege to her. One year after the BBC had been televising the Grand National for a while she chucked us out and decided that the commentary would be done by the *Daily Mirror*. It was a total disaster and next year we were allowed back in. What helped the BBC was the great commentators – O'Sullevan, Maskell, Dorian Williams. Lew Grade tried, ITV started *World of Sport* but in the late 1950s and early 1960s it was sewn up by Dimmock. He's the hero of this story.

The one sport which remained resistant to the lure of television was football, which annoyed the television executives because it had exactly what their schedules demanded – wide popularity with endlessly repeatable content. Wimbledon was transmitted for seven hours a day but it was only for twelve days a year. The Grand National lasted just twenty minutes. League football had forty-two matches a year but the Football League wasn't selling its precious fixture list. Alan Hardaker, secretary of the Football League, sat in his office at Lytham St Annes and rejected approaches from both the BBC and ITV. Not even the fabled charm of Peter Dimmock could persuade him to change his mind. Stanley Rous might have been a gentleman but the gruff Hardaker assuredly was not.

Instead of football, what BBC Sport got was rugby league which, along with a mud-splattered sport called moto-cross – involving a bunch of unidentifiable motorcycles scrambling up and down mud banks – dominated the Saturday-afternoon sports programme *Grandstand* until 4.40 p.m. when David Coleman grabbed the lip mic and read out the football results as the teleprinter clattered out the news from grounds across the country. When *Grandstand* was first broadcast in 1958 the ubiquitous Dimmock had been the presenter, but he had to read his script off a teleprompter (the only one in the country at the time) because he couldn't remember a word. Coleman was younger and more in keeping with the presenters of the new decade.

The hunger for football on the small screen was palpable, but Hardaker's fear that televised football would result in crowds deserting the terraces for the telly was sufficient to prevent anything beyond the Cup Final and the occasional representative game from being shown live. During the 1950s it was reported that attendances at Football League grounds declined by 3.8 million, a huge drop from the admittedly unsustainably high crowds of the immediate post-war years. Various explanations were offered: it was now the age of the family, the five-day week, the saloon car and the television set. Billy Wright was always convinced that television would be a help to the growth of football in England, not a hindrance. In *The World's My Football Pitch* he wrote: 'During the 1960–1 season, BBC and ITV both tried to do deals with the Football League but failed. Figures as high as £150,000 were bandied about. A live game every third Friday would be good. Soccer cannot fight television; it must therefore use it.'

In fact, Wright was not quite correct. A deal was indeed done between ITV and the Football League to show the second half of twenty-six matches. The first match to be thus broadcast, between Blackpool and Bolton Wanderers in front of a half-empty Bloomfield Road, was shown to a small audience on the evening of 10 September 1960. Unimpressed, Arsenal and Tottenham Hotspur then refused to allow the cameras into their grounds to televise their matches against Newcastle United and Aston Villa respectively. ITV then withdrew from the deal and broadcast *The Nat King Cole Show* instead. There was no appetite on either side for a renewal.

Match highlights were shown on TV even before the advent of *Match of the Day* in 1964. The Saturday-night television programme *Sports Special*, introduced by Kenneth Wolstenholme, included coverage of three matches which could not be announced in advance, just as the identity of the matches for which second-half commentary was broadcast on the radio on Saturday afternoon could not be revealed until 3.45 p.m. in case people chose to listen rather than pay to go to the ground and watch. The film of the matches was flown by helicopter to a laboratory which had to develop the film before it could be edited so, with sweat trickling down their collars, the production team and presenter frequently started the live programme without the edited film having been threaded on to the telecine machine.

Such was the success of *Sportsview* that the BBC with that sense of originality that has always marked it out as the finest public service broadcaster in history came up with another programme in the same genre. It was designed to appeal to children, so they called it *Junior Sportsview*. Not even Peter Dimmock with his Battle of Britain pilot's moustache could pretend that he was a natural presenter of a programme for children from six to sixteen, so the BBC went looking for a new face. The first one they tried, on Paul Fox's recommendation, was the Tottenham Hotspur captain, Danny Blanchflower. Unfortunately, as Fox recalled,

> Danny Blanchflower didn't want to do it. Blanchflower was the best, a natural TV performer. He had the face, the personality and the nous but he was never that interested in television so we chose Billy Wright who was. It helped that he was married to Joy who understood TV. He wasn't that good and at ATV they got him off camera as soon as possible.

Marriage to Joy Beverley changed Billy's life. He claimed later that he had not even thought seriously about marriage until 1954, when he was thirty, and it took him another four years before he eventually tied the knot. They had met when he had been asked to show Joy's son by a former marriage round Molineux. He admitted that, to his own surprise, he had kissed Joy goodbye on their first meeting. 'That putting it mildly was quite out of character with my normal self.' Football, to say nothing of society as a whole, was not as devoted to the formal farewell kiss as it is today.

Nevertheless, the possibility of a blossoming relationship between the captain of the England football team and Joy

Beverley – who, along with her twin sisters Teddie and Babs, made up the popular singing trio known as the Beverley Sisters – sent the press into the sort of frenzy we certainly would recognise today. To the couple's dismay one newspaper decided to splash a story about Joy's first marriage which angered both of them because 'that story represented journalism at its worst'. The couple eventually decided to get married on Sunday 27 July 1958 at Poole Register Office when the sisters

were appearing in a summer show in Bournemouth. Despite their best attempts at maintaining the secret, somehow it leaked out. By the time the bridal party of two cars got to the register office on the Sunday morning the whole press pack along with hundreds of curious onlookers were waiting outside. To the bride's dismay, the aerial was snapped off her car. The honeymoon took place in Stratford-upon-Avon and lasted precisely twenty-four hours. Joy went back to the show in Bournemouth and Billy returned to pre-season training in Wolverhampton.

For the last season of Billy's career he and his new wife were the Posh and Becks of 1958. Victoria Beckham might have risen to fame on the back of a singing career but there the parallel with Joy Beverley Wright disappears. Posh Spice's first big hit as a member of the Spice Girls was 'Wannabe'. Joy's was the sisters' cover version of 'I Saw Mommy Kissing Santa Claus' and, six years later in 1959, 'Little Drummer Boy'. Brian Glanville was not a fan: 'You couldn't have been the showbiz couple of the decade if you were married to one of the Beverley Sisters. They were dreadful. Give me the Andrews Sisters any day.'

However, for all the vocal limitations of the Beverley Sisters there was an undoubted glamour now attached to the captain of the England football team which went beyond the realm of football. It was nothing compared to what was yet to greet the other three captains but it certainly indicated the way in which the England football captain could be recognised by more than just his achievements on the field.

In that 1958–9 season, Tom Finney and Nat Lofthouse both made their last appearances for England. In April, Billy Wright won his one hundredth cap as England defeated Scotland 1–0 at Wembley with an acrobatic header from Bobby Charlton. At the end of the game Wright was carried towards the dressing room on the shoulders of Ronnie Clayton and Don Howe, but still he showed no inclination to call it a day. The time when an England player would retire early from the international game in order to concentrate on extending his club career was many years distant, which meant that when England went on their summer tour of North and South America Billy Wright was still in the firing line as they lost all three matches against Brazil, Peru and Mexico.

Jimmy Armfield made his debut in the match in the Maracanã and Jimmy Greaves in the 4–1 defeat by Peru. Greaves, inevitably, scored the England goal but when the team arrived in Los Angeles for the final match of the tour against the United States, they were under siege from withering criticism in the press. Only too aware that the memory of the 1950 World Cup fiasco was fresh in everyone's minds, England began as if determined to repeat it. The Americans had an early goal disallowed but then took the lead after eight minutes through a goal scored by their captain Eddie Murphy. As the teams emerged for the second half the score was only 1–1, but a further seven goals in the last forty-five minutes, including a hat-trick by Bobby Charlton, ensured there was to be no repeat of the Belo Horizonte nightmare. It was Billy Wright's last match for England though not even he knew it at the time.

In June 1959, Billy was invited to open a new leisure complex in Saffron Walden by the town's MP and current home secretary, Rab Butler. It was Butler, according to Wright in *One Hundred Caps and All That*, who raised the question of retirement. Butler thought it was a jolly good idea to go out at the top though, of course, he didn't, losing the prime ministerial selection process in 1957 to Harold Macmillan and in 1963 to Alec Douglas-Home and not retiring from politics until after Labour was returned to power in October 1964. Of course, Butler never played in a pre-season match and found he no longer had the pace that he had formerly been able to command. Wright played in the Wolves pre-season match, traditionally the Whites v. the Colours, and told Stan Cullis soon afterwards that he was retiring with immediate effect. As the home secretary knew, it was the right decision.

Wright left the game with gratitude for the memories and the opportunities it had given him. Born in Ironbridge, the son of a worker in the nearby Coalbrookdale iron foundry, Wright lived a life of glamour and excitement that would not have been available to any other boy:

> I've heard the calypso boys of the West Indies in their right and proper setting, watched the Mountains of Mourne slope down to the sea from my bedroom window, drunk the health of Her Majesty the Queen under a spreading palm tree, bargained with smooth tongued spivs in Rome, been buffeted around in a plane by gale-force winds over the Alps, climbed the Eiffel Tower, bathed in the fabulous five-mile sweep of the millionaires' Copacabana Beach, ridden on the Big Wheel of the Harry Lime film in Vienna, gazed upwards at the skyscrapers of New York and been driven by a speed-crazy coach-driver through little Portuguese villages. All this I owe to football.

Billy Wright left school at fourteen and did not have the opportunity to become upwardly socially mobile through what became the conventional working-class method of escape of the Eleven Plus examination and the grammar school. Football was one of the few avenues open to him to progress and certainly one of the very few that could provide him with the opportunity to enjoy the lifestyle described above and the mixed blessings of a celebrity marriage.

However, Billy Wright's career was significantly different from that of a regular first-team player at a First Division club of the era. Whatever the level at which he played, an English footballer in the 1950s could not, legitimately, exceed the maximum wage. A year after winning the FA Cup at Wembley in May 1959, Nottingham Forest were involved in a First Division relegation dogfight alongside Leeds United, Luton Town and Birmingham City. Before Forest's vital match at

Stamford Bridge, the Chelsea captain Peter Sillett gathered the other ten players together in the snooker room, away from management eyes and ears. He informed his team-mates that he had been approached by two Forest players who were prepared to give the Chelsea players £500 to deliberately lose the match. It would have worked out as a tax-free sum of £45 a man; that was more than two weeks' wages for the Chelsea players. They took a vote. The result was an 11–0 verdict in favour of rejecting the offer out of hand. The match ended in a genuine, hard-fought 1–1 draw. Forest finished the season just one point above Leeds United who were relegated along with Luton Town.

Honest in respect of the illegal bribe, for some professional footballers who were desperate to supplement their meagre wages petty theft was nevertheless a way of life. As a ground-staff boy, Jimmy Greaves worked for John Battersby, the Chelsea secretary, who was in charge of issuing the luncheon vouchers worth two shillings and sixpence (12.5 pence). The brothers John and Peter Sillett, so admirable in their refusal to countenance the illegal offer from the two Forest players, suggested to the young, impressionable Greaves that he liberate a few luncheon vouchers, which Greaves did from time to time in return for a few welcome shillings. Greaves knew that the Silletts would then trade the stolen vouchers down at a café called Charlie's for cigarettes. Battersby was a heavy smoker so the young ground-staff boy's first job every morning was to run down to the local café and buy forty Senior Service for Battersby. 'Snozzel' Sillett would then waylay him and give him the black market packets of Senior Service bought with the luncheon vouchers liberated from Battersby's desk drawer in return for the cash Battersby had just handed to Greaves. Life at Stamford Bridge in those days was, Greaves later said, 'like Harry Lime's Vienna'.

According to the prime minister, Harold Macmillan, the winds of change were blowing through the continent of Africa at the start of 1960. Different but equally significant winds of change were starting to sweep through class-conscious Britain. Underpaid, resentful English footballers were about to initiate their own startling social and legal revolution.

CHAPTER TWO

THE AGE OF BOBBY MOORE

THE AGE OF BOBBY MOORE

The England football team did not go into a steep decline when Billy Wright disappeared from the international stage he had graced since 1946. In fact, for a brief period it was both settled and successful, before, of course, the World Cup came along and England once again failed to perform.

The leadership of the side was initially taken over by Ronnie Clayton, the Blackburn Rovers captain and right-half, who had already played alongside Wright in thirty games for England. However, despite being ten years younger than the Wolverhampton Wanderers centre-half, Clayton's international career ended after just five games as captain when Bobby Robson displaced him as the England team's right-half. The captaincy now passed to Johnny Haynes, who had been an adornment of the English game since 1950 when, as a diminutive fifteen-year-old schoolboy, he had dominated a game at Wembley against Scotland Schoolboys, watched by an admiring television audience. It was another small harbinger of the growing fateful relationship between football and television.

Despite playing Second Division football for Fulham, by October 1954 Haynes had progressed to the full England team, where he became the creative hub of the midfield, stroking long elegant cross-field passes with either foot. Wright admired him enormously.

> I think [he] is destined to become one of England's great captains. His leadership has grown in leaps and bounds in a very short space of time, and now we find him emerging as a constant source of inspiration not only to the young players in the England side but to youngsters all over the country.

Haynes's greatest moment probably came at Wembley in April 1961 when he was the captain of an England side that put nine goals past the hapless Scotland goalkeeper Frank Haffey. That was the England team that suddenly seemed to have found itself. Ron Springett in goal; Jimmy Armfield and Mick McNeil of Middlesbrough at full-back; a half-back line of Robson, Peter Swan and Ron Flowers and a forward line that boasted the skills of Douglas, Haynes, Greaves and Charlton together with the Spurs battering ram of a centre-forward, Bobby Smith. For the first time since the days of the Busby Babes, England had a settled, successful team and could look forward with some optimism to the World Cup in Chile in 1962.

Johnny Haynes was not only the captain of England but the highest-earning footballer in the land. Tommy Trinder, the Fulham chairman, had publicly announced that he would very much have liked to have paid Haynes £100 a week but unfortunately the maximum wage was capped at £20 by the Football League. In 1961 the pay cap was abolished and Trinder was obliged to put his money where his mouth had been. Haynes's new-found riches did not immediately change his lifestyle, however, as the football journalist Patrick Barclay noted:

When Beckham became one of the first £100,000 a week footballers I went up to Edinburgh to talk to Johnny Haynes because he'd been the first £100 a week footballer. He said even when he was on that £100 a week and the highest paid player in Britain he was still travelling to matches by Tube to Hammersmith, then he would get a bus up the Fulham Palace Road. Occasionally fans would say, 'Have a good game today, Johnny!' The irony is that even though they were 'one of us' I regarded the players of those days as being on a pedestal in a way that I never regarded the Beckhams and players of today.

The maximum wage crumbled in the face of a threatened strike by the players. Britain was already getting so used to the increasing incidence of strike action that 'the British disease' eventually became the term associated with low industrial productivity and irresponsible industrial action. A BBC television sitcom called *The Rag Trade*, written by Ronald Wolfe and Ronald Chesney, first appeared in 1961. It focused on the lives of a group of working-class women who were employed in a clothing factory named Fenner Fashions, run by the permanently harassed Harold Fenner, played by Peter Jones, and his much put-upon assistant, played by Reg Varney. As in the recently successful Boulting Brothers film *I'm All Right, Jack* (1959), management was painted as either venal or incompetent and the workers were shown to be self-centred and ideologically hidebound.

In the film, there was a brilliant performance of no little depth by Peter Sellers as the shop steward, Fred Kite, in awe of the workers' paradise known as Soviet Russia ('all them cornfields and ballet in the evening'), but in *The Rag Trade* the character of the shop steward was played strictly for laughs. The belligerent Paddy Fleming (Miriam Karlin) revelled in the power she wielded over the bosses with the blast on her whistle and the screech of 'Everybody out!', a catchphrase which caught on quickly. Invariably, the girls all responded instantly and production stopped entirely while some petty labour dispute was resolved. Both *The Rag Trade* and *I'm All Right, Jack* worked because the audience recognised the reality of Britain's current industrial relations behind the comedy.

In 1956, Johnny Haynes's Fulham colleague Jimmy Hill was voted chairman of the Players' Union in succession to Jimmy Guthrie and soon changed the name of the organisation to the more white-collar-sounding Professional Footballers' Association. Everyone in the game knew that at this time, after five years with one club, a player qualified for a benefit worth up to £750 which was taxed at the standard rate – unlike professional cricketers, whose benefits were not taxable. In 1948 Cyril Washbrook collected the tax-free sum of £14,000 at Lancashire and in 1961 Brian Statham was awarded a similar amount. In those days, footballers looked at cricketers with financial envy.

This was just one of the twenty-two points of outstanding difference between the PFA and the Football League who represented the clubs, the players' employers. In 1960, the maximum wage was £20 a week during the season and £17 in the summer. The clubs also controlled their players' destinies through the 'retain and transfer' contract system. If at the end of his contract a player did not wish to re-sign on the terms offered to him, his club could simply retain his contract and not pay him anything. He could not be transferred except with the club's consent. In the wage negotiations of 1960 it was later revealed that the PFA would have settled for a maximum wage of £30 but the intransigence demonstrated by the Football League pushed them towards strike action. The PFA also wanted their players to have the right to move at the end of their contract but, unlike the situation that arose after the

Bosman decision in 1995, they did not expect freedom of contract to come without a fair fee being paid to the selling club by the purchasing club.

Hill and the PFA Secretary, Cliff Lloyd, feared that if the Football League and the clubs accepted a small increase in the maximum wage, the overwhelming majority of players would sign and forget about the principles behind the strike. When the Football League refused to negotiate seriously the members of the PFA started to see the sense in a strike. The PFA, like Actors' Equity, was at the time a weak union because its members knew that their services were far from indispensable. A 'bolshie' actor could be replaced as easily as could a 'bolshie' football player. Actors and footballers *wanted* to work, whereas workers on an industrial assembly line did not necessarily feel similarly. As the character Arthur Seaton says in Alan Sillitoe's contemporary bestseller *Saturday Night and Sunday Morning*, 'All I'm out for is a good time – all the rest is propaganda.'

The crucial PFA meeting took place in Manchester in December 1960. Jimmy Armfield was the Blackpool PFA representative:

Cliff Lloyd rang me at home the night before and just said, 'Make sure you get him there tomorrow.' I knew what he meant. I had to get Stan [Matthews] to the meeting because all the players looked up to Stan. The fact that he and Tom Finney were there changed the meeting. We were all British and we'd been through the war and through the hard times. Not everyone was committed to the strike at first. A lad got up and said, 'My dad's a miner in Chesterfield; he works five and a half days a week for £8 a week. I'm on £12. I'm earning half as much again as my dad. I can't go on strike.' Tommy Banks [the infamously hard Bolton Wanderers left-back] got up and said, 'Son, thee, me and

all on us can do thi father's job. You come and ask thi dad
to come and play against Brother Matthews in front of
35,000 people on a Saturday afternoon.' We all laughed
and everyone started cheering. In my opinion that changed
the meeting. Players went into that meeting not sure they
should go on strike. By the time the meeting had finished
we all were united behind the strike.

The PFA gave the Football League one month's notice of
strike action. At Belle Vue in Manchester, northern players passed
the resolution by 254 to 6. The final countrywide vote was 694
to 18. Ted Hill, then chairman of the TUC, declared his support
for the PFA. In January, he asked all members of every trade
union not to attend 'blackleg matches'. There was still considerable pressure against a strike from the football pools companies,
so the PFA tried to arrange alternative matches for people to bet
on. The players had been frightened by the prospect of alienating
their supporters by depriving them of their Saturday-afternoon
entertainment. In the end, they need not have worried.

The strike that was due to start on Saturday 21 January 1961 was called off on the Wednesday before when the Football League offered to abolish the maximum wage and make concessions on retain and transfer. The latter principle still held until the revolutionary judgment in the Eastham case which the PFA brought when the Football League started to backslide on the agreement made with the PFA at the Ministry of Labour. George Eastham was a skilful inside-forward who had asked his club, Newcastle United, for a transfer in 1959. When Newcastle used the retain-and-transfer system to prevent him from leaving, the player refused to play for the club and took Newcastle to the High Court for restraint of trade and unpaid wages. Eastham's situation became a test case for all players in contractual dispute with their clubs. The player noted:

> Our contract could bind us to a club for life. Most people called it the 'slavery contract'. We had virtually no rights at all. It was often the case that the guy on the terrace not only earned more than us – though there's nothing wrong with that – he had more freedom of movement than us. People in business or teaching were able to hand in their notice and move on. We weren't. That was wrong.

The decision in the case was announced on 4 July 1963 by Mr Justice Wilberforce:

> The system is an employers' system, set up in an industry where the employers have succeeded in establishing a united monolithic front all over the world, and where it is clear that for the purpose of negotiation the employers are vastly more strongly organised than the employees. No doubt the employers all over the world consider this system

to be a good system, but this does not prevent the court from considering whether it goes further than is reasonably necessary to protect their legitimate interest.

The judge's ruling that the retain-and-transfer system was unreasonable led to reforms in the transfer market, with players who were looking to re-sign for their clubs receiving fairer terms, and a transfer tribunal being set up to resolve disputes between players and clubs. In 1963, football was finally starting to move with the times.

The life of Jimmy Hill seemed to symbolise those times and, had he been captain of England, he would have made a persuasive case for inclusion as one of the five significant captains of the post-war era. He was born in 1928 in a two-up, two-down terrace house in Balham in south London, to parents who struggled to make ends meet and were obliged to take in lodgers and other paying guests. Hill's father was frequently unemployed but found occasional work, first as a milk delivery man ladling out milk from a churn door to door, then in a bakery in Blackheath for £4 a week. His day started before dawn and Hill rarely saw his father before 7 p.m. on those days when he was working. Hill passed the Eleven Plus and went to Henry Thornton School in Clapham. In 1949, after national service with the Royal Army Service Corps at Cirencester, which he spent, like many national servicemen who were talented sportsmen, mostly playing football and cricket, he joined Brentford, for whom he made eighty-three appearances. Three years later he moved to Fulham where he would spend the remainder of his playing career.

His entrepreneurial talents revealed themselves early on, although they were undoubtedly encouraged by financial insecurity. Ossie Noble, an accomplished drummer and local mime artist, with whom Hill regularly played golf, shared his own fears about future penury and informed Hill that he had started the Immaculate Chimney Sweeping Company, having invested in a vacuum machine that boasted that it could suck the soot from the chimney without depositing it on the sitting-room floor. Noble invited Hill to join this revolutionary start-up and use his persuasive and articulate powers to attract new customers. The charge to the householder was seven shillings and sixpence (37.5 pence) of which Hill kept one shilling (5 pence). So well did he perform his duties that the Immaculate Chimney Sweeping Company soon had more orders than it could fulfil and Hill was invited to join as a full active partner by donning the overalls and doing the sweeping himself. However, Hill could only devote his time to the business during the summer months and since he suffered from hay fever at that time he was soon rendered ineffective by constant sneezing and withdrew. Nevertheless the Immaculate Chimney Sweeping Company affair demonstrated the lengths to which professional footballers had to go in the 1950s to supplement the family budget.

> So there we were – the Immaculate Chimney Sweeping duo wanting to play golf much, much more than sweep chimneys but imprisoned by the constant rumblings of insecurity arising from the fear that one day our art would no longer feed the family – the nagging insecurity of professional sport.

Hill's story continued to thread its way through the narrative of English football for another thirty years.

Johnny Haynes, Jimmy Hill's team-mate at Fulham, led England into the 1962 World Cup, but the settled team which had looked so impressive in 1960 and 1961 was badly affected by injuries. Not for the first – or last – time the England football team failed to do justice to their talents at the end of a gruelling domestic season. The dependable and accomplished right-back Jimmy Armfield remembers the sad decline of that England team only too well:

> The expectancy of the England team was greater in 1960 than it is today. Then we really did think we were going to win every match. We lost Bobby Smith who did his ankle before we left for the 1962 World Cup and he was a key player. We had an excellent team, the best I ever played in for England. It was a very attacking team. The balance of the team was good. Jimmy Greaves was like Messi, his close control was so good and he had quick feet. But eventually we lost Bobby Smith and Peter Swan and Johnny Haynes. Gerry Hitchens came in for Bobby Smith, and then they brought Bobby Moore in and he reminded me of when I first played against Brazil, but he did better than I did and I told Walter he's going to be OK. His temperament and his positional play were excellent.

Bobby Moore had been making a reputation for himself for a few months before his first selection for England. On Friday 4 May 1962, Moore gave an outstanding display in a Young England v. England game played at Highbury. The match, which was one of the very few games of the era to be televised, took place the evening before the 1962 FA Cup final between Tottenham Hotspur and Burnley. Ron Greenwood, Moore's manager at West Ham, had been telling his friend Walter Winterbottom of Moore's blossoming for a few months. Shortly after the Cup final, which Spurs won 3–1, the party for the World Cup in Chile was announced and Moore was in it.

The England party that went to Chile for the World Cup was based at the end of a single-track railway line in Coya, a remote mining community run by the Braden Copper Company. It reminded Armfield of a barracks in his National Service days. Most of the squad had done their National Service and were not disconcerted by the basic nature of their accommodation: 'The country had been through hard times. There was a lot of austerity and players today simply wouldn't put up with what we had to go through. National Service had prepared us for anything.'

England lost 2–1 to Hungary in their opening group game, then beat Argentina surprisingly but convincingly 3–1 in the second match, before grinding out a scoreless draw against Bulgaria in the knowledge that the result would be good enough to assure them of a quarter-final place. Unfortunately, it was to be against the World Cup holders, Brazil, but Armfield believes that the England team was unlucky on the day to lose 3–1.

If we'd taken our chances against Brazil in the quarter-final we could have won it. We lost to that Garrincha free-kick. We'd been in a mining camp 8,000 feet up in the Andes for three weeks. That's where we played our games but then we didn't have the time to readjust to playing in the quarter-final. I was round about my best then.

Armfield himself had a superb tournament and was recognised widely as one of the best full-backs in world football, but his view of England's performance wasn't necessarily one shared by the press and the public. The British public's perception of the performance of the England team was largely shaped by the press coverage. In 1962, television viewers did not have the luxury of live broadcasts of England's games from which they could draw their own conclusions as to the quality of their team's performance. The matches were recorded on film, the negative of which was then taken to Santiago, whence it was flown to Lima and then to Panama, entering the United States at Miami before travelling on to New York where it was processed. The film was then flown across the Atlantic and was transmitted by the BBC forty-eight hours after the matches had been played. When viewers finally got to see the black-and-white television pictures, they were fuzzy and – because they were sourced from just one or, at most, two cameras, whose operators did not always manage to follow the flight of the ball – hardly gave an accurate sense of the progress of the game.

The significance of the role played by television in the English reaction to their football grew by leaps and bounds only after this tournament held in a faraway country about which we knew less than we knew about Czechoslovakia in 1938.

Johnny Haynes never played for England again after that match against Brazil. Shortly after his return to England he was badly injured in a car crash on the promenade in Blackpool in which he broke both legs. He was only twenty-seven at the time and he recovered to offer Fulham another eight years of sterling service but it seems that, for all his cultured defence-splitting passing, he was not Alf Ramsey's kind of player because he never picked him after he became England manager in 1963. It is undeniable that Haynes, whom Brian Glanville still describes as 'petulant', had had two disappointing World Cups, but he had been an outstanding player nonetheless. Ramsey thought that his natural ability was offset by his tendency to be witheringly contemptuous of players of lesser ability. It was not a character trait that would be likely to find favour with a new England manager who was looking to build an indomitable team spirit and a feeling of collective achievement. In Haynes's absence after his Blackpool accident, Jimmy Armfield became the regular captain of England in the autumn of 1962, having already led out the national side in a World Cup qualifying game against Luxembourg in September 1961, played at Highbury, which England won 4–1.

Armfield's early life was even more deprived than that of Jimmy Hill. Born in 1935, he grew up in a very poor community in the Denton district of Manchester. When the war started and Manchester was subjected to Luftwaffe bombing, his mother moved to Blackpool, although his father remained temporarily in Denton and visited Blackpool when he could. But then an opportunity opened up:

> He heard about a shop near where we lived that was available for rent. I remember going in there for the first time. When we opened the door we could hear the mice scattering. We opened the cash tills and the drawers were full of mice. We then got a shop that had accommodation above it and he started a small grocery there and he stayed

there till he was sixty-seven and I stayed there till I got married. My mother carried on being a machinist until she was seventy-six. She started cleaning when she was thirteen years old. Where we came from in Denton was rock-bottom. There was no electricity, there was no mattress on the bed; there were no curtains and no carpet on the stairs. You took a candle upstairs to the bedroom with you.

Life improved for the Armfields when they moved to Blackpool, although Jimmy's mother worked as hard and as long as she had in Manchester, leaving the house at 7 a.m. and not returning until the evening. The work ethic in the Armfield family was extremely strong. Jimmy, an only child, was alone for long periods of the day in the single room they called home. For the first year in Blackpool they didn't have a radio so Jimmy read and read and read. It paid off in the sense that he passed the examination for Arnold School and, like so many bright working-class children, he now benefited from the excellent teaching and cultural opportunities that became available to him.

I was one of the lucky ones. We had good teachers who were too old to be in the war and they had their heads screwed on. We had a man called Joe Brice who was a Doctor of Divinity who had started selling newspapers on the streets of Wolverhampton when he was fifteen. It's a socialist ethic.

I had no ambition to be a professional footballer. I'd done my O levels and I went on to do A levels in History, Geography and Economics plus a General Studies paper and I won a place at Liverpool University to read Economics. I thought the latter was common sense made difficult. I'd had the habit of reading because I was an only

child. I must have read Hans Christian Andersen's fairy
tales twenty times. I still need to read.

Liverpool University's loss was Blackpool and England's
gain. Having developed rapidly through his National Service
days in the mid-1950s, alongside Eddie Coleman, Duncan
Edwards, Trevor Smith from Birmingham City and the
Sheffield United pair Graham Shaw and Alan Hodgkinson,
Armfield soon came to the attention of the England selectors.
The manner in which he was informed of his first international call-up says much about the hierarchical nature of
football at that time.

> When I first got picked for the Young England team, the
> trainer told me that the manager Joe Smith was looking for
> me so I went to see him in his office at the back of the
> stand. 'I've been told you want to see me' – I thought I was
> going to get a pat on the back but he said, 'No. Why should
> I want to see you?' Talk about being put in your place. So
> I started to walk out and as I reached the door he said,
> 'Oh, there is one thing.' He picked up a piece of paper from
> his desk. 'I've got a letter here from the Football Association.
> They want you to play against Denmark in Copenhagen in
> about two weeks. I want you to go and thank Stan
> [Matthews]. Anyone can play behind him.' Not a word of
> praise. I went back to find Stan and said the manager had
> asked me to thank him. He said, 'Why?' I said, 'I've been
> picked to play for Young England against Denmark and
> the manager said it was because of you.' Stan looked and
> me and smiled. 'Quite right', he said, 'quite right.'

Armfield believes that his grammar-school education made
it easier for him to understand the somewhat bookish Walter

Winterbottom than some of his colleagues. Jimmy Greaves, who made his full England debut on the same 1959 tour as Armfield, always claimed that he never understood a word of the tactical briefings that Winterbottom was so fond of imparting to his mostly bewildered players.

Greaves didn't pass the Eleven Plus and went to a secondary modern but his social background was not dissimilar from that of Armfield. He was born in Manor Park in east London in February 1940, but the family was forced to relocate to Dagenham when their house was bombed. Like most boys of his age and class he was brought up on powdered egg and milk and tinned corned beef. He was thirteen before he saw a banana. His family was fortunate to have an indoor bathroom, but actually filling the bath with water involved his father using a Heath Robinson contraption that pumped the water up the stairs from the downstairs boiler. For that reason a bath was a once-weekly occurrence. Summer holidays in the days of rationing were spent hop-picking in Kent. Being small and agile, Greaves was frequently woken by his father in the middle of the night to scrump apples from a neighbouring orchard which his uncle Fred loaded into his sidecar and drove back to London to sell on the black market.

Nineteen fifty-five, the year that the fifteen-year-old Greaves was due to leave his secondary modern school, was a time of almost full employment. His parents, who had lived through the Depression of the 1930s, were therefore delighted at the prospect of young Jimmy being taken on as an apprentice joiner or plumber. His father came home one night to tell his son that he had had a word with a friend at *The Times* and there was a job waiting for him there as a compositor. Fortunately the Chelsea scout Jimmy Thompson, a diminutive man in a bowler hat who had been closely following Greaves's schoolboy football career, arrived at the Greaves's home in a red Sunbeam Talbot and took Jimmy and his father out for tea at the Strand Palace Hotel. Neither father nor son had previously seen such magnificent furnishings. Shortly afterwards, Jimmy signed forms with Chelsea with the reluctant approval of his father who felt his son would have been set for life with a job as a compositor in Fleet Street or an apprenticeship with a plumber or a joiner.

Greaves and Armfield, like Johnny Haynes, were part of a generation of players who still walked to work or took public transport. Greaves made his debut for Chelsea in the match against Tottenham Hotspur at White Hart Lane in the first match of the 1957–8 season. He travelled to Stamford Bridge from his home in Dagenham by bus and Tube. Chelsea had declined from the Championship-winning side of 1954–5, which had inevitably frustrated the fans. Following a 3–1 home defeat at the hands of a rapidly improving Burnley, John Sillett – who had been responsible for two of the goals – made his way to the bus stop a hundred yards from Stamford Bridge. His hope that all the Chelsea supporters had dispersed by the time he left the ground was dashed when he found four middle-aged fans waiting at the same bus stop.

'Been to the match?' one of them asked.

The Chelsea defender nodded silently, knowing what was to come.

'What about that bloody John Sillett?'

'Yeah, bloody rubbish, wasn't he?' asked another one rhetorically.

Sillett could only nod in agreement once again. The abuse heaped on Sillett intensified, to which the man himself could only keep nodding in eager agreement and pray for the merciful arrival of the bus. What makes the anecdote so revealing is that fans who had been watching Sillett play for several seasons didn't recognise him when they met him in the flesh. They were used to seeing him from the terraces, fifty yards away. Without televised football to make the close-up of his face familiar to them, Sillett's anonymity could be preserved.

Jimmy Armfield could walk to Blackpool's Bloomfield Road ground from the family grocery store:

> When I was living in the shop before I was married, my two best friends came to pick me up and we all walked together over Bloomfield Road bridge. I went into the Players' Entrance, they went into the Paddock. After the game we walked back over the bridge and everyone'd be in the shop and my mother would point at me and say, 'You! Inside! Now!', particularly if we'd lost.

Even after the maximum wage was abolished in 1961, Armfield's wages were far from astronomical.

> I went up from £20 a week to £40. Johnny Haynes told me he was on £100 a week so I went back to my chairman and told him and they put it up to £50. I felt like a millionaire. My dad said that deciding not to take up that place at Liverpool University wasn't a bad idea now. The most I ever earned was £55. It was that kind of wage that kept me in touch with the common man.

The common man's world, however, was also changing. By the middle of the 1960s it was estimated that five million Britons were taking their summer holidays abroad. Because of the post-war baby boom, half of the population was under thirty-five, a ticking time-bomb for the cost of social care at the start of the next century. The expansion of the economy and the general rise in the level of disposable income were leading to an increase in social mobility. Britain's highly stratified class system certainly did not collapse, but there were perceptible shifts within it as the power of the new money began to make itself felt. Thanks to the grammar schools, which offered opportunities to bright children from working-class backgrounds, and the building of new universities, Britain was slowly becoming a more meritocratic country, even if the prevailing class system militated against the emergence of a truly egalitarian society.

This revolution in society and in football was paralleled by a similar one in cricket. Cricket is frequently, and some-times quite rightly, seen as a game administered by blinkered reactionaries. However, to put it in perspective, cricket made two significant innovations in the early 1960s which the Lawn Tennis Association, the Royal & Ancient, the Amateur Athletic Association, the Rugby Football Union and even the Football Association and Football League would have regarded as seismic. On 26 November 1962, to the surprise of nearly everyone and certainly that of the Duke of Norfolk and Ted Dexter, manager and captain respectively of the MCC party then on tour in Australia, the Advisory County Cricket Committee passed by twelve votes to seven a pro-posal by Glamorgan that the status of the amateur cricketer be abolished entirely. Given the fact that only four years previously the committee, which MCC had set up to examine the threatened status of the amateur cricketer, had returned a verdict that the preservation of the status quo was vital to the good health of the game, this rapid reversal reveals how far changes in British society had gone that even MCC was obliged to take note of them. From the start of the 1963 season, there would be no amateurs and no professionals in the old sense of the word. All the players would simply be cricketers and the absurd anomalies of amateurism were thankfully consigned to the grave.

Nineteen sixty-three saw not only the first season without amateur 'gentlemen' on the cricket field but another, perhaps even more significant, change to the structure of county cricket. It was decided to experiment with a new limited-overs knock-out competition that would last one day only. Each side would have a single innings of up to sixty-five overs. Weather permitting, anyone who came to watch and stayed until the end of the day's play would see a result. One-day cricket, like T20 cricket forty years later, was to be the salvation of the game for some time to come.

It was also a landmark year in British social and cultural history. There is a well-advanced theory among historians that the disastrous invasion of Suez in 1956 prompted seven years of cultural turmoil which culminated in the extraordinary events of 1963, the year that effectively divides the British twentieth century in two. In those seven years, so the theory goes, Britain shuffled off the constricting attitudes of a class-ridden society and embraced a new social order that scorned the conventional notion of social deference.

In 1963, the Beatles emerged in their full mop-top glory, most of the public took the side of the audacious Great Train Robbers against the police who were trying to capture a gang of thieves and revelled in the scandals revealed by the Profumo affair. That year, too, the now much-reviled and out-of-touch Harold Macmillan, though forced to leave office by illness, appeared to have resigned in the face of a satirical broadside issued by the stage revue *Beyond the Fringe*, the magazine *Private Eye*, the Soho-based nightclub The Establishment and ultimately the most powerful weapon of all, the television series *That Was the Week That Was* which began transmission in November 1962. The influence of this satirical programme, transmitted late on Saturday night, grew at the same rate as its delighted audience. Macmillan, parodied mercilessly by Peter

Cook on the stage and slightly more kindly by Willie Rushton on *TW3*, resigned in favour of yet another Old Etonian, who still sat in the House of Lords, but in accordance with fashionable theory agreed to renounce his peerage. This change was symbolised politically the following year when plain Mr Harold Wilson from Huddersfield, with his stated predilection for H.P. Sauce and St Bruno pipe tobacco, led the Labour party to an electoral victory after which the Conservatives replaced Sir Alec Douglas-Home with Ted Heath, a man who had been to a grammar school.

If Billy Wright had been the epitome of 1950s conformism and deference, a new spirit was starting to engage the captains of England in the 1960s, a decade in which much changed – though rarely to the extent promoted subsequently by popular myth. History, especially English history, tends to be the product of evolution rather than revolution. It is received wisdom that the 1960s was the decade of change, but the developments of that time would not have been possible without the changes that had taken place in the middle of the 1950s. Certainly the 1950s was a decade of social conformism, illustrated perfectly by the fate of the Wolfenden Report in 1957, which recommended significant liberalisation of the current legislation dealing with homosexuality. An outraged popular press called it a 'Pansies Charter' and the Conservative government, which had no doubt commissioned the report with the best of intentions, quickly buried it. It was to be another ten years before the country was thought to be ready for the reforms that appeared at the end of the 1960s but it seems unlikely that homosexual relationships between consenting adults over the age of twenty-one would have passed into law as early as 1967 had it not been for the innovative efforts of Wolfenden in 1957.

Even so, the changes came slowly. A private member's bill introduced by the Labour MP Sydney Silverman in 1965 abolished capital punishment, but it would not have been confirmed by the public had a referendum been held on it. When England won the World Cup in 1966, homosexuality and abortion were still illegal. It was just over twenty years after the end of the Second World War and English society had, of course, changed but not to the extent that is popularly suggested by current television documentary film-makers who did not live through those times. The pill certainly changed women's lives but most teenagers in the 1960s were as virginal as their parents had been at the same age. Only married women were permitted to be prescribed the pill by their family GP. Unmarried girls who went to their doctor to ask to be put on the pill because they were in a relationship with a boyfriend were not only refused, but the doctor frequently told the girl's parents of the request, to her utter mortification. The friends of girls who had been through such humiliation were hardly in a rush to experience it themselves. Teenagers in the 1970s certainly benefited from the pill, but that was another decade.

The 1960s were the decade of the BBC's *The Wednesday Play* – a series of TV plays which included *Cathy Come Home* and Dennis Potter's *Stand Up for Nigel Barton* – and of the campy spy series *The Avengers*, a clever mixture of the stereotypical Englishman played by Patrick Macnee with his bowler hat and rolled umbrella and the sexually predatory Honor Blackman and Diana Rigg. At the start of the decade Ken Russell and John Schlesinger broke new ground with their films for the arts series *Monitor*, whose one hundredth programme, broadcast in 1962, was Russell's celebrated drama documentary about the composer Edward Elgar. The previously unmentioned north of England became chic in television as well as films with the success of *Coronation Street*, set in a fictional version of Salford, and *Z Cars*, set in a fictional suburb of Merseyside. Pop music was showcased in the BBC's

Top of the Pops, which was first broadcast in January 1964, and on ITV with *Ready Steady Go!*, which had begun in August 1963, but which would last only until December 1966.

However, despite these real innovations, some historians looking back at the decade tend to notice the elements of continuity as much as the more obvious breaks with the past. *Dixon of Dock Green* achieved bigger audiences than *Z Cars* and lasted for years beyond George Dixon's official retirement age. The big film of 1965 was *The Sound of Music*, the television ratings were dominated by *The Black and White Minstrel Show* and *Sunday Night at the London Palladium*. People in 1966 would doubtless have been astonished to have been informed that within twenty years *The Black and White Minstrel Show*, which featured performers with blacked-up faces, would be regarded as embarrassingly racist. Despite the steady flow of Caribbean immigrants into the UK, and the beginnings of a similar movement of people from the Indian subcontinent, Great Britain in the 1960s remained overwhelmingly a white nation.

The younger generation of television programme makers in the 1960s were dominated by the product of Rab Butler's grammar schools and a university – if not an Oxbridge – education. The programmes they wanted to make reflected their interests and so comedy now included Peter Cook and Dudley Moore in *Not Only... But Also* as well as *The Dick Emery Show*. The successful magazine programme *Tonight* spawned a twenty-six-part documentary series *The Great War* as well as *That Was the Week That Was*. At the end of the decade co-production money from Time Life subsidised Kenneth Clark's personal view of the historical development of ideas and the arts, *Civilisation*. If these were the shows that historians eagerly seize upon to demonstrate the fact that television was growing up and that the medium could innovate in the 1960s where it had found it difficult to do so in the previous decade, it should not be forgotten that most people who rented their sets from Granada or Radio Rentals or DER wanted to watch Charlie Drake as much as Hancock, Harry Worth rather than Monty Python, *Take Your Pick* or *Double Your Money* rather than *Hamlet in Elsinore* or *The Year of the Sex Olympics*. *Perry Mason*, *The Dick Van Dyke Show* and *Batman* made a much bigger impact on audiences than *An Age of Kings* (a fifteen-part adaptation of Shakespeare's history plays produced by the BBC in 1960) or *The Spread of the Eagle* (a nine-part BBC adaptation of Shakespeare's three major Roman dramas).

In 1965, the BBC introduced two bi-weekly half-hour soap operas whose subject matter reflected some of the social changes that were taking place in 1960s Britain. Two nights a week viewers could watch *The Newcomers*, produced by the rising star Verity Lambert who had won her spurs on *Dr Who* and who was now trailblazing a path as a television executive for future generations of women. *The Newcomers* centred on a London family who moved to a housing estate in the fictional country town of Angleton. Exterior sequences were filmed in Haverhill in Suffolk, a town which, after a rapid post-war expansion to incorporate families moving out from London, had undergone similar social changes to those depicted in the soap opera itself.

The Newcomers ran in conjunction with a soap opera with a similar format called *United!*. This series followed the travails of a fictional Second Division team called Brentwich United. The football scenes were filmed at the Victoria Ground in Stoke with the ubiquitous Jimmy Hill, now the manager of Coventry City on their climb from Third Division anonymity to First Division status, acting as a technical adviser. His efforts to achieve authenticity unfortunately ran into heavy criticism from the then management of Wolverhampton Wanderers who complained that the storylines followed too closely their own unavailing struggles to avoid relegation. *United!* was less successful than *The Newcomers*, and was cancelled after only two series. The show was generally considered to be too soft to appeal to male viewers, and too male-oriented for the female audience who preferred *Compact*, a soap opera set in the world of a fashion magazine which had been taken off the air to provide breathing space in the schedule for *United!* and *The Newcomers*. The devastated writers of *Compact*, Peter Ling and Hazel Adair, wrought a terrible revenge on the callous BBC by moving across to ATV Network and creating *Crossroads*. The cultural hooligans who ran the BBC in the 1960s insisted that the Corporation save money by reusing the original two-inch videotapes on which *United!* had been recorded, as a consequence of which none of the programme's 147 episodes are believed to have survived. It is not the act of short-sighted philistinism that wiping the tapes of *Not Only... But Also* undoubtedly was, but at the very least it denied future historians the chance to check their teenage memories.

Nevertheless, the very fact that cautious BBC programme executives who have always been risk averse and are probably more so today than ever before, had accepted the fact that football was a suitable topic for a BBC1 drama series in peak viewing hours suggests that both football and television were changing. *United!* appeared at almost the same time as *Match of the Day* made its transfer from the tiny initial audience on BBC2 to its unquestioned status as a fixed point in BBC1's Saturday-night schedule. The relationship between football and television was then still in its early, fumble-in-the-back-row-of-the-cinema stage, but it would blossom in spectacular fashion, the shy virgin of the 1960s medium becoming the unhealthy predator of the twenty-first century.

The change from the schoolmasterish Walter Winterbottom, who accepted the fact that he had to play with a team selected by men who knew little about football, to Alf Ramsey, who only took on the job on the understanding that he would have complete control of the selection process, is another indication of the changes that the new decade brought. In a parallel move, the enthusiastic Billy Wright, with his unkempt, schoolboyish shock of blond hair, gave way to the stylishly groomed Bobby Moore, a man who rarely revealed what he really thought to anyone. 'Ask me to tell you about Bobby Moore, the footballer,' Ron Greenwood, his West Ham manager, once said, 'and I will talk for days. Ask me about Bobby Moore the man and I will dry up in a minute.'

Matt Dickinson, Moore's latest biographer, writes perceptively that Moore was a child of post-war austerity. Children born during the war years and having very little memory of them were heavily influenced by the years of rationing and austerity. George Best, who was born in 1946, just five years later than the future England captain, was a symbol of a different age. Moore's appearance had something of the Spitfire generation about it: he was always neat, compulsively tidy and socially polite to everyone. He came from an upstanding socialist background where there was no drink, no swearing and significant working-class solidarity. His mother, known as Doss, would wash and iron the laces in Bobby's boots before every schoolboy football match. His shirts were never folded but placed on hangers and hung in the wardrobe in colour order, from dark to light. Moore, not unlike Ramsey, nursed a constant anxiety that he might be exposed for his lack of social skills. He inherited his hatred of fuss and attention from his mother, while his father, Bob, was no socialiser either and shunned the drinking culture of the pub. It was a regimented upbringing, Dickinson concludes, but not a joyless one. Moore knew that his parents were his firm supporters and he understood why they eventually retreated from the reflected limelight of being the parents of the captain who held aloft the World Cup.

Although he eventually gave way to Bobby Moore before the start of the 1966 World Cup, Jimmy Armfield was the England captain when Alf Ramsey took over. His first match in charge was the second leg of a qualification fixture for the 1964 European Nations Cup against France in Paris at the end of February 1963. Britain, like most of Europe, was enduring its worst winter since 1946–7 and most players hadn't played a competitive match since the turn of the year. Armfield recalls the night with a shudder:

> We should never have played that first game in France. The floodlights were awful. The pitch was covered in snow and ice. We lost 5–2. The last goal they scored I was the only England defender in the penalty area and there were three French forwards with the ball. Springett had slipped and the left-back was still trying to get back. On the bus afterwards Alf sat next to me and said, 'Do we always play like that?' He rang me up at home and carefully went through the strengths and weaknesses of every player asking me what I thought. I was captain for a couple of years, maybe fifteen games, and I lost the captaincy through injury. I ruptured my groin in the last match of the 1963–4 season. Alf was in the stand and I had my suitcase with me. I was going to fly off with him for the mini World Cup they called it but instead I was on my way to hospital. I rang Alf on the Monday morning and said I wasn't going to make it and that's how Bobby Moore got the captaincy.

Ramsey's second match in charge saw an equally humiliating 2–1 defeat by Scotland at Wembley and a mistake by Armfield when he dallied on the ball and was robbed by Jim Baxter on the edge of his own penalty area. Baxter continued unhindered and thumped the ball past debutant Gordon Banks. Ramsey, an Englishman who at core loathed the Scots, felt humiliated by his team's general display, and he was particularly unimpressed by Armfield's laxity. Eventually he preferred George Cohen at right-back, which would have limited Armfield's games as captain, but the Blackpool skipper continued to lead the side in Moore's absence as late as the warm-up games before the start of the World Cup in 1966. This, however, was probably the result of Alf Ramsey's reluctance to let Moore think he had a divine right to the captaincy. Despite his legendary, and ultimately fatal, loyalty to his players, Ramsey was always keen to emphasise that he was in complete control of the selection process. No matter how well a player had performed the last time he pulled on an England shirt he was not guaranteed a place in the next squad until Ramsey had informed the FA of its composition.

At the end of the 1962–3 season, Jimmy Armfield was injured and for the first time Bobby Moore was asked to lead out the side for England's match against Czechoslovakia in Bratislava on 29 May. At just twenty-two he was the youngest captain in England's history. England won the game convincingly by 4–2, two of their goals coming from Jimmy Greaves. It was the first indication that England might indeed win the World Cup in 1966. After the defeat in Paris in February, Ramsey had also spent some time talking earnestly with Bobby Moore, who was still a relative newcomer to international football. Jimmy Armfield was sharp enough to realise that, despite Moore's youth, Ramsey had found his natural lieutenant in the West Ham United left-half. Although he was determined to maintain his own presence in the national side for as long as possible, Armfield could not help but recognise that the young man from Barking had an extraordinary maturity for one so young.

Bobby Moore, like Armfield and Jimmy Hill, had also passed the Eleven Plus examination. R. A. Butler's 1944 Act had laid down three types of school – grammar, secondary modern and technical – but of the last named there were few in operation. One of them, however, was Tom Hood Technical College in Leyton which Moore attended from the age of eleven, working towards his four O levels in woodwork, geography, art and technical drawing. He had been born on 12 April 1941 and raised in Barking, only a symbolic few miles from Alf Ramsey's Dagenham and David Beckham's Leytonstone. He was the only one of his friends to pass the

Eleven Plus and attend Tom Hood. Moore's journey to his new
school required him to get up at 7 a.m., catch a bus to Barking
station, then take the train to Wanstead and the trolleybus to
Leyton, followed by a long walk to the school. He hated the
journey and the attendant loneliness so he went to his doctor
to ask for a certificate for transfer to a school nearer home in
Barking on the grounds of travel sickness.

In the end Moore stayed at Tom Hood because he was
swept along on a tide of footballing success. He joined West
Ham United in 1956 and made his debut for the first team at
the age of seventeen in an early-season encounter with
Manchester United in September 1958. His rival for the shirt
was his mentor, Malcolm Allison, who had finally recovered
from a debilitating bout of tuberculosis that had kept him out
of the game for over a year. Allison had never played in the
First Division and was desperate to do so. He had spotted
Moore's potential as soon as the youngster appeared on the
same training pitch. It was Allison who had taught Moore to
adopt that distinctive upright gait, who had told him constantly to ask himself the question, 'If I get the ball now who
am I going to give it to?', which gave Moore that extra second
of awareness as an opponent tried to close him down.

Confronted by the dilemma of whom to pick, the West Ham
manager, Ted Fenton, consulted Allison's best friend, the Irish
left-back Noel Cantwell, who advised that the manager select
the young lad over the desperate veteran. On learning of the
decision Allison walked out of Upton Park and effectively finished his playing career. He never played in the First Division,
although he would go on to become a famously successful and
innovative coach. Moore, meanwhile, played his part in an
exciting 3–2 win over a Manchester United side that was still
struggling in the post-Munich era. Had Allison remained to
watch the game he might well have gained the place he so

coveted in the West Ham first team. A few days after the victory over Manchester United, West Ham went to Nottingham where Forest beat them four-nil. Bobby Moore was taken apart by the skilful Forest inside-forward Johnny Quigley but Allison was no longer around to take advantage of Moore's subsequent demotion to the reserves. Much as Moore admired Allison, he despised the self-destructive streak that so tormented his fellow defender. Moore would endure two difficult seasons playing as a centre-half or a traditional wing-half, but he learned from these early struggles and developed a mental strength. In February 1962 Ron Greenwood asked him to play in the back four alongside Ken Brown, the regular centre-half. It was the catalyst for Moore's transformation into a player of exceptional class, and his career took off from this point. The invention of the second central defender killed off the old WM formation, in which one centre half marked one centre forward. Liverpool adopted it with Tommy Smith alongside Ron Yeats, and Harry Catterick at Everton did the same when he also gave the number ten shirt to John Hurst but played him at the back alongside Brian Labone. Nobody, however, performed more gracefully and effectively in the role than Bobby Moore.

As Moore rose through the ranks to become captain of his country, his predecessor Billy Wright was taking his first and, as it transpired, his only job as a Football League club manager. After his retirement as a player, Wright had turned down the chance to be groomed as Stan Cullis's eventual successor at Molineux, as well as offers of management jobs in the Midlands and London. He preferred the atmosphere at Lancaster Gate where the FA continued to show their great admiration of a footballer who knew his place in their world. Wright was duly appointed to manage the England Under-23 and youth sides. In the summer of 1962, Arsenal sacked their manager and former goalkeeper George Swindin for not being

as successful as Bill Nicholson was across north London at
Tottenham. The job was offered to Billy Wright who, unfortunately for all concerned, accepted.

As a manager Wright took his cue from Walter
Winterbottom rather than Stan Cullis. He simply did not
have the toughness that a good manager needs: after a bad
defeat he would excuse his players rather than criticise them.
When he did eventually get round to dropping a well-known
player who was badly out of form, the player responded by
hammering on the manager's door, which was firmly bolted
against all intruders. Gary Newbon, who knew Wright well
when they both worked for ATV Network in Birmingham,
relates the story as told to him some years after the event by
Wright: 'He used to put up the team list then run away and
hide. There was a big bruising centre-half who also occasionally played centre-forward who would bang on his door
which was locked and he would scream, "I know you're
fucking in there!"'

The general consensus was that Billy Wright was simply
too nice a man to be a good manager. In 1965–6, the last of
his four unsuccessful seasons at Highbury, Arsenal finished
fourteenth in the league, having earlier been knocked out of
the Cup in the fourth round by lowly Peterborough United.
The hostility of the fans and the careless incompetence of the
players, who were by no means untalented, literally drove
Wright to drink. It was to be many years before he emerged
from a debilitating battle with alcohol. The match which
sealed his fate was a 3–0 home defeat to Leeds United, a
match played, through inept scheduling, on the same night as
Liverpool lost 1–2 to Borussia Dortmund in the final of the
European Cup Winners' Cup, a match shown live on television. At the same time, just 4,554 spectators trickled into
Highbury.

For all the fact that he could spot a talented youngster (most of the home-grown players who won the Double for Arsenal in 1971, including Charlie George, had been signed and developed by him), he was mercilessly dismissed by the chairman Denis Hill-Wood. Wright was on holiday when he was accosted on coming out of the sea by a newspaper reporter who wanted Wright's comment on his dismissal. Prior to this unwelcome confrontation Wright had no idea that he had been sacked, although he could hardly have been unaware of the possibility. Brian Glanville was less than impressed by the behaviour of Arsenal's Old Etonian chairman towards England's former captain:

> He was betrayed by Denis Hill-Wood. Supporters shouted Wright must go, he responded Wright must stay – and then stabbed him in the back. I wish I had the talent to draw the cartoon of Hill-Wood backing Billy Wright to the hilt and then showing the dagger sticking out of his back.

The successful captain of Wolves and England had proved a signal failure as a manager. Ironically, it was a fate that also eventually awaited Bobby Moore. Wright, however, unlike his successor as England captain, was to find his salvation in television.

The power of live television and its influence on sport was a growing factor in the 1960s. Paul Fox, Bryan Cowgill and Ronnie Noble, along with Peter Dimmock, had created a thriving BBC Sport department in the 1950s, acquiring the rights to the Olympic Games through the European Broadcasting Union, Wimbledon tennis, the Grand National and other horse races, the cricket Test matches, the Boat Race, the Open golf championship, rugby league, and rugby union's Five Nations championship. However, the best they could do with live football was the FA Cup final and the occasional England match.

The 1960s saw two major developments in British television – the launch of BBC2 in April 1964 and the arrival of colour transmissions at the end of the decade. Each innovation produced an increase in the number of television sets sold and a consequent boost to the BBC's income through the licence fee. BBC2 was conceived as a channel that catered for minority interest groups, so – taking its cue from the new UHF transmission on 625 lines – the audience was soon presented with *Jazz 625*, *Theatre 625* and *Cinema 625*, as well as strands which would became staples of future broadcasting schedules – *Call My Bluff*, *Man Alive*, *Chronicle*, *The Old Grey Whistle Test*, *One Pair of Eyes* and *The Money Programme*. One of the minorities thus catered for was football supporters in a new programme called *Match of the Day*, which began transmission on the first day of the 1964–5 season with a match between Liverpool and Arsenal at Anfield. The audience was estimated to be around 20,000 viewers, which was roughly half the number of spectators at the ground who had paid to watch the match. Such figures must have come as a great comfort to the wary Alan Hardaker at the Football League, but the audiences soon began to grow. The following season the programme transferred to BBC1, where it has continued to thrive ever since.

Hardaker was not alone in his suspicions. A large minority of clubs actually voted against renewing the existing deal with the BBC for fear of television's impact on ground admissions. The BBC, meanwhile, possibly through gritted teeth, accepted that part of its remit was to show matches from outside the First Division and during that inaugural season on BBC2 the audience was treated to edited highlights of the Fourth Division game between Oxford United and Tranmere Rovers.

As the decade progressed, ITV started to compete with the

BBC as a sports broadcaster, but it was a slow process. While the BBC was transmitting the British gold medal successes of Lynn Davies, Mary Rand and Ann Packer from Tokyo in 1964, ITV was transmitting Frank Keating reading the results to camera in the studio from the stop press of the *Evening Standard*. ITV tried to compete with *Grandstand* by introducing *World of Sport*, their Saturday-afternoon magazine of different sports in January 1965, but their trump card was wrestling, which seemed to belong more properly to show business rather than sport. Michael Grade remembers that *World of Sport* might have been the flagship of ITV Sport but it caused endless factional arguments.

> Sport was networked so the only argument within ITV was about budgets, not about how it was carved up on the network. Most of the arguments were about *World of Sport*. Every year there was an argument and we all went fifteen rounds over the *World of Sport* budget. Both BBC and ITV covered the Cup final. We both had full crews and commentators and our own cameras but the pictures were pretty much identical and coverage would start at ten o'clock in the morning. It was always a case of who could get their cameras on the team coach... it was all mad. The BBC maintained its traditional ratings superiority because it had no commercial interruptions. If you've got the choice of watching without breaks, even though you wouldn't cut away from the play, you'll choose BBC because you couldn't be sure when there would be an ad break so the BBC tended to win the ratings battle 3:1.

London Weekend Television did briefly win the right to broadcast the Gillette Cup final between Warwickshire and Sussex from Lord's in 1968 and transmit it across the ITV network in the face of outrage from the BBC. The one-day competition had captured the public imagination very quickly and the first Saturday in September at Lord's was to become cricket's equivalent of the first Saturday in May when the FA Cup final was played at Wembley. In fact, LWT's association with the Gillette Cup lasted for that one game only. *Frost on Saturday* went out live on LWT at 6.45 on Saturday evenings and had to be preceded by a commercial break since that was how LWT was funded. In order to fit in the adverts, LWT had to end its transmission of the Gillette Cup final in the last over, before Dennis Amiss and A. C. Smith had scored the runs that won the game for Warwickshire by four wickets. The public was frustrated and the cricket authorities, particularly MCC and the Test and County Cricket Board, were outraged. ITV lost the contract. The fact that the BBC frequently cut away from coverage of Test matches to show horse racing from Sandown Park was for some reason not considered equally reprehensible. Commercial television was simply not welcome in the Long Room at Lord's. The BBC retained control of nearly all cricket for another twenty years until the arrival of satellite broadcasting.

The United States set the trend for sports presentation on television. BBC and ITV were public service broadcasters and, although they were both motivated by the need to achieve high ratings, they did not emerge from the same landscape as American broadcasters who were, with the almost irrelevant exception of PBS, commercial organisations. Their job, as ITV soon realised, was to sell products and the programmes they aired were basically the vehicle for the sales drive. The man who realised this as quickly as anyone and thereby solved the equation of sport, broadcasting and commerce was an American lawyer – and pioneering sports agent – called Mark McCormack.

McCormack graduated from Yale Law School and went to work for the prestigious law firm of Arter, Hadden, Wycoff & Van Duzer in Cleveland. The client who helped him change the world of sports broadcasting was the golfer Arnold Palmer, who had won the Canadian Open in his rookie year of 1955 and his first Masters at Augusta in 1958. After an initial meeting in 1959, during which the two men shared collegiate reminiscences of playing golf in a match between the lawyer's College of William & Mary in Virginia and the golfer's college at Wake Forest in North Carolina, McCormack became convinced that his quickest route to the top was via the role of a personal manager. Sam Snead from an earlier generation of golfers had been represented by the Boston sports promoter Fred Corcoran but not to anything like the extent that McCormack envisaged.

Arnold Palmer's growing success as a professional golfer soon generated the need for decisions of a financial rather than a strictly sporting nature – there were contracts and commercial endorsements to negotiate, and public appearances to manage. Initially McCormack was content for the firm that employed him to handle everything but Palmer was resolute in his wish for McCormack to handle him exclusively, one on one. In the wake of Palmer's success on the golf course, all the commercial advantages of sporting prestige soon presented themselves. A first book led to talk of Arnold Palmer golf schools, driving ranges, golf tips in periodicals and a syndicated column. McCormack soon abandoned his other commitments to concentrate exclusively on Palmer. He examined the contract that the sporting goods company Wilson had persuaded Palmer to sign. It paid the golfer a mere $5,000 a year and prevented him from working for anyone else until 1963.

After Palmer won his second Masters in 1960, the commercial pressures built up but, despite McCormack's reasonable approach, the irascible Wilson chairman, Judge James Cooney, said he would not renegotiate the terms of the contract while it was still valid, a threat which Wilson maintained until Palmer's contract expired on 1 November 1963. This response made Palmer and McCormack all the more determined to sell themselves dearly and to exert considerably more control over future agreements. They agreed initially that Palmer would only endorse products he personally used – Coca-Cola, Liggett & Myers (L&M) cigarettes and Heinz tomato ketchup. Within a few years Palmer would lend his name to ice skating rinks, insurance companies and 110 branches of a dry cleaners. A chain of motels was planned, but – like plans for Arnold Palmer shaving cream, suntan oil, talcum powder and deodorant – it never got off the ground. Nevertheless, Arnold Palmer was the first elite sportsman to become a million-dollar corporation while still in the prime of his playing career.

McCormack now wanted to spread his own wings, which made Palmer insecure. Nevertheless, the International Management Group (IMG) which he started in Cleveland in 1960 would grow into a global sports and media empire. Out of it emerged Trans World International (TWI), a television company which in 1963 and 1964 made a TV series called *Challenge Golf* featuring McCormack's two big clients, Palmer and the South African Gary Player. When McCormack signed the new star Jack Nicklaus he controlled the commercial lives of a trio of golfers who became known collectively as the Big Three. For three seasons in the late 1960s Palmer, Player and Nicklaus made *Big Three Golf* for the television network NBC. In 1970 Nicklaus left IMG to go his own way, but by then the standard for the commercial exploitation of sports stars had been set. Between 1960 and 1967 those three together won a total of fifteen majors while no other golfer was able to win two.

Sam Snead and Ben Hogan, the big stars of US golf in the decade after 1945, did not come near to matching Arnold Palmer's income, popularity and prize-winnings. It was McCormack's involvement that produced big television purses, big galleries and the idea of golf as a sport with an international audience. Arnold Palmer came from Latrobe, a modest town thirty-five miles east of Pittsburgh, and his small-town origins were the key to understanding his appeal. He was, McCormack insisted, an ordinary man who liked steak dinners and the television series *Bonanza*. His strict Scots-Irish father had been the golf professional at Latrobe Country Club and the young Palmer grew up very aware of the socially inferior position of the humble golf pro who ate his meals in the club kitchen or at home and never entered the locker room, bar or members' lounge unless specifically invited by a member. Arnold himself was not allowed to play with the members' children or to swim in the club pool. His earliest career plan had been to become a businessman because he could not face the prospect of being a servant and second-class citizen.

McCormack believed that Palmer's appeal to the common man all over the world lay in five particular assets: first was his relatively modest background (his father had been a green-keeper before rising to be club professional and Latrobe was a humble club); then there was his good looks, which widened his appeal with women; there was also the way he played golf, taking risks and wearing his emotions on his sleeve; there was his involvement in a string of exciting finishes in early televised tournaments; and, finally, his affability. Taken together, these positive characteristics made Palmer a highly marketable product.

Palmer had been astonished that Wilson would not do the honourable thing and let him out of a contract that clearly undervalued his new-found star status. At the end of the contract Wilson offered an increased deal but at the price of a ten-year contract which allowed the golfer to make up to $75,000 p.a. Palmer himself valued his relationship with Wilson, so McCormack worked on the best possible deal while staying within the Wilson fold which led to the evolution of the Arnold Palmer Golf Company making its own branded clubs and balls.

Before the end of the decade American men could shave with Arnold Palmer lather, spray on his deodorant, drink his favourite soft drink, fly his 'preferred' airline, buy his approved corporate jet, eat his candy bar, order stock certificates through him and do their DIY around the house with his power tools. When the chain of Arnold Palmer Dry Cleaners became visible all over America, the professional golfer Dave Marr said in a joke that would not be broadcast or printed today, 'The only pro golfer I would send my laundry to is Chen Ching-po. If you have two new cleaning businesses in town and you don't know either and one is called Irving Schlepperman and one is called Arnold Palmer, you're going to go with Palmer.'

McCormack and Palmer were both visionaries and saw in the Open Championship a way to expand their business beyond the North American continent. The British Open – as American golfers always refer to it – had, since Bobby Jones's triumph in 1930, declined in status compared with its American equivalent and with the Masters in Augusta. Palmer certainly felt a kinship with the history of golf so that it gave him great pleasure to compete on the great British courses on which the Open was played. However, he like Nicklaus did not much like being referred to as A. Palmer or J. Nicklaus while amateurs were dignified with the title 'Mr' before their names. In this respect golf followed the lines of social stratification laid down by cricket. Until 1963, cricket scorecards would present the initials of amateur players before their names (as in P. B. H.

May or M. J. K. Smith), and those of the professionals after (as in Washbrook C. and Hutton L.). That in itself was an improvement on the practice of Cricket's Golden Age which printed scorecards with Mr C. B. Fry the amateur and Hobbs the professional who was deprived of the dignity of any initial.

When Britain was trying its hardest to persuade the Americans to join in the fight against Hitler in 1940 and 1941, propagandists soon discovered that one of the biggest obstacles to acquiring American sympathy was the strong feeling that Americans were not prepared to send their boys off to die in a foreign war to preserve the British Empire and the British class system. Palmer and Nicklaus retained traces of those feelings and in addition, they did not greatly care for antiquated British plumbing which left locker rooms cold and sometimes without hot running water. Their attitude was shared by other American golfers. Indeed, apart from Sam Snead in 1946 and Ben Hogan at Carnoustie in 1953, the American golfers who dominated the world game in the post-war era could not be bothered to travel all the way to Britain to play in the Open.

When Arnold Palmer arrived at St Andrews in 1959 it was generally assumed that he would win at the first time of asking as there was no real competition, but it was the Australian Kel Nagle who won by a stroke from the American. However, the Old Course worked its charm on Palmer as it has done over the years on so many other golfers from beyond the British Isles. Palmer returned the following year and won at Royal Birkdale, at the same time winning over the British press and a legion of fans. Palmer was able to hit long, low shots which played well on links courses and, just as importantly, he was a great scrambler. Palmer won again at Troon in 1962, but now he was accompanied by Nicklaus, Gene Littler, Sam Snead and Phil Rodgers. It was the greatest Open field for twenty-five years. Palmer shot successive rounds of 71-69-67-69 and won,

to great acclaim, by six strokes. He returned to the UK later in
the year for a new tournament founded by Mark McCormack,
the World Match Play at Wentworth, winning at the first time
of asking. In total, Palmer would play twelve major British-
based tournaments in seven years. He achieved something
similar in Japan, establishing his status as a world star.

The relationship between Arnold Palmer and Mark
McCormack and their television and commercial ventures is
treated in such detail because it set the trend for the way in
which sport would develop in the second half of the twentieth
century. Television played such a large part in Arnold Palmer's
life that by the mid-1960s he was the best-recognised athlete
in the United States, although a case could certainly be made
for the boxer Muhammad Ali. Mickey Mantle and Joe
Namath, the biggest stars in baseball and American football
respectively, were largely unknown outside the United States.
The tournaments that established Palmer's fame were the
Masters and US Open of 1960 which were both televised and
won by Palmer with sensational finishes in front of audiences
of millions.

It was the success of the Big Three that transformed golf and
the earning capacities of professionals on the USPGA golf tour.
In 1950, the twenty-fifth leading player on the tour made $5,152
whereas by 1965 the twenty-fifth leading player made $36,692.
The trend has continued upwards in recent years but at a
much more rapid rate, due partly to inflation and partly to the
recognition that elite sportsmen are valuable commercial
assets and need to be rewarded accordingly.

Palmer's rapid expansion as a corporate entity was in large
part, of course, the result of the burgeoning prosperity of the
1960s. The wages of professional footballers in England also
benefited from the expansion of the economy but their wages
and their commercial income from endorsements were

minuscule compared to their American counterparts in golf and tennis. Team sports in America like football and baseball were far less lucrative, as Jim Bouton's seminal work *Ball Four* indicates, but American values had not significantly penetrated British cultural life in the 1960s. If Billy Wright in the 1950s, like every other English professional footballer of the time, had no option but to accept the offerings of the maximum wage, Bobby Moore was part of the post-abolition generation. Six years older than Moore, Armfield might have felt like a millionaire in 1961 at £50 a week but if he never earned more than £55 it suggests that for the final decade of his career, for half of which he remained an England player, his wages rose by no more than £5.

There were not yet any agents in the English game to take on the clubs for him; in fact the Football League had taken legal measures to prohibit any third-party representation. Moore himself, having experienced the unwelcome realities of footballers' remuneration at the start of his career in the late 1950s, was to adopt a much more aggressive approach to wage negotiation than many of his contemporaries. His first wage on the West Ham ground staff as a school leaver was £6 15s 0d, which was supplemented by a one pound note if he were chosen to play for the reserves in the Football Combination. Playing away, young players would also receive five shillings for tea money. Moore made careful plans for the distribution of these riches:

> Fifty bob to Mum, set aside for fares and Saturday night out and the three bob you could save from the tea money was profitable especially if you played two or three times a week for the reserves and youth team. Otherwise it was sweeping terraces, cleaning out the stands, set out clean kit, clear away dirty kit, clean first team boots, knock on

door, clean toilets, paint the back of the stand and even help prepare the pitch, schlepping heavy roller. I was relieved to be sent back to polish taps on baths and showers. Even on Fridays all I could do was to stagger home after 6pm because I had to be up early for the Saturday match. There was no time to answer back or get into much mischief.

On his seventeenth birthday in April 1958, Moore signed a professional contract at £12 a week but, four years later at the tender age of twenty-one, he was involved in a standoff with West Ham who had, post-abolition, offered all their players £28 a week. All of them signed in the docile manner that clubs expected of their employees; all, that is, except Moore. Apart from gossip and rumour nobody really knew what any other player was earning so the principle of 'divide and rule' remained the easiest way for clubs to retain absolute power. Moore decided he was worth £30 a week and refused to be cajoled or bullied. He had justifiable confidence in his own ability and thought that £30 was what he was worth and he wouldn't sign a contract for anything less.

Moore held out for six weeks and in the end he got his way. The club, unwilling to break what would now be regarded as a salary structure, saved face by raising the wage level of the whole first team squad to £30 a week. Moore always retained a strong belief in his own talent and was determined to stand up for what he thought was right, or at least what was right for him. The other players now looked at Moore with a new respect. Perhaps unwittingly he had taken a significant first step on the trail that would lead to the captaincy of club and country. Equally unwittingly, he had demonstrated that the socialist principles of his father were not necessarily for him as he would presumably have been quite happy to have taken the

£30 for himself even if the others remained at £28. He was fighting the battle of individual enterprise and was setting off on the ideological expedition from traditional working-class Labour to aspiring middle-class Tory. It was a journey made by many footballers in the 1960s and 1970s as Hunter Davies demonstrated when he wrote *The Glory Game*, which offered an insight into the dynamics of the Tottenham Hotspur dressing room in 1971.

Moore's assumption of the captaincy in April 1962 seemed almost taken for granted. When Ron Greenwood took over as manager of West Ham from Ted Fenton in April 1961, he promised to build a new team around the twenty-year-old Bobby Moore. Nobody does that unless he is quite sure that the player is outstanding and that he will be able to gain the respect of his team-mates, particularly those more senior to him. Moore later commented on the captaincy:

> In boys' teams the captain is generally the outstanding player simply because boys are impressed purely by ability and very little by knowledge. But in professional terms the captain – if he means anything at all – must be a natural leader, the kind of individual whose play and conduct sets an example to the others. If he is slack and cynical and doesn't seem to care much about training then the rest of the team will take the hint. I try to be the other kind.

Moore was never a shouter, never a fist-pumper in the manner of future England captains like Robson, Adams, Pearce, Butcher and Terry: he did not fit the traditional image of the battling central-defender-as-captain. When England and West Ham were winning this was an attitude that provoked nothing but admiration, but when results started to turn against the team Moore's generally perceived air of insouciance irritated fans. Results started to go wrong at West Ham at the end of the 1960s and the Upton Park faithful were quick to criticise Moore's reluctance to yell at his failing team-mates. They wanted a more visibly vocal presence which Moore was unable to provide because it simply wasn't in his nature to do so.

We find it hard to think of Moore as anything other than the captain of any side he played for but, of course, Armfield was captaining the England football team as late as June 1966. In many ways Ramsey and Armfield were a better-suited pair than Ramsey and Moore. Armfield was abstemious where Moore decidedly was not. Armfield had a quiet and dignified Christian faith which would have appealed far more to Ramsey than Moore's cynicism and irrepressible urge to rebel against authority. To that extent Armfield was a grown-up and Moore a teenager. Moore would have no hesitation in leaving his hotel room, sliding down a drainpipe and setting off in the evening in search of a bar. Ramsey, who knew all about Moore's nocturnal proclivities, quietly seethed at such behaviour. Armfield would never have embarrassed him in this manner. In terms of character then, there is no doubt which of the two players the England manager respected more. But Ramsey had dedicated himself to ensuring that England won the World Cup in 1966, and every decision he took was with that end in mind.

That is why the public myth endures, and why we find it hard to think of Ramsey and Moore as anything but a loving couple, two men who respected each other and found in each other the perfect manifestation of what Moore looked for in a manager and what Ramsey wanted in a captain. Ramsey was happy to proclaim his confidence in his young captain:

> He was my captain and my right-hand man. Bobby was the heartbeat of the England team, the king of the castle,

my representative on the field. He made things work on the pitch. I had the deepest trust in him as a man, as a captain, as a confidant... I could easily overlook his indiscretions, his thirst for the good life, because he was the supreme professional, the best I ever worked with.

The reality is that the relationship was much more uneasy than Ramsey's laudatory words suggest. In fact, Moore had nearly lost the England captaincy within a year of his leading his country for the first time in May 1963. At the end of the 1963–4 season, ten days after Moore had held aloft the FA Cup after a dramatic 3–2 win over Preston North End, he was part of the England squad that was due to fly out to Lisbon for a match against Portugal. The England party stayed at White's hotel near the FA headquarters in Lancaster Gate. On the Wednesday night before the match on the Sunday, after training at the Bank of England ground in Roehampton, a party of seven players left White's to stroll along Bayswater Road – Moore, Charlton, Wilson, Banks, Eastham, Byrne and Greaves. Moore, Greaves and Byrne were part of the heavy-drinking brigade, but the presence of Charlton suggests that this was no wild night out. Nevertheless, all of them ended up in the Beachcomber, a club that was a favourite haunt of Jimmy Greaves.

The seven players had a few drinks in the West End but when they got back to their rooms they found their passports on their beds – a clear sign that Ramsey knew who had left the hotel and why they had done so. Management invariably held the travel documents of players when they were travelling abroad. The implication was clear – these seven might not be travelling to Lisbon after all. Ramsey was clever. He allowed them on to the plane and watched as the seven miscreants took part in training, all of them knowing that some kind of retribution was inevitable. The thunderclap didn't erupt until after the final training session on the Saturday. Ramsey dismissed all the players with the words, 'You can all go and get changed – except for the seven players who I think would all like to stay and see me.' Ramsey then let rip in a burst of concentrated fury, but he still played all seven on the following day: 'Budgie' Byrne scored a hat-trick and Bobby Charlton the other goal in a 4–3 victory. Moore was not spared the lash of Ramsey's tongue because of his privileged position as captain. Moore's taste for alcohol and his refusal to be the mouthpiece of his managers does not correspond very accurately with the traditional image of the captain as the embodiment of the conformity expected by the manager.

The reality was that Moore suffered badly from insomnia and, as far as he was concerned, it was better for him to go out in the evening, unwind by drinking, and then get his eight hours of sleep from 1.30 a.m. to 9.30 a.m. These were not hours that would generally find favour with his managers but it was the best solution for Moore who would otherwise have been up all night. Moore's other argument was that he could hold his drink. He might be the last one out of the bar and the last one into bed, but he would also be the first one into training the following morning to sweat it off – and the last to leave the training field. George Best and Jimmy Greaves were both badly affected by alcohol. Bobby Moore was not.

The social backgrounds of Moore and Ramsey were not dissimilar. Both were born in east London and in their behaviour on the field, cool, calm and thoughtful, short of pace but clever anticipators of the ball, they had much in common. Off the field, however, the two men were chalk and cheese. Ramsey loathed publicity of any sort and felt uncomfortable when not in the company of football men or his wife, Vicki, on whom he greatly relied. By contrast, Moore enjoyed the limelight and, as his career soared upwards, he and his wife Tina revelled in the trappings of wealth and fame.

Their marriage was much more typical of footballers' marriages than Billy Wright's had been or Beckham's was to be. They had met, as so many couples did in the 1950s, on the dance floor of the Ilford Palais when Tina was fifteen and Bobby was sixteen and were married five years later in the summer of 1962 after Bobby's return from the World Cup in Chile. It wasn't quite the childhood sweetheart romance beloved of saccharine gossip columns. Tina found Bobby very resistible at first and was only persuaded to give the polite young man from Barking another chance after intervention on his behalf from her mother. Bobby's mother, Doss, inevitably saw Tina as a threat. 'My Bobby's a good boy,' she was reported as warning the young woman. 'You'd better not be getting him into any trouble.' It was an odd thing to say since that phrase was used constantly at the time but only in reference to the possibility of the boy getting the *girl* into trouble. It echoes the relationship between Alan Bates and Thora Hird in *A Kind of Loving* mentioned previously but from the reverse perspective, as if June Ritchie were throwing up over the back of the sofa in Alan Bates's home. The wedding went ahead as planned at the Valentine pub in Gants Hill with Bobby in his dark blue mohair suit looking as handsome as the bride looked radiant. After a honeymoon in Majorca, the happy couple set up home together in a three-bedroom semi-detached house in Gants Hill which cost £3,650, but they moved up the housing and social ladder as soon as they could afford to do so – to the mock-Tudor splendour of Manor Road in Chigwell.

They could afford to do so because Bobby's career was progressing so well. The FA Cup win in 1964 was followed a year later by a 2–0 victory over Munich 1860 in the final of the European Cup Winners' Cup which was played, fortuitously, at Wembley. After the FA Cup had been won each man in the West Ham team received a £25 bonus from the club but £175 from the commercial pool, suggesting that outside endorsements might provide a greater part of a player's wages than the salary he received for playing football. For many years, however, the biggest perk attached to reaching the FA Cup final was the twenty complimentary tickets each player received. They were obviously intended as gifts for the players' close friends and relatives, to allow them to attend the match of the season, but inevitably some of them ended up on the black market affording players, who were still not particularly well paid despite the abolition of the maximum wage, a very welcome financial bonus. The West Ham winger Johnny Sissons was reputed to have made £600 which he used to buy a Morris 1100. Football celebrity was starting to have a commercial value.

As the FA Cup-winning skipper, captain of England, blond and good-looking, Moore was constantly in demand for commercial photographs and endorsements. He was an obvious client for Bagenal Harvey, the man who had virtually invented the role of the sports agent in England when he got a lift from Denis Compton, on the back seat of whose car lay a bag with unopened letters spilling out of the top. Harvey told Compton, whose distaste for correspondence, administration and organisation was legendary, that he would open them and sort them out, suspecting that there would be commercial offers in at least one of them. According to legend, in one of them there was the offer from Brylcreem which turned England's most exciting batsman into 'The Brylcreem Boy'.

Moore's encounter with the Bagenal Harvey agency turned out to be of brief duration during which the agent secured only one contract, ironically from Brylcreem for a poster worth £450. Instead Moore turned to Jack Turner, West Ham United's property manager, a well-known figure around the club, a man who was impeccably honest and trustworthy, who wore grey suits and polished shoes, a man whom young footballers, untutored in the ways of the world away from the football field, could trust to acquire a mortgage or complete a tax return. He was a man of sound advice and calm reassurance who did the best he could for a grateful Bobby. A weekly column in *Tit-Bits*, a mass-market magazine with undemanding content aimed mostly at men, paid Bobby £80 a week for twenty-six weeks. Moore chatted for half an hour each week with his ghost writer Roy Peskett who received £15 of the fee, leaving Bobby with a clear profit of £65 at a time when his weekly wage from playing football was £35. At the start of the 1964–5 season his wages went up to £60 a week, far in excess of what most of his team-mates were earning but, compared to what Mark McCormack was doing for his clients, it was small potatoes.

The real money, of course, was to be made on the back of the 1966 World Cup. Moore entered the tournament in the middle of yet another contractual dispute with his club. As a result, technically speaking Moore was out of contract on 30 June 1966, and therefore legally unqualified under FIFA rules to play any kind of football – either league or international. A frustrated Ramsey, who could well have done without this aggravation, consulted the FA and told Greenwood to come out to Hendon Hall Hotel where the England squad was staying. Allegedly, Ramsey told Greenwood that he could have his captain for just one minute and sent them both into a dark-panelled room. Moore, exchanging barely a word with or a glance at the man who had said he would build his team around him, signed a one-month contract with West Ham United that was sufficient to permit him to perform on the stage of the 1966 World Cup and to enjoy his greatest moment.

The England team had been slowly progressing since the disastrous start to the Ramsey regime. A prestigious 2–1 victory at Wembley over the Rest of the World in an exhibition match to mark the centenary of the Football Association in October 1963 meant less than a more important win in Madrid on a bitterly cold night in December 1965 against a Spanish team who were the current holders of the European Nations Cup. The 2–0 scoreline did scant justice to the manner of the England victory. What made it all the more significant was that it was achieved with the help of Ramsey's new 4-3-3 formation. The press had been scandalised by Ramsey's decision to abandon conventional wingers and instead use a front three of Joe Baker, Roger Hunt and Alan Ball, who had made his debut as a nineteen-year-old six months earlier, backed up by a midfield of Charlton, Nobby Stiles and George Eastham. Nine of the players who were to feature in the World Cup final the following year played in that game; only Hurst and Peters were missing. It was the first time that the English press, which had been largely sceptical of Ramsey up to this point, expressed support for his belief that England could win the World Cup in 1966.

The fact that the World Cup was to be played in England had apparently taken the then prime minister unawares. Harold Wilson had been seven years old when his local team, Huddersfield Town, clinched the first of the three consecutive First Division titles that they would win under the leadership of their innovative manager, Herbert Chapman. It was perhaps not surprising that one of Wilson's party pieces in later years was to rattle off the names of the team that won those three championships in the 1923–4, 1924–5 and 1925–6 seasons. What is more surprising is that when Denis Howell – the football league referee who became a Birmingham Labour MP in 1955 and Britain's first minister of sport in October 1964 – reminded the new prime minister that England was the venue for the 1966 World Cup, Wilson indicated that it was the first he had heard of it. In the event England hosted the World Cup four months after Wilson was returned to office in March 1966 with an overall majority which had increased from an almost unworkable four seats – after the 1964 election – to a resounding ninety-six. Wilson could now welcome the approach of World Cup Willie with a lighter heart.

It is possible to argue that there is a synergy between Wilson, Ramsey and Moore even if, as seems likely, the latter two never voted for the former. One of Wilson's primary tasks was to change the image of Britain from that of a country run by men who spent too much time on the grouse moors to one of a country that was prepared to incorporate the full extent of recent technological changes. At the Labour party conference in Scarborough in 1963, Wilson, in his first conference speech as leader, warned his audience that if the country was to prosper, a 'new Britain' would need to be forged in the

'white heat' of this 'scientific revolution'. It became one of his more memorable soundbites even if it did echo the passionate appeal for modernisation which had been made by Hugh Gaitskell at the 1959 conference in the same location.

In their own ways, Ramsey and Moore were doing something similar. Ramsey's constant battles with the FA reflected the wider ongoing war in many areas of British social and economic life between the amateur and the professional. Cricket was the most visible sporting stage on which this battle was fought and the abolition of the amateur cricketer followed by the adoption of the highly commercialised one-day knock-out competition sponsored by Gillette suggested that even in the corridors of the MCC there was a recognition of the need to move with the times. Ramsey had persuaded the FA to abolish its much-despised selection committee so that the manager had complete control over the playing side of the England team. His assiduous attention to the detail of where the team was to stay and train when playing matches abroad was matched by his determination not to allow a repetition of the gastronomic catastrophe of 1950. When England set out for Mexico to defend their World Cup in 1970 they would take with them endless supplies of tinned goods like baked beans with which the minds and stomachs of the players would be comfortable.

These battles were being fought as football in Great Britain was going through a period of decline. At the height of its post-war popularity in 1948–9 Football League matches had attracted more than forty-one million spectators. By the 1964–5 season that number had declined to just twenty-eight million. Cricket had suffered similarly. The traditional Saturday, when men had gone to the football and thence to the pub or had spent all day at the cricket, was fast disappearing. Increased leisure time, increased disposable income and an increase in the affordable and practical range of leisure activities hastened what seemed to be a long-term decline in attendances. Men who needed only a sixpenny fare on a bus to go to the nearest Football League or county cricket ground now had a car and the chance to take the family out on a Saturday afternoon. The desire for home improvements and the resulting growth of DIY stores provided alternative weekend entertainment.

It wasn't just sport that felt the impact of these socio-economic changes. The cinema, which had paralleled the major sports in its post-war boom, also suffered badly from a steep decline in audiences throughout the 1950s. High streets and local neighbourhoods which had boasted a Regal, a Plaza, a Gaumont, an Odeon and a Rialto saw these former pleasure palaces looking shabbier and shabbier until they were finally closed and turned into bingo halls or blocks of flats. Women who had formed the bulk of the audiences for matinée showings started to return to work and no longer spent their afternoons like Celia Johnson in *Brief Encounter* returning their books to Boots Lending Library and sitting in the circle to watch the matinee of a Hollywood film. In the late 1950s, Hollywood began to lose its touch as the big studios failed effectively to counter the growing threat of television. Many of the men who had made Hollywood great – Harry Warner, Louis B. Mayer and Harry Cohn, the founder of Columbia Studios – died and in the following decade their studios were swallowed up by multi-national corporations like Gulf & Western, which took over Paramount, Transamerica Corporation, which swallowed United Artists, or Kirk Kerkorian, the Armenian who developed much of Las Vegas and who seized control of MGM. Twentieth Century Fox had nearly gone out of existence after the fiasco of its production of *Cleopatra* (1963), starring Elizabeth Taylor and Richard

Burton, which had been budgeted at $2 million but which eventually cost the studio $44 million.

From football to DIY, from cricket to a day out in the country in the family car, from cinema to television, the shift from the collective activity of the late 1940s and early 1950s to the individual activity of the late 1950s and 1960s was ubiquitous and growing. Use of public transport declined as car ownership increased. In 1963, the physicist and engineer Dr Richard Beeching, a former technical director of the chemicals giant ICI, and chairman of British Railways since 1961, produced a report entitled *The Reshaping of British Railways* which called for the closure of 5,000 miles of track and a third of Britain's 7,000 railway stations. Seventy thousand jobs were to be lost in order to create a saving of £18 million a year. A bitter rearguard action by the unions proved to be of little avail as, before Beeching returned to ICI, he had indeed drastically reshaped Britain's railways.

The Titfield Thunderbolt (1953), one of the last of the Ealing comedies, had dramatised an almost identical situation ten years before the Beeching report was published. It told of the efforts of a group of villagers to keep open a country branch railway line after British Railways had decided to close it down. Full of lovingly photographed rural scenes and quaint eccentric characters, it was written, like *Passport to Pimlico*, by T. E. B. Clarke and it culminated – inevitably – in the triumph of the amateur enthusiasts and lovable villagers over the unlovable, humourless professional bureaucrats. Ironically, Clarke and Beeching were neighbours in East Grinstead and it was rumoured that the latter had contributed some technical details to an earlier Ealing comedy, *The Man in the White Suit* (1951). *The Titfield Thunderbolt* was almost the swansong of Ealing Studios, which a few years later were taken over by the BBC for use by its film department.

The celebration of the amateur over the professional made for a pleasantly nostalgic diversion in a comedy film and it struck a chord with the sort of audiences who were starting to abandon the cinema as a primary form of recreation in favour of television. It ran, however, contrary to the direction in which British society, and even British cinema, was slowly moving. The Rank Organisation had maintained a firm grasp on the British film industry through its ownership of the Odeon chain of cinemas and Pinewood Studios, but, by the mid-1960s the sort of films that the public had demonstrated it wanted to see were neither the Second World War adventures which had proved so popular in the previous decade nor the sort of films that were populated by girls from the Rank charm school like Susan Beaumont in *Innocent Sinners* (1958) or Belinda Lee in *Nor the Moon by Night* (1958). Outside that uniquely British phenomenon the *Carry On* films, the national cinema was moved forward in the 1960s by independent companies like Woodfall Films, which produced such classics as *Look Back in Anger* (1959), *Saturday Night and Sunday Morning* (1960), *A Taste of Honey* (1961), *The Loneliness of the Long Distance Runner* (1962) and *Tom Jones* (1963) which won the Academy Award for Best Film, returning a profit of $39 million on a budget of $350,000.

The film series which carried the image of the new Britain around the world, however, was the James Bond franchise. Sadly, global audiences were less delighted by *Carry On Constable* and *Carry On... Up the Khyber* than by *Dr. No* (1962), *From Russia with Love* (1963) and *Goldfinger* (1964). The box office grosses of the Bond series grew exponentially from $59.5 million for *Dr. No* to $141.2 million for *Thunderball* (1965). Bond himself offered a seductive blend of patriotic traditionalism and swinging modernity. The early Woodfall films might have appealed to British audiences who

recognised the truth of their gritty, frequently northern, set-
tings, but they held little appeal abroad outside of arthouse
cinemas. Bond was different. Bond was cool. Bond might have
been British but he reflected the Britain of Harold Wilson
rather than the Britain of Harold Macmillan, the Britain of the
white heat of technology not the Britain of the grouse moor. If
there were ever a passage of dialogue that illustrated this
transformation it is the exchange in *Goldfinger* between Bond
and Q as the latter demonstrates the iconic Aston Martin DB5.

Q: You see the gear lever here? Now, if you take the top
        off, you will find a little red button. Whatever you do,
        don't touch it.
Bond: Yeah? Why not?
Q: Because you'll release this section of the roof and
        engage and then fire the passenger ejector seat.
Bond: Ejector seat? You're joking!
Q: I never joke about my work, 007.

At the same time Bond found a way of making the traditional Britain an object of contemporary attraction. The Union
Jack, most memorably seen in the astonishing parachute jump
that opens *The Spy Who Loved Me* (1977), was reclaimed
from the flag that stood for nineteenth-century imperial conquest and instead symbolised a Swinging Britain which the
rest of the world found seductive even if it was essentially a
simple but commercially potent mixture of style and camp.
Bond was part of the outpouring of fashion, photography and,
above all, music which led to a new British cultural invasion.
James Bond wasn't played by an Old Etonian, as he probably
would have been had the series started fifty years later, but by
a former milkman from Edinburgh. The CIA and the White
House doffed their caps to this new British professional who

regularly saved the world from the evil intentions of SMERSH and SPECTRE. James Bond wasn't the amateur spy of popular myth whom the novelist John Buchan would have recognised. James Bond was a professional agent of the security services.

The amateurish nature of the FA was demonstrated even before the World Cup tournament began when they managed to lose the Jules Rimet trophy. On 20 March it was on display at a Stanley Gibbons stamp exhibition at the Central Hall in Westminster; on 21 March it wasn't. For seven days the newspapers covered the story relentlessly with endless speculation. On the eighth day it was found by a dog called Pickles, under a garden hedge in Norwood, south London. Pickles briefly became very famous and in dog terms very rich, being awarded a medal by the Canine Defence League and a year's supply of dog food. Nobody ever discovered who had stolen it or how and why it had turned up under a hedge in a south London garden. If the FA had had a PR agency it might have been seen as a masterpiece of brilliantly organised publicity. The FA didn't have a PR agency and the stolen trophy seemed more symbolic of British incompetence and bumbling than British entrepreneurial flair.

Fortunately for all concerned the trophy was on display at Wembley as the World Cup reached its climax. The story of the 1966 World Cup is too well known to bear much repetition. The first England game was a damp squib, a goalless draw against Uruguay in front of a crowd that was 13,000 short of capacity and which booed the negative South Americans off the field. If the crowd at the game was smaller than might have been anticipated the numbers watching on television were considerably greater. More than thirty-two million people watched the match on fifteen million television sets. The pattern of football in the future was being set, and television was to play an increasingly large part in it. Condensed as it was into just nineteen days, the tournament was given blanket coverage but the Portugal v. Bulgaria match attracted only 25,000 to Old Trafford and even a game as attractive as Portugal v. Hungary drew only 29,000 to the same stadium. Television would provide the missing millions.

England's second game, a 2–0 win over Mexico, sparked into life only after a nervous first forty minutes when Bobby Charlton opened the scoring with a spectacular Roy of the Rovers goal from twenty-five yards out. It lifted the entire country, never mind the players and the Wembley crowd. The third game was an even duller 2–0 victory over France, most notable for a tackle by Nobby Stiles on the skilful Jacques Simon which would undoubtedly have earned him a red card in today's climate but produced not a booking from the referee but a demand from the FA to Ramsey that he omit Stiles voluntarily from the next match. Ramsey threatened his own resignation if the FA continued to insist. The FA backed off, Ramsey stayed and Stiles played. It was an early demonstration of the importance Ramsey placed on loyalty and of his contempt for the FA. Walter Winterbottom would never have dared to adopt such a truculent stance. Ramsey's steadfast and publicly proclaimed faith in Stiles confirmed the bond that had been growing between the manager and his squad. It was to be a vital ingredient of success in the next match.

It was the narrow, fortuitous victory by a single goal over Argentina that changed the dynamic of England's tournament. The English public had not been apathetic but it hadn't been particularly optimistic about England's chances of winning the tournament. The press felt similarly. During the course of the quarter-final against Argentina the national mood changed. Jimmy Greaves, one of the greatest natural goalscorers in the history of English football, an automatic selection since he had made his international debut seven years earlier, was badly injured while playing against France and was replaced for the match against Argentina by Geoff Hurst. It was a selection that had been on Ramsey's mind for a while. Greaves had not scored in any of the first three games; Hurst was prepared to run himself into the ground for the good of the team. It was to be a significant substitution for both men.

Argentina were one of the favourites to win the cup and one of the few teams England genuinely feared. In the 'Little World Cup' tournament of 1964, played to mark the fiftieth anniversary of the Brazilian Football Confederation, the England party had watched from the stands as the Argentinians destroyed Brazil 3–0 in a frightening display of the brutal and the skilful. The outstanding player by far was the tall, imposing midfield pivot Antonio Rattín. After England lost 1–0 to Argentina in the next match in the competition Ramsey told his players that he thought that Brazil would not win the World Cup in 1966 for the third time in a row. Argentina, however, were another matter. They had already demonstrated their streak of cynical ruthlessness in a scoreless draw against West Germany in which Rafael Albrecht had been sent off for openly kicking the German central defender Wolfgang Weber in the stomach. Their uncompromising aggression would be a challenge in itself but when their technique – which was superior to that of most of the England players – was also taken into account, Argentina posed a significant threat to the host nation's desperate desire to advance further in the competition.

From the kick-off, Argentina let England know they would be in for a remorselessly physical encounter. The pompous, fussy German referee Rudolf Kreitlein took so many names in the first twenty minutes that Kenneth Wolstenholme wryly observed that if he wanted to know the names of so many of the players he should have bought a programme. Had Argentina chosen to contest a match of footballing skills they might very well have won, but they tried the patience of Herr Kreitlein too sorely. Their tactics involved cynical fouls and blatant dives which only confirmed in the mind of the patriotic crowd that the Latins had brought with them their usual bag of tricks which mostly included thuggery and cheating. The English crowd jeered but Rattín seemed an immovable object at the heart of the Argentinian team until he tried it on with the referee once too often and was sent off. Rattín claimed he had only been asking the referee for an interpreter, which might have been useful since he spoke no German and Kreitlein no Spanish. Kreitlein simply pointed to the touchline.

Rattín's outraged team-mates surrounded the official but after nearly eight minutes of histrionic pleading, the decision stood. It took Rattín a long time to leave the pitch and even longer to make his way round the perimeter towards the tunnel. His slow exit evoked catcalls from the crowd particularly when he wiped his hands on the corner flag bearing England's colours. They responded by hurling beer cans at him, many of them unopened, an expensive symbol of their contempt. It was, as Hugh McIlvanney observed, less of a football match and more of an international incident. After Rattín's departure the Argentinians started throwing themselves to the floor after every English tackle. The English players were no helpless victims. Even Bobby Charlton had his name taken for the first and only time in his career as he attempted to come to the aid of his elder brother after he had been assaulted in a manner that would have caused the perpetrator to be bound over to keep the peace in a court of law. When a game of football sporadically broke out, Argentina's remaining ten men defied England to break them down.

As long as the game remained scoreless a breakaway goal
by the visitors remained a strong possibility. Finally, twelve
minutes from time, a curling cross from the left wing by Martin
Peters was met at the near post by his West Ham colleague
Geoff Hurst, who twisted his head to send the ball beyond the
Argentinian goalkeeper and into the far corner of the net, a
staple West Ham training ground routine that had brought
many goals for their club side. The celebrations at the final
whistle were halted as Ramsey, in a highly uncharacteristic
public display of emotion, raced on to the field and prevented
George Cohen from exchanging shirts with the Argentinian
forward Alberto González. The German referee had to be
escorted from the field by the Metropolitan Police.

After the match the Argentinians urinated in the corridor
outside their dressing room and threatened to break down the
door to the England dressing room. An incensed Jack Charlton
bellowed to let them in because they would get what was
coming to them but he was the only Leeds United player on

the team and his bellicosity was not echoed by his team-mates. In his interview with Kenneth Wolstenholme for BBC Television half an hour later, Ramsey was still fuming with rage: he told the world that his side would not be able to produce their best football until they 'met the right kind of opposition and that is a team that comes out to play football and not act like animals'. It was to be a fateful choice of words. In Mexico in 1970 England were to pay dearly for the events of that day.

Although in Britain people felt that the 1–0 result was a triumph for honest British pluck over Latin American deceit, in most parts of the world it seemed like an imperial stitch-up. Over forty years later, the seventy-year-old Rattín still spoke emotionally of how the referee was so biased that Argentina had no chance of winning. Had England not scored, Rattín claimed, the European referee would have given them a dubious penalty. He was banned for four international matches and his team was fined £85. The British Ambassador in Buenos Aires had to be given a special police guard. Everyone knew that it had been 'fixed' that England could play all their games at Wembley because technically the winner of the quarter-final at Wembley was due to play the semi-final at Goodison Park. At the last minute, however, FIFA announced that the England v. Portugal semi-final would be played at Wembley, allegedly because of its bigger capacity. Wasn't the Englishman Sir Stanley Rous, who had been secretary of the FA, now the president of FIFA? England would not have that sort of protection four years later.

Meanwhile, the country had belatedly caught World Cup fever and the Tuesday-night semi-final brought a further spike in the temperature. Portugal, who had kicked Pelé and Brazil out of the tournament in the group stages and who had found themselves 3–0 down to North Korea in the quarter-final before the European Footballer of the Year Eusébio rescued them, presented their most attractive aspect in the match at Wembley. Two goals by Bobby Charlton gave England a lead they would not relinquish despite a consolation penalty converted by Eusébio three minutes from time. To the surprise of many Englishmen who had not given the host nation a chance, the national football team had reached the World Cup final. The Union Jack fluttered from every flagpole in the country. It was to be another twenty-five years before the cross of St George would be seen flying from the nation's white vans. For all the understandable reservations of the Scots, Welsh and the Northern Irish, Great Britain and England were interchangeable in the minds of many and certainly in the eyes of most foreigners.

Most of the players who wore the red shirt with the three lions on that last Saturday in July 1966 have written their own accounts of what transpired during the tournament. One element of Ramsey's personality that always shines through is his love of westerns and the players were subjected to the manager's cinematic preferences whether they cared for them or not. Staying as they did for six weeks at the Hendon Hall Hotel, without the comfort of the company of their wives, they spent a lot of evenings and free afternoons at the Hendon Odeon. George Cohen observed that after six weeks without his wife, Daphne, even Jack Charlton was starting to look attractive although every time he makes this good joke he tends to change the name of the player. The entire squad, the manager, his assistant Harold Shepherdson and the trainer Les Cocker would arrive together at the box office; Ramsey would ask for twenty-five tickets in the upper circle and hand over the cash. In fact Ramsey was usually in such a rush that he would set off without the players who were left scrambling for their coats and could be seen running through the streets of

Hendon in pursuit of their manager who was determined not to miss a minute of any western featuring his favourite film star, John Wayne. The players got rather bored with Ramsey's choice of film but any polite requests to sample other genres were invariably rejected. The day after the opening game against Uruguay, Ramsey had arranged a visit to the set of *You Only Live Twice*, the new James Bond film being shot at Pinewood. They were shown around by Sean Connery whom Ramsey thanked at the end of the visit, pronouncing the Scots actor's name – quite incredibly – as 'Seen'. It gave the players the giggles, but it was a puzzling error coming from such a confirmed film fan.

On the morning of the final, a Saturday, the Jewish Sabbath, the good Catholic boy Nobby Stiles set off from the hotel in search of a Catholic church in Golders Green, aided no doubt by the many Orthodox Jews who lived in the area. It is not clear if he found one or ended up in the Golders Green Beth Hamedrash synagogue but his performance that day suggested a spiritual peace amid the war on the turf. Bobby Charlton and Ray Wilson went shopping that morning and Gordon Banks recalled that he went for a walk with a few of the others down Hendon High Street to stretch his legs and buy a news-paper. The place, he said, was buzzing and a number of people came up to the players to wish them luck. The restraint of people compared with the pandemonium that would occur today is what is noticeable. A fair-sized crowd gathered outside the hotel to cheer them off, but it was only when the coach left the North Circular Road and started to edge its way towards Wembley Stadium that they realised the extent of the World Cup fever they had created.

The game was won, as the Second World War was won, after an initial reverse and a helpful intervention by Soviet Russia. Geoff Hurst's second goal, the shot which hit the underside of the bar and came down either on or just over the line, was validated by Tofik Bakhramov, the official from Azerbaijan but known thereafter as 'the Russian linesman', giving England a 3–2 lead. As a teenager, Bakhramov would have been part of the resistance to the Nazis in the Battle of the Caucasus, fought bitterly for control of the vital resources of oil and gas. Could the linesman's decision possibly have been influenced, if only subconsciously, by his memory of what he had experienced more than twenty years previously? Providing their own patriotic contribution, the crowd broke into a rousing rendition of 'Rule, Britannia!'. If fortune favoured England then, it had not done so when the Germans had equalised in the last minute of normal time. Jack Charlton can be seen gesticulating angrily that his foul on Sigi Held, for which he was penalised in a dangerous position just outside the England penalty area, was a fair challenge. Certainly, Moore and Peters appealed immediately when, from the free-kick, the ball appeared to be handled by Schnellinger just before Weber poked it into the net. The Swiss referee was as firm in his decision to award the second German goal as he would be to confirm England's third.

It is a tribute to Alf Ramsey's thoroughness and his care for the whole squad that he had thought about what the players who were not selected might be feeling as the match drew to its close. Jimmy Armfield recalls:

When you don't play it's not the same but I genuinely wanted them to win. We had to sit in the stands because we weren't allowed to sit on the bench, FIFA rules, but Alf said to me, because I was the leader of the reserves group, that someone would come to us just before the end of the match and I had to make sure we all came down and sat on the bench behind him. 'Win lose or draw we'll all be together at the end.' And of course as soon as we got there the Germans equalised.

As time ran out, with England clinging on to their 3–2 lead, the composure of Bobby Moore became increasingly visible. As he gained control of the ball in his own penalty area, he ignored the screams of Jack Charlton to boot the ball as far as possible over the touchline and into the stands to gain a precious few seconds and instead played a one-two with Alan Ball, looked up, saw Geoff Hurst in space and played the most glorious and accurate of forty-yard passes. Hurst, shaking off the valiantly pursuing figure of Wolfgang Overath, hit the ball as hard as he could, hoping it would go forty yards past the goal and with a bit of luck by the time the goalkeeper Hans Tilkowski had retrieved it, the final whistle would have blown. Instead, as the three interlopers on the pitch who thought it was all over would have seen, the ball ripped into the roof of the German net. Looking at the extraordinary manner in which Moore had dealt with the danger in his own area, Jack Charlton observed wryly, 'I remember looking at my captain and thinking, "I will never be able to play this bloody game!"'

As all England supporters rose to their feet to acclaim the certainty of victory and the England bench erupted with delight mixed with relief, Ramsey remained sitting stoically on the bench. 'Sit down, Harold,' he said sharply to Shepherdson who was obscuring his view. In his excellent biography of the Yorkshire bowler Bob Appleyard, Stephen Chalke writes about the great Yorkshire side of the 1930s, a team blessed with exceptional talent but one moulded in the harshness of pre-war Yorkshire life. He tells the story of how the young Ellis Robinson once held a spectacular slip catch, diving full stretch, only for Arthur Mitchell alongside him to growl, 'Gerrup, lad. Thar't mekin' an exhibition of thissen.' It was a suppression of emotion that would have sat well with the England football manager at this supreme moment. The players tried to involve Ramsey in their celebrations on the field but the manager demurred. Ramsey stood and watched anonymously as his players climbed the thirty-nine steps to the Royal Box and Bobby Moore carefully wiped his hands before shaking hands with the Queen.

Ramsey said it was the players' day but he was being unduly modest. However, if there was one player to whom the day did belong it was the captain. Perhaps because of his sadly early death and because his life after he finished playing was not lived in the media spotlight, the image that everyone retains of Bobby Moore is of that day in July 1966 as he held aloft the trophy that symbolised that England had reclaimed her place at the top of world football. It would be impossible to imagine a more suitable captain for that England. It was not just how he looked; it was also how he played. At all times he exhibited an air of calm authority. When England were struggling and the players looked to their captain for reassurance Moore would show no sign of desperation.

When England had gone behind to an early goal by Helmut Haller following Ray Wilson's uncharacteristically weak defensive header, Moore went forward looking for the equaliser. After being brought down by Overath, the England captain got up immediately, ignoring the foul, his eyes scanning the German penalty area for Hurst. The free-kick landed on Hurst's forehead as he sought the space on the edge of the six-yard box at the near post that Moore would always expect him to find, and in a split second England were level. Moore trotted back to the centre circle, pleased but displaying little emotion.

Moore, for all his membership of the Spitfire generation and his upbringing in the world of austerity, was now associated

with Carnaby Street and James Bond – the superficially modern
images of a Britain that, in reality, still watched *The Black and
White Minstrel Show* and treated foreign food with suspicion.
Indeed, it was all about image now. And the image of Bobby
Moore seated on the shoulders of his beaming team-mates,
holding the Jules Rimet trophy aloft, was the most iconic
image of them all. He won the BBC Sports Personality of the
Year in 1966, the way the nation conferred its favours without
the need to involve Buckingham Palace or 10 Downing Street.

In the streets of London that night, the joyous crowds celebrated as if it were VE Day all over again. The men of the
English Football Association congratulated themselves on
hosting a perfect tournament in which England had defeated
West Germany in the final. They hosted the perfect banquet
after the game to which only the wives of the FA officials and
no other women, certainly not the players' long-suffering
wives, were invited. The night before the final, the wives who
did not live in London were allowed to stay at the FA's expense
at the Royal Garden Hotel in Kensington where the victory
banquet would be held the following night, but the players
who had not seen their families for nearly two months
remained incarcerated in Hendon until after the match. On
this matter the manager and the FA were in perfect agreement.
The role of a footballer's wife, they firmly believed, was to
offer constant support to her husband and not make emotional or any time-consuming demands that might interfere
with his football. That night the wives were permitted to eat
in the hotel's chop house as their husbands enjoyed the com-
forts of the plush reception and banquet in the principal dining
room, attended, of course, by the wives of the FA officials.

This was not just an example of appallingly sexist behaviour, it was a display of class snobbery; and as such it serves
as a depressing reminder that even during England's transition

from the country of Eden and Macmillan to the country of Wilson and Callaghan, old habits died hard. Jimmy Greaves recalled that he and the Manchester United left-half Wilf McGuinness were once flying out to play for the England Under-23 side, accompanied by the usual number of FA officials. The stewardess on the plane served canapés to the latter and asked if she should serve the same to the players. 'Canapés?' repeated the FA official in evident surprise and well within the hearing range of Greaves and McGuinness, 'No, no. It would be like feeding strawberries to donkeys.' Only *Yes Minister's* Sir Humphrey Appleby could match a line dripping with such class-ridden contempt and he was a fictional character.

The day before the final the players' wives had been given an envelope containing £50 in cash to spend on something nice to wear that evening. They were naturally delighted and made the reasonable assumption that they would be wearing their new clothes sitting next to their husbands whom they hadn't seen for two months. It was only when they reached the ground floor that the players found themselves ushered one way and their wives another. The women did not feel mollified by the spending money or by the food laid on in the chop house but they recognised that being the wife of a professional footballer, even one of the most famous and successful footballers in the history of the English game, did not automatically confer on them any rights or privileges. They might resent it, but they knew their place and not only was their place not at the top table, it was not even in the same room. To that extent little had changed since Billy Wright had enjoyed his misty-eyed celebration arranged by the FA in 1952. News of the sexual revolution had not yet reached Lancaster Gate.

There was professionalism in evidence in the television coverage and in the preparation of the team but the commercial exploitation of the event, which was the FA's prerogative, rather passed it by. The official mascot was World Cup Willie, a cartoon lion wearing a Union Jack. The World Cup song, also entitled 'World Cup Willie', was performed by Lonnie Donegan, the skiffle artist whose biggest hit, *My Old Man's a Dustman*, had been recorded in the previous decade. It was as if the FA had never heard of the Beatles, which was a distinct possibility. They turned a decent profit – how could they not with a captive audience and a monopoly? – but they simply did not perceive any of the commercial possibilities that stemmed from the global television coverage. The British soldiers in the First World War were memorably described as 'lions led by donkeys' (although the phrase has a rather earlier provenance). In 1966 the performance of the FA compared to the meticulous planning in evidence elsewhere made it look like professionals led by amateurs.

Had they bothered to glance at what was happening in Coventry they might have learned something. In partnership with his innovative chairman, Derrick Robins, Jimmy Hill made Coventry City in the mid-1960s the most enterprising club in the Football League, the first to appreciate the power of public relations. A Sky Blue song based on the 'Eton Boating Song' was well received by the fans and when the supporters' coach left at 7.30 a.m. for an FA Cup tie against Lincoln City a catering coach went with them providing tea, coffee and hot dogs. Hill started a number of community activities including a pop and crisps party for children, but the idea of letting off fireworks to celebrate each home goal had to be abandoned on health and safety grounds. In an attempt to replicate match-day fitness peak in a circadian rhythm, he had the players train at 3 p.m. instead of following the traditional morning routine. Coventry also commissioned a 'Sky Blue Special' train service to transport fans to away matches; the trains remained full until results declined and the service became uneconomical to run.

Crowds responded positively to Hill's initiatives. In Division Three Coventry City averaged an attendance of 26,000 compared to the 10,000 they had attracted only two seasons before. After promotion, the club's first home game in Division Two brought in a crowd of 37,782 for a match against Ipswich. Coventry also started a Sky Blue supporters club where fans could eat a meal, take the wife and family and generally feel part of the club set-up. Hill and Robbins also experimented with closed-circuit TV at Highfield Road when the team was playing away, thereby pulling in an extra 10,000. In the 1966–7 pre-season the team travelled to Europe to play four matches promoting Coventry-manufactured Rover cars in Frankfurt, Vienna, Zurich and Brussels. At the climax of that same season, the crowd that watched the Second Division promotion decider against Coventry's West Midlands rivals Wolverhampton Wanderers numbered 51,500. Coventry were promoted as Second Division champions and stayed in the top flight for thirty-four consecutive seasons – an astonishing achievement when one looks at the identity of some of the clubs that were relegated from English football's top tier between 1967 and 2001. Jimmy Hill left Coventry after the club was promoted to Division One, when Michael Peacock offered him the job of Head of Sport at the new London Weekend Television, which was to go on air the following year. His salary would be £10,000 per annum, compared to the £7,500 he had received as a successful football manager. Hill's move from football to television was a trailblazing one, to be followed in due course by other former professional footballers from Bob Wilson to Saint and Greavsie and then to Gary Lineker. Hill's imaginative thinking and commercial enterprise stood

in marked contrast to the sclerotic attitudes that still prevailed in FA headquarters at Lancaster Gate.

Nevertheless, London was *en fête* that Saturday night at the
end of July 1966. Whatever the fragility of Britain's economic
position (there had been a damaging seamen's strike just before
the World Cup started), the country had succeeded against the
odds and emerged triumphant, forcing the rest of the world to
admire our skill and fortitude. Even people who had little or
no interest in football could not help but be caught up in the
tide of emotion that swept the country. It was much the same
as what happened when the Olympics came to London in
2012 and suddenly the nation became passionate about cycling
and rowing in a way that would have mystified them a week
before the opening ceremony.

Politicians now saw the possibility of reflected glory. On the
day of the World Cup final, Harold Wilson, James Callaghan
and George Brown arrived at Wembley before the players
emerged and offered their self-serving comments to the television cameras. Wilson, it was later revealed, had to be discouraged
from appearing on television at half-time and offering his
expert opinion on the match. Still, he would probably have
made more sense than Phil Neville generally does. Another
cabinet minister, Richard Crossman, noted in his diary that
there was a big upswing in Wilson's personal popularity ratings
after the World Cup was won and that it might be the precur-
sor of a change in the fortunes of the government as well.

> When I told Anne [his wife] over lunch today that the
> World Cup could be a decisive factor in strengthening ster-
> ling she couldn't believe it. But I am sure it is. Our men
> showed real guts and the bankers, I suspect, will be influ-
> enced by this and the position of the government
> correspondingly strengthened.

However, the Labour government, despite its best efforts, did not manage to surf the World Cup wave for much longer as industrial strife and the increasing balance of payments deficit continued to exert pressure on a weakening pound. At the time that Crossman wrote his optimistic diary entry, the country was just fifteen months away from Wilson's devaluation of sterling.

The historian Peter Hennessy understands the relationship between football and the Labour party:

Labour people after the war frequently enjoyed an identification with football. Michael Foot was fanatical about Plymouth Argyle. J. P. W. Mallalieu was Spurs. Harold could recite the 1923–4 championship-winning Huddersfield Town team as his party piece. In 1975 at the Dublin summit as part of the renegotiation of our membership of the EEC as it then was Harold began his speech by saying something like 'First the most important business' and then gave the score in the match England were playing that day as if to say, 'All right, Johnny Foreigner, you might think we are supplicants but we've got our priorities right. You might think Britain's membership of the EEC is of great importance but there are some things that are even more important.' Jim Callaghan was sitting next to him and looking a little puzzled because I don't think Jim was a football supporter. Nico Henderson was the British Ambassador in Bonn when Harold returned to power in 1974 and if you read his diaries you can see that he's horrified by Harold wanting to talk to him about where Billy Bremner should be played in the 1974 World Cup. For Tony Crosland, watching *Match of the Day* on a Saturday night became something of a fetish as he tried to piss off the *bien pensants* who were gathered round his dinner table. Harold had been the sort of schoolboy in Yorkshire who would have talked endlessly about the scores the previous Saturday and bored people rigid. He took it seriously and he enjoyed being photographed with Bill Shankly.

In the next series of *Till Death Us Do Part* the 'Scouse git' made great play of the fact that England had won the World Cup playing in the red of the Labour party. Alf Garnett's only response was to invoke the names of his beloved West Ham players, Hurst, Peters and, of course, Bobby Moore.

Although the commercial endorsements were nothing compared to what became available in later years, Moore's name appeared on football boots, footballs, books and newspaper columns written by somebody else. His earnings from football shot up to £8,000 a year but that figure was dwarfed by the £15,000 he made from off-field activities. He bought a new Jaguar and a holiday home in Marbella. He and Tina ate in the best restaurants and a friend observed that Tina's oven wasn't used in the year after the World Cup. Almost daily their postman delivered invitations to the homes of the good, the great and the celebrity-obsessed. In the course of the social whirl that followed the events of July 1966, Moore liked to be seen out and about in the latest fashions. Indeed, his wife would later say that Moore had a touch of the feminine about him. By this she did not mean to impugn his heterosexuality, but she recognised that Bobby took an interest in clothes that was not necessarily widely shared by other footballers at the time. His obsessive neatness, which would now be categorised as OCD, ensured that if he did appear in those fashions he would be immaculately dressed.

Tina, much to her surprise – as she was used to being seen as Bobby's appendage – was asked to appear in a television commercial for Bisto gravy without standing next to Bobby. Of course, when she and Martin Peters's wife were asked to promote the concept of the local pub ('Look in at the local') it was firmly in the company of the two World Cup stars. Nevertheless, just as World Cup glory cast more stardust on Bobby Moore than it did on the other players so Tina Moore benefited from being the wife of the country's great hero.

Billy Wright, captain of England for eleven years and for ninety matches, was never seen as a man whose endorsement could sell products. Denis Compton was the only sportsman of those post-war times whose name and appearance appeared to have a commercial value, but that all changed in the atmosphere after the World Cup win. The remaining years of Bobby Moore's career have been described as England football's golden age between the post-war working-class solidarity of the years of austerity and the point in the 1970s when the game started to suffer the torments of hooliganism. It was a revelation that more footballers than just Bobby Moore and George Best could sell products. The Manchester City midfielder Colin Bell became, briefly, the human face of Kellogg's sugary breakfast cereal Frosties in partnership with the more durable mascot Tony the Tiger. Bell's appearance in television commercials for Frosties revealed the distinct influence of the mumbling 'Method' acting style made famous by Marlon Brando in *A Streetcar Named Desire*. Bell looked as though he would have been much happier being brought down from behind by Norman Hunter and was soon replaced in front of the camera by Bobby Moore, whom Kellogg paid £3,000 for a single Corn Flakes commercial.

For Bobby Moore these were the lotus years. After 1966, he, Martin Peters and Alf Ramsey were all honoured by the London Borough of Barking where they were born at the confluence of east London and Essex. West Ham United more than doubled his wages to £150 a week on a three-year contract with an option to extend for a further three years. Best, Law and Charlton were on more than he was but Manchester United's home crowds, which frequently touched 60,000, were double those who paid to go through the turnstiles at Upton Park. Moore, along with the other twenty-one players in the squad, was awarded a £1,000 bonus for winning the World Cup, but it was taxed at 40 per cent so the final sum was £600. It was another step on his journey from the Labour-voting, working-class solidarity of his childhood to being an aspiring member of the Tory-voting middle class. There were failures along the way. Bobby Moore Jewellery went out of business in 1968, as did Bobby Moore Shirts & Ties – and a later investment with Mike Summerbee in a suede and leather company making menswear also collapsed – but by the time of the World Cup in 1970 his company, Bobby Moore Ltd, was turning over £22,000 per annum.

In 1966 Tottenham Hotspur tried hard to sign him, but West Ham would not sell and Moore remained in east London. Although Spurs won the FA Cup in 1967, they never regained the dominance they had displayed at the start of the decade and the teams that won the honours at the end of it were largely northern – the two Liverpool clubs, the two Manchester clubs and Don Revie's rising Leeds United. From holding aloft a trophy at Wembley in three consecutive years Bobby Moore played out the rest of his ten years as a footballer with no silverware to show for his efforts. His visible achievements were his captaincy of a feared and respected England football team, and as a smiling, confident symbol of the time.

Like Ramsey, Moore was plagued by feelings of social inferiority. Ramsey dealt with the problem by appearing and speaking in public as little as possible. But Moore liked the limelight, so he had to develop a different strategy for dealing with the attendant nuisances of celebrity. With journalists he deflected their questions by getting in first with questions of his own. Patrick Barclay recalls:

> When he looked at you, his eyes went straight into yours and he would say, 'How are you? How's the family?' and so on. And when he asked you those questions he would wait for a reply. It was only when I read Matt Dickinson's biography of Moore that I realised that he was such a private man that he was trying to deflect attention from

himself, as well as being instinctively polite. He was the most charming man imaginable.

Nevertheless, Moore had to endure the daily attentions of bores who thought that their limited knowledge of the England captain – gleaned from the press and the broadcast media – entitled them to intrude into his private life. Time and again he was obliged to deny that he was dedicated only to the pursuit of money and pleasure, or that he was cold, aloof and insincere. Matt Dickinson has revealed that Moore suffered a daily barrage of rudeness, insults and snide comments and that he spent his life biting his tongue. On the field or off it, he almost never lost his composure, which is why his heroic status remains untarnished despite later revelations surrounding his private life.

Moore's celebrity was even reflected in the cinema of the era, his name appearing on the side of a van in Peter Collinson's film *The Italian Job* (1969). Slightly more surprisingly, the name on the other side of the van is that of Colin Bell, the young Manchester City player who had made his England debut as recently as 1968. The film tells how a gang of English thieves steal $4 million in gold bars from a security van in the centre of Turin and, having reduced the city's traffic to gridlock, make their escape in the aftermath of an Italy–England football match. Although the game is never seen, it is reported that England have won ('Look happy, you stupid bastards. We won, didn't we?') and, of course, the Turin setting recalls the famous 4–0 victory there in the salad days of 1948. The casting of Benny Hill as the expert who reprograms the master computer that controls all the traffic lights in Turin suggests that the film is nothing more than an enjoyable caper, but there are elements in it that are highly revealing of the Britain of 1969. Peter Hennessy maintains that *The Italian Job* is a work of genius and it concludes with Britain's gold and currency reserves teetering over an abyss. Fred Emney carrying a Union Jack bag puts a series of electrical devices in street bins in Turin designed to aid the confusion allowing the Minis to get away. He asks for directions and gets a torrent of impenetrable Italian in response and he just mumbles, 'Bloody foreigners'. It's built round the glories and the anxieties of the British people and football is central to that.

Charlie Croker, played by Michael Caine, develops the concept of the robbery but it is Mr Bridger (Noël Coward) who finances it from his cell in Wormwood Scrubs. Croker, who has just been released, returns to waylay Mr Bridger on his way to the lavatory having been handed a soft toilet roll and that day's copy of the *Daily Express* by a deferential prison warder. Bridger affects disdain for the Italian job and Croker tries hard to summon up the words that will motivate him – 'Mr Bridger, this is important – four million dollars, Europe, the Common Market, Italy, the Fiat car factory!' 'Croker,' responds Bridger slowly, 'this... is... my... toilet!'

Bridger goes to see the prison governor to complain about the outrage of someone breaking into his toilet. He waves the governor (the traditionally befuddled John Le Mesurier) to a seat and tells him in no uncertain terms that

> There are some things, Mr Governor, that to an Englishman are sacred. You are not doing your job properly. Her Majesty's prisons are there not only to prevent people from getting out but to prevent people from getting in. You are symptomatic of the lazy, unimaginative management that is driving this country onto the rocks.

It is old-fashioned patriotism that finally convinces Bridger to give the Italian job his blessing and his support. An acolyte hands Bridger copies of the balance of payments reports for 1966 and 1967 along with the latest edition of the *Illustrated London News* which contains a photograph of the Queen. We follow Bridger back to his cell where we see that his walls are decorated with photographs of the Queen from her earliest days as a princess. He tells the acolyte that he has noticed that some of the younger criminals in E Block are not standing to attention when the national anthem is played. They are warned to do so unless they wish to incur his displeasure. Somehow, in Bridger's mind, the Italian job is, as Croker suspected, an opportunity to show the world that British is best.

The symbols are the respective cars. The daring, skilful English getaway drivers pilot their Mini-Coopers up and down steps and through busy shopping arcades. The three cars are patriotically coloured red, white and blue. Pursuing them is a creaking, rust-coloured Fiat that is left for dead by the English Minis. It is a repeat of Francis Drake and the Sea Dogs in their manoeuvrable ships routing the unwieldy galleons of the Spanish Armada, only this time the purpose is not to save the realm but to proclaim the triumph of British engineering, or, rather, the spectacular success of the Greek-born designer of the Mini, Alec Issigonis.

Oddly, Fiat are thanked in the final screen credits because they co-operated with the film-makers, unlike the British Motor Corporation which did not, even though *The Italian Job* was the best piece of free product placement advertising it could have wished for. Managed successfully by the Agnelli family, Fiat continued to prosper in the 1970s and 1980s, helping its local Turin club Juventus to a position among the European footballing elite. The British Motor Corporation, which had been created out of a merger between Austin and Morris, was joined by Jaguar in 1966. The year before *The Italian Job* was released, BMC merged with the Leyland Motor Corporation to form British Leyland, which would eventually sink beneath the waves of its own troubled industrial relations created by militant trade unions and weak, incompetent management.

As news of the success of the daring raid filters back to Wormwood Scrubs, the entire prison joins in the celebrations. Mr Bridger makes his way down the iron staircase waving regally to the crowd as they bang their enamel plates rhythmically on the tables to the chant of 'Eng-land Eng-land', as the chant of 'Bra-zil' had been heard on the Football League grounds where Brazil had played in their group games in 1966. Although he is descending the stairs rather than ascending them, the triumphal roars that accompany him are naturally reminiscent of those that greeted Moore and the other England players when they went up to the Royal Box to receive the Jules Rimet trophy.

The Italian Job was, as the film's producer Michael Deeley has freely admitted, the first Eurosceptic film. The English lads might have been rapscallions and thieves but they were English and they were daring and successful. The opposition were portrayed not as the sleek, stylish, licentious Italians seen in the films of Fellini, De Sica and Antonioni but as stereotypes who could have stepped out of a wartime propaganda film. The ending with the coach's back half precariously balanced over a vertiginous drop down the Alps is one of the reasons that the film is so well remembered nearly fifty years after its making, although Troy Kennedy Martin, who wrote the script, didn't write it and Peter Collinson didn't direct it. It is a tease to the audience, perhaps a moral reminder that crime doesn't pay such as might have been issued from the Hays Office in Hollywood in the 1930s. If that ending has a contemporary significance it is, as Peter Hennessy suggests, a warning that Britain's gold and currency reserves were disappearing so rapidly they were almost out of reach. One of David Frost's favourite jokes on *The Frost Report* was 'The drain on Britain's gold and currency reserves has stopped. They've all gone.'

Noël Coward symbolised the Britain in which Billy Wright had grown up. During the war Coward wrote, produced and starred in *In Which We Serve* (1942), which he co-directed with the debutant David Lean. The film is a hymn of praise to the wartime naval commander Lord Mountbatten, the future Queen's uncle, to Mountbatten's ship HMS *Kelly* (renamed HMS *Torrin* in the film) – and to the Royal Navy. Michael Caine symbolised the new Britain: he was young, blond, talented and good-looking and as such would have evoked memories of the England football captain. He was also the star of *Alfie* (1966), the film of a play by Bill Naughton about a flawed womaniser, which was released at the time of the World Cup and whose theme song, written by Burt Bacharach and Hal David and performed by Cilla Black, was an instant hit. Moore delighted in sitting on the back seat of the team coach and singing it loudly, much to the discomfiture of the England manager sitting grim-faced at the front. Billy Wright would never have dared to display such lèse-majesté in the presence of Walter Winterbottom. The torch had indeed been passed to a new generation from Coward to Caine as it had been from Wright and Ramsey to Moore.

No matter how much they genuinely respected and needed each other, and how much they declared their admiration for each other in public, the relationship between Ramsey and Moore was always a slightly wary one. Never was the relationship subjected to a greater test than during the days of Moore's incarceration on a trumped-up charge of shoplifting before the start of the World Cup in Mexico in 1970. The England party that left these shores after recording the World Cup song 'Back Home' was arguably stronger than the 1966 squad. In the first eleven Brian Labone, centre-half of the newly crowned champions, Everton, replaced Jack Charlton, while the two full-backs of 1966, George Cohen and Ray Wilson (possibly England's finest ever such pairing), had given way to Keith Newton, also of Everton, and Terry Cooper of Leeds United. Tottenham's Alan Mullery had come into the side instead of Nobby Stiles, and Manchester City's Francis Lee, who was in the form of his life, played up front with Geoff Hurst instead of Roger Hunt. The squad itself had strength in depth with Peter Osgood, Colin Bell, Norman Hunter and Allan Clarke – who might have expected to play regular international football for another country – buttressed by the experience of Stiles and Jack Charlton. Ramsey knew that to defend the title of world champions in the hostile environment of Mexico, particularly bearing in mind what had happened after the Argentina game in 1966, was never going to be easy, but his preparations had been meticulous and he believed he had thought of everything.

In the summer of 1969, when *The Italian Job* was on general release in England, Ramsey had taken the England team on a tour of South America to give them some experience of the heat and the problems of playing at high altitude which they would face the following year. After a 0–0 draw with Mexico, the party flew to Montevideo where they beat Uruguay 2–1. It was an excellent result, the gloss of which was tarnished when it emerged that the England players had refused to eat any of the food at the barbecue laid on by the host's football federation. Jack Charlton had tried to digest something which turned out to be sheep's kidneys and was vomiting for the whole of the following day. Finally, in Rio, against the team which would be their main rivals in Mexico, England lost somewhat unluckily, having held on for most of the game to a 1–0 lead given them early on by Colin Bell. The Brazilians scored twice against an exhausted England in the last few minutes. Ramsey was by no means dissatisfied.

Mindful of the horrors of the food in Brazil in 1950 and the unfortunate confrontation in Montevideo in 1969, Ramsey ensured that his 1970 World Cup squad would eat and drink nothing but food that had been shipped to Mexico from England. Ramsey's most recent biographer, Leo McKinstry, revealed that 25,000 bottles of Malvern water were sent and Ramsey negotiated with the frozen food company Findus to transport 140 lb of beefburgers, 400 lb of sausages, 300 lb of frozen fish and ten cases of tomato ketchup. Unfortunately, the Mexicans got wind of the importation because Findus were too keen to boast of their part in England's future success and the hosts were predictably insulted. The Mexican authorities refused to allow any meat or dairy products into the country and the England team doctor had to go down to the quayside and watch his carefully planned supplies of steak, butter, sausages and beef burned in front of him. It might have been done on the grounds of public health but it must have felt like a twentieth-century version of a sixteenth-century religious persecution.

For the rest of their stay in Mexico, the frustrated England players subsisted on a diet of fish fingers and chips as if they were adult versions of their five-year-old children. Ramsey's meticulous preparations did not extend to the provision of a Spanish-speaking press officer, as a result of which the cultural divide between the stoic British and their allegedly excitable Latin American hosts widened still further. Ramsey's fear and loathing of the British press was significantly increased when he was confronted by local journalists. Ramsey was a past master at alienating foreigners and the press. The combination of the two meant that England were as popular in Mexico City as Louis Napoleon's troops had been a hundred years before when they tried to make the Habsburg prince Maximilian into the new Emperor of Mexico. They lost just as badly. Louis Napoleon ended his days in anonymity, living in a three-storey house in the village of Chislehurst in Kent; Ramsey faded away in a semi-detached in Ipswich.

More traumatic than the bad public relations or the unvarying diet were the events that had taken place in Bogotá at the end of May during England's pre-tournament trip to Colombia and Ecuador. The purpose of the visit was to play two friendly matches to acclimatise the England squad to the high altitudes of Mexico, but things took an unfortunate turn when Bobby Moore was accused of stealing a bracelet from the gift shop in the hotel where the England party was staying. It seemed at first as if the incident was the result of a misunder-standing and would be quickly sorted out. Moore duly played in England's victories over Colombia and Ecuador, but when the team returned from Quito to Bogotá he was arrested for theft. As the judicial procedure dragged on, the England party had to leave Colombia to fly back to Mexico in time for their first game against Romania, leaving Moore in Bogotá. Thanks to the efforts of the British Consul, Moore was allowed to remain under house arrest at the home of the Director of the Colombian FA rather than languishing in a Colombian prison.

At home Harold Wilson was in the middle of a general election campaign. The idea that the England captain would be dragged through a foreign court like a common criminal might have done untold damage to Britain's prestige and the government's popularity. Wilson remained in close contact with the President of the FA and even offered to telephone the president of Colombia. Moore, who never lost his dignity throughout the humiliating process, was eventually released because of a lack of evidence, although the case was not closed for some years, much to his silent fury. There was no more relieved man in Guadalajara than Alf Ramsey when the unflappable but mentally exhausted Moore walked into the Hilton hotel to rejoin the England party. But the affair of the 'Bogotá bracelet' meant that, despite four years of careful planning, England were going into the World Cup in 1970 in a highly disconcerted state.

Back home, Moore's temporary incarceration only served to increase public interest in the World Cup, already fuelled by blanket coverage on television. This started with an hour-long breakfast show, an hour and a half of interviews, and then continued with discussions and highlights of the previous day's games at lunchtime, a preview of the night's matches during the children's tea time and five hours of live transmission in the evening. On 15 November 1969 BBC1 and ITV television started to transmit in colour, but, because many still watched in black-and-white, audiences for *Match of the Day* and *The Big Match* were solemnly advised by commentators, 'For those of you watching in monochrome, Spurs are in the dark shorts'. In 1970 ITV was beginning to offer real competition to the BBC as a football broadcaster. BBC Sport had existed for years in a state of complacency, with the rights to most of the prestigious sporting events sewn up thanks to the efforts of Paul Fox and Peter Dimmock in the 1950s. In the case of the FA Cup final, which was broadcast by both BBC and ITV, the corporation could simply point to the audience figures; the BBC consistently outstripped ITV's ratings by more than 3:1. When it came to sport, the BBC sniffed, the public clearly preferred the BBC.

Not in 1970 they didn't. In 1968 Charles Hill at the IBA created a revolution when he restructured the ITV system. ATV lost the franchise for London at weekends to the new London Weekend Television and instead became a seven-day-a-week operation in the Midlands. Associated Rediffusion merged with ABC, who had lost their weekend franchise for the north of England to Granada in the north west and Yorkshire Television across the Pennines, to create Thames Television, which broadcast to the London area on weekdays. Out of the confusion emerged a much stronger ITV Sport under the aegis of the widely popular former *Daily Mirror* sports journalist John Bromley. It was Bromley who invented the World Cup panel which was the innovation of the 1970 World Cup. The often heated studio debates were chaired by Jimmy Hill, displaying a natural ease in front of the cameras. The key panellists were the Manchester City coach and assistant manager Malcolm Allison, the voluble Northern Irishman Derek Dougan, Pat Crerand – whose Manchester United career was ending – and the rather more reticent Bob McNab of Arsenal who had been one of the six men left out when the original England squad of twenty-eight had been reduced to twenty-two just before the tournament started. Allison, who wanted Ramsey's job, launched into a diatribe at almost every session, criticising his tactics and demanding that Colin Bell replace Alan Mullery, whom he thought ineffective. Allison's obsession with Mullery and Bell became a modern version of Cato the Elder's repeated advocacy of the destruction of Carthage, in which 'Play Bell not Mullery' became the new 'Carthago delenda est'. Bell didn't actually need Allison's support: he was a good enough player for Ramsey to select him on his own merits. The debates did exactly what Bromley wanted – they absorbed the country and boosted ITV's ratings above those of the despised establishment BBC.

The 1970 World Cup was another staging-post in the developing relationship between sport and the broadcast media, and in particular between football and television. Mexico had benefited from a rehearsal in 1968 of transmitting black-and-white pictures of the Olympics. In the meantime, transcontinental satellite broadcasting had improved considerably and England supporters settled back after dinner to watch what they fondly imagined would be a successful defence of their title. It was still a World Cup with global audiences estimated at approaching 600 million but the commercial power of television in Western Europe had persuaded FIFA to schedule its matches with maximum convenience to those audiences. It was a sure sign that power was starting to shift away from the football authorities and towards the television companies.

World Cup coverage fought for exposure in newspapers and on radio and television with news of the general election. There seemed to be a symbiotic relationship, encouraged no doubt by Harold Wilson, between the holders of the World Cup and the government, both of whom were looking to repeat the success of 1966. In the consistently warm weather of early summer, Wilson displayed the same unflappability that Ramsey constantly strove for. The election was certainly not being fought on issues as Wilson took off his jacket, literally rolled up his sleeves and went on walkabouts through the friendly crowds, shaking hands with all and sundry and chatting happily. The issues that had led to Barbara Castle's White Paper *In Place of Strife*, an attempt to control the power of the unions which had been voted down the previous year, were never mentioned. Devaluation and inflation seemed a distant memory as Moore was released from custody. England laboured to a hard-fought 1–0 victory over a tetchy, negative Romania in the first group game with a goal by Hurst, and in the opinion polls the Labour lead over the desperate Tories continued to rise as Ted Heath struggled to make an impact. One pressman commented that covering Heath's campaign was the equivalent of being sent out to Mexico to report on El Salvador. The Central American state was playing in the World Cup finals for the first time in its history. It exited at the group stage having lost all three games, secured no points, scored no goals and conceded nine. As election day approached, Ted Heath's Tories appeared to be heading in the same direction.

After the Romania game, England were scheduled to face their sternest test since the World Cup final in 1966 – a group stage encounter with the feared Brazilians. Brazil had demolished Czechoslovakia 4–1 in their first match and in Pelé, Jairzinho, Tostão, Gérson, Rivellino and Carlos Alberto appeared to have a core of players who successfully combined the virtues of hard work and application associated with European teams with the equally stereotypical South American skill and flair. The highly anticipated game kicked off on Sunday 7 June in scorching midday heat. England, playing in utterly alien conditions and beset by the seemingly unending travails that had plagued them since they had left Heathrow – and despite enjoying little sleep the night before the game thanks to a concerted attack of noise deliberately orchestrated by the locals – produced arguably their finest performance for many years. They demonstrated that they had learned the value of keeping the ball and not expending pointless energy under the merciless sun. Considerable pressure was placed on the full-backs Tommy Wright, replacing the injured Keith Newton, and Terry Cooper to get down the wings, but in the event they were mostly involved with stemming the relentless tide of Brazilian attacks. Cooper was left for dead by Jairzinho as he hurtled down the right flank and pulled the ball back from the dead-ball line for Pelé to head it down towards the left-hand side of England's goal. Banks had been covering the near post as Jairzinho crossed the ball and it seemed impossible to Pelé that he could scramble back to get a hand to the header. Pelé yelled 'Golo!', expecting to see the ball bounce up into the roof of the net. Instead, Banks made what became known as 'the save of the century', somehow turning the ball over the bar for a corner.

Francis Lee threw himself into the attack but Geoff Hurst, his partner up front, seemed unaccountably lacklustre and the memories England supporters took from the game were mostly of resolute English defence. Apart from the Banks save, the dominant image was that of the captain who, having under-gone the most traumatic week of his life, displayed a preternatural calm at the centre of the defence. Above all, there was one tackle on the flying Jairzinho that is forever exhumed and exhibited to demonstrate the magnificence of Moore. Jairzinho was running at the defender who was back-pedalling desperately towards his own penalty area when he saw the perfect moment to pounce. His right leg extended and trapped the ball against his opponent's foot as he went down on his left knee. The Brazilian winger went over the body of the England captain who rose calmly to his feet, the ball under perfect control, as he looked up, just as Malcolm Allison had taught him to do fifteen years earlier, and set up another attack.

Jairzinho eventually got the better of him after an hour when Pelé rolled the ball sideways for the winger to drive the only goal of the game across Banks and into the far corner of the net, but England were by no means out of it. Surprisingly, instead of the ineffectual Hurst, Ramsey took off the ever-dangerous Lee and replaced him with Jeff Astle who caused considerable trouble for the Brazilian defenders by winning everything in the air. Unfortunately his control on the ground was less impressive and what everyone subsequently remembered, apart from the Banks save and the Moore tackle, was the Astle miss. It was a sitter which it seemed unlikely that any other of the England strikers would have failed to put away, but Astle missed it.

England's World Cup was not over on 7 June despite the defeat. It was popularly believed that Moore had said to Pelé 'See you in the final' as they memorably exchanged sweat-soaked shirts. In the light of England's impressive display, supporters believed even more strongly that their team had the potential to be World Cup finalists for a second succes-sive tournament. Four days later they scraped past Czechoslovakia thanks to an Allan Clarke penalty. He and Astle started the game instead of Lee and Hurst, Bell took Ball's place in midfield and Jack Charlton, looking far from the dominant defender he had been in 1966, gave Brian Labone a rest before the coming encounter with Gerd Müller. A draw would have been enough to have seen England into the quarter-final so, although the performance was a come-down after the previous Sunday's heroics against Brazil, everyone back home was perfectly happy to accept that the result was, in the usual managerial doublespeak, more impor-tant than the performance.

Harold Wilson continued to beam benignly on the team
from his lofty position in the polls. On Thursday 11 June, a
week before election day, as England qualified from the group
stage, two opinion polls put Labour 7 per cent clear of the
Conservatives, which suggested a Labour majority at least as
large as the ninety-eight seats they had acquired in 1966. On
Saturday 13 June NOP published a poll that gave Labour an
astonishing 12.5 per cent lead over the rapidly wilting Tories.
Wilson could sit down and watch the West Germany quarter-
final knowing that his pre-election nightmare would not be

realised. Richard Crossman's diaries reveal clearly that when the cabinet discussed the timing of the 1970 election, Wilson was very conscious of the fact that a bad World Cup for the England side might well impact adversely on the government's campaign for re-election. He thought that to go to the country in June 1970 was taking an unnecessary risk, but the cabinet convinced him it was the right time and that the result of a football match couldn't possibly matter that much. As election day approached, polls unanimously proclaimed the certainty of a third consecutive Labour victory.

In *Whatever Happened to the Likely Lads?*, the 1973 BBC sitcom written by Dick Clement and Ian LaFrenais (both football supporters), Terry Collier, played by James Bolam, returns to Newcastle after five years in the British Army on the Rhine and a failed marriage to Jutta, a German woman. When his best friend Bob Ferris (Rodney Bewes) asks him why the marriage disintegrated he is told that it had all been going so well until 14 June 1970. Bob is puzzled. What could have happened on 14 June, he wonders. Terry is astonished that the date isn't seared into Bob's brain the way it is in his:

Terry: What happened? I would have thought the date was printed indelibly in the mind of every Englishman worthy of the name. England two, West Germany three! That's what happened!

Bob: Oh my God, of course!

Terry: Have you any idea what it was like to be in West Germany that night? Especially after being two up. After the second I was standing on the sideboard singing 'Rule Britannia' and 'Land of Hope and Glory'. Their faces! And then... The shame! The humiliation! To have them all leaping up and down, eyes glazed with national socialist fervour... I thought they were going to rush out and invade

Poland again... I just got up quite unnoticed and left... Just
got my bag and walked out of her life for ever.
Bob: I would have done the same. It was bad enough here.
I can't say I blame you, mate. I had to go to bed and lie
down. For two weeks. Mind you, I think Chivers has made
a difference.

It wasn't just Bob who instantly understood how Terry had
felt: the ten million viewers who watched *Whatever Happened
to the Likely Lads?* would have felt exactly the same way.

Maybe if England hadn't gone two-nil up after fifty minutes
and played the Germans off the park it wouldn't have felt so
shocking. Maybe if England had been three-nil down after
twenty minutes and scored two scrappy goals in the last few
minutes to offer a late burst of vain hope it would have been
easier to have accepted that defeat. Maybe if Ramsey had left
Charlton on the pitch, Beckenbauer would not have felt able
to go on his marauding forward runs, but then the substitution
of Bell for Charlton happened *after* the Beckenbauer goal.
Charlton himself always said that Ramsey had done the right
thing in the belief that no England team gave away three goals
in twenty minutes and there was a semi-final to be played in
three days' time. Bell, in fact, was brought down in the penalty
area by Beckenbauer, but the referee refused to award what
looked like a certain penalty. All the luck that had accompanied England in 1966 deserted them with a vengeance in 1970.

In the end it probably came down to whatever Gordon
Banks ate or drank that gave him food poisoning and kept him
out of the game. His replacement, Chelsea's Peter Bonetti, had
played two pulsating Cup finals against Leeds United at the
end of April so he wasn't short of big-match experience, but
on the day he seemed to freeze. Unlike Banks, who gave extra
comfort to his defenders, Bonetti's nerves caused Moore and

Labone to be forever casting anxious backwards glances. After sixty-nine minutes, he allowed Beckenbauer's weak shot to slip under his falling body and thirteen minutes later, when Seeler stumbled but managed a back header, Bonetti remained flat-footed as the ball looped into the net. The third German goal, in extra-time, was a foregone conclusion. England were out on their feet by then and the Germans were rampant. Even before Müller volleyed home to clinch victory every England supporter could see that defeat was looming.

For Harold Wilson the defeat must have caused some tremors, but he picked up the telephone and called Ramsey in León to congratulate the stunned manager on England's magnificent if unlucky performance. He certainly remembered the general election of 1945, when the newspapers had all predicted a Churchill victory. He must, too, have remembered the 1948 US presidential election when the Republican candidate Thomas Dewey was mistakenly proclaimed President of the United States by the *Chicago Daily Tribune* in the notorious headline DEWEY DEFEATS TRUMAN. The day after the calamity in León, the Board of Trade released the latest trade figures. The visible trade balance for May showed a deficit of more than £31 million. In the election post-mortem those figures were credited with turning the tide against Labour although, like England supporters after the first German goal went in, it was still believed that the lead could not be overturned. Just as England might have had to settle for a 2–1 rather than a 2–0 victory, Labour might have to settle for a fifty-seat, rather than a hundred-seat, majority.

As Bonetti fumbled Beckenbauer's weak strike that Sunday evening, senior Tories were meeting and appointing Willie Whitelaw as the man to carry the box containing the asp to Ted Heath. On the Labour side, according to Crossman's diary, the expectation of victory disappeared within an hour of the first result being announced on election night. It came from Guildford, where the Conservatives took the seat with a swing of more than 5 per cent. Wilson's nightmare had become a reality. It appeared at the time to be the most surprising of election results, which probably gave the Board of Trade announcement on the Monday morning more importance than it deserved. Certainly, Peter Hennessy discounts the significance of the trade figures, preferring to concentrate on what had happened in the months leading up to June 1970:

> Elections measure the flow of a stream that has been long in the changing and I think you can trace the Labour defeat in 1970 back to the unpopularity following the devaluation of October 1967 along with the cuts that followed and, of course, *In Place of Strife*. Harold was setting his stall out as the transformer of Britain's economic performance and in all the areas where he did that he did badly on the terrain on which he had chosen to fight in 1964 and 1966, and I think that's far more important than Germany stealing the 1970 quarter-final. It was an unpopular government by this time. It had lost badly in the local elections the previous year. From devaluation onwards Harold was being done over by the very factors where he claimed his supremacy lay. Ted wasn't any good at working the public so the forty-four-seat majority was in spite of rather than because of him. It was because people were disillusioned with Harold. Losing to West Germany put people in a bad mood but why should they vote for Ted because they're in a bad mood? I was in Luton on a council estate in 1970 trying to get the core Labour vote out late in the evening and it was very hard.

People continued to draw a parallel between Ramsey and Moore and the Labour party for a few more years. For manager and captain, professional glories now lay in the past. Moore was still in his twenties; Ramsey was just fifty. Both would continue to play a part in England's football history but, like Harold Wilson and his party, they were, in the title of the infamous BBC documentary that followed their journey into the wilderness of the first year of opposition, *Yesterday's Men*. Wilson would come again, briefly, but for Ramsey and Moore there was only the sad spectacle of decline in prospect.

That decline came as a surprise to everyone who sympathised with the unlucky heroes as they flew back to England without the trophy they most cherished. There was a belief in the minds of Ramsey and Moore that the England team had performed so well in the match against Brazil that the scoreline was unjust and irrelevant. Similarly, the defeat by Germany was simply unfortunate and could be explained away entirely by Gordon Banks's ill-timed illness. If the match had been played two days later England must surely have won. Drastic surgery on the England team seemed unnecessary. Such was the strength of the English First Division and the quality of the squad of players available for selection that alarm bells did not ring again until the match against West Germany in April 1972. Bobby Charlton retired from international football after Mexico but, to Malcolm Allison's relief, Colin Bell was now ready to stake a claim for a permanent place in the England midfield. The Tottenham Hotspur forward Martin Chivers made a strong start in an England shirt, as did Derby County's Roy McFarland, but the World Cup veterans Banks, Peters, Hurst, Moore, Lee and Ball continued to play in the England campaign for the European Championships of 1972.

Ramsey was a cautious, conservative man and he made his selections accordingly. It wasn't just that he was loyal, arguably for too long, to the players who had served him so well in the 1960s, it was more that, as Wilson gave way to Heath, the Beatles broke up and Britain prepared to join the Common Market he found his outlook, shaped by depression, war and austerity, out of tune with the mood of the country and, more importantly, with the changing attitudes of English footballers. In most cases, managers are always a generation older than their players but the gap is not unbridgeable. The manager might affect distaste for the musical preferences of his players or their hairstyles or their choice of clothes but it is usually expressed in tolerant and good-natured banter. Indeed, when managers are too close to their players in age or wish to be 'one of the lads' they are usually unable to exercise the necessary measure of objectivity. Distance can lend enchantment.

Ramsey knew and liked the character of the men who had won the World Cup. They were, by and large, modest and mature at an early age, nearly all having been through the rigours of National Service. They had started their careers when the maximum wage was still in force and they felt privileged to be allowed to earn a living by playing professional football when their fathers had probably struggled to find a job at all. They might have grumbled at the poor wages but they knew that almost every young man of their age in the country would have willingly swapped places with them. They were not well treated by their clubs, but they recognised the hierarchical, class-ridden nature of English society and they knew their place in it. They loved Alf Ramsey because they knew he was loyal to them and they reciprocated that loyalty. They respected his knowledge of the game and, even when his tactics were not working, Bobby Moore would not change anything on the field until the team had specific instructions to do so from the manager. They might find Ramsey's strangled enunciation and social gaucheness a subject for mockery but they knew who was in charge of the England set-up. Moore was the captain but Ramsey was the boss.

At the start of the 1970s some of these attitudes were changing as the idea of deference started to come under threat. A gap was opening up between parents and their children that previous generations had not known and parental authority was diminished accordingly. Schoolteachers had to work hard to elicit the respect that had previously been automatically their due. The police in the turbulent 1960s had become 'pigs'. Wild youth were not a new phenomenon in the 1970s. The 1950s had produced cosh boys and Teddy boys; the 1960s gave us the bank holiday coastal town battles between Mods and Rockers but the majority of law-abiding people sympathised with the police. In the 1970s the troubles in Northern Ireland were played out on the streets of England in the form of bombs which killed innocent people and the authorities seemed incapable of doing anything about it. The police now seemed as helpless as the rest of the anxious population.

Wilson's lauded white heat of technology did not produce the classless, meritocratic, modern Britain he so desired as relations between labour and management worsened. The balance of power between them swung towards the trade unions as industrial action now simply meant strikes. In the nineteenth century Britain had been known as the workshop of the world. In the second half of the twentieth century British industrial production was immobilised by the chaos which culminated in the three-day week.

Ramsey did his best to move with the times, but the sort of footballers who stole the headlines in the early 1970s were simply not his sort of men. It wasn't just the common criticism that he distrusted flair. There have been plenty of English managers who have distrusted players who were more intent on performing party tricks for the instant gratification of the crowd than doing the hard, unselfish work that successful teams need. Ramsey felt deeply reluctant to select crowd and press favourites such as Stan Bowles, Alan Hudson, Peter Osgood, Charlie George and Rodney Marsh. When Frank Worthington, the tricky forward from Huddersfield Town, was selected to play for the England Under-23 side in the summer of 1972, he arrived at Heathrow Airport dressed in black leather trousers, a red silk shirt topped with a lime velvet jacket and walking in high-heeled cowboy boots. Peter Shilton later reported that Ramsey was palpably astonished by the player's appearance. He turned to his trusted aide Harold Shepherdson and said, 'Oh shit, what have I fucking done?' The idea of Bobby Charlton or Roger Hunt turning up to play for England in such attire was simply inconceivable.

To the extent that so many of the 1966 World Cup winners had done their National Service, they had more in common with their parents than they did with this new generation of players who were starting to take their places at club and national level. The last National Servicemen had been called up in 1960 and many of them went to basic training reluctantly. There seemed no good reason to give up a relatively comfortable domestic life and the start of a financially rewarding career for two years of boredom, allegedly serving Queen and Country. That attitude automatically made them different from the men who were called up at the start of National Service in the late 1940s, and who understood that the preservation of a hard-won peace required their temporary inconvenience and commitment to a cause and an idea more complex than their own physical comfort. In the late 1960s there was an anxiety among the student population that Britain would be dragged into the war in Vietnam by its economic and military dependence on the United States, and the young men whose parents had gone off to war to defend their country's security and honour now marched through the streets yelling 'Hell, no, we won't go!' There was no idea big or important enough to convince them that dying in the jungles of South East Asia was to be meekly accepted as their patriotic duty. The end of deference entailed a new definition of patriotism.

For the men of 1966 the meaning of patriotism was quite clear. If your country needed you, you packed up your things and served. Alan Hudson was selected for that Under-23 tour of Eastern European countries in the summer of 1972 for which Frank Worthington arrived looking more like Jason King than Bobby Moore. However, Hudson telephoned the England manager and told him that he preferred to spend the summer at home and on the beach with his family. The England manager was incandescent with rage. Such insouciance was an insult to his country as well as being an insult to the country's football manager. Hudson was never selected for any England side as long as Ramsey was manager. When Don Revie took over, Hudson played superbly in a 2–0 win over West Germany, took part in a 5–0 demolition of Cyprus and then, in contradiction of the strict orders of the manager, indulged in the sort of refuelling that finished off the career of Paul Gascoigne. Greaves and Moore might climb out of their bedroom windows and down the drainpipe to consume a few pints before returning by the same route but neither would have flaunted their disobedience. Greaves and Moore had the added benefit of being world-class players. Hudson was talented but not in their class. Ramsey knew that he could do very well without Alan Hudson but most of the seven players whose passports he laid out on the beds of their hotel rooms in 1964 were fundamental to his plans for winning the World Cup. They did not need more than that one warning. Ramsey knew his players, their qualities and their essential reliability.

It is understandable, then, why five of the team that won the World Cup in 1966 were still playing for England six years later. In the first leg of the European Championship quarter-final at Wembley against West Germany, Ramsey chose three creative players – Bell, Ball and Peters – in midfield, but there was no Stiles, no Mullery, no Storey. It was certainly a team full of good players but, worryingly, Bobby Moore had been chosen at centre-half with Norman Hunter playing alongside him in the role Moore usually took. Moore had started at West Ham as a centre-half but his career had only taken off when Ron Greenwood switched him to the defensive left-half position he made his own. Günter Netzer ran England ragged that night. Germany won 3–1 but it could have been six. Moore had a stinker, robbed while dribbling in his own penalty area for the first and conceding the third when he tripped Siggi Held inside the box. For the second leg in Germany, Ramsey chose Peter Storey in place of Martin Peters, pushed Hunter into midfield alongside him and played 4-4-2 instead of 4-3-3, including, surprisingly, the dilettante Rodney Marsh up front with Martin Chivers, dropping both Lee and Hurst. The goalless draw and an exit from the competition was the most England deserved.

The European Championship had not yet imprinted itself on the mind of the English football public. Defeat in a European Championship quarter-final was hardly welcome, but it wasn't as if they had been knocked out of the World Cup and when the draw was made for the 1974 tournament, England would only have to finish ahead of Wales and Poland to go to the finals in Germany. The difficult game was away to Poland in Katowice in June 1973, but England had emerged unscathed and triumphant from many such matches over the course of the previous ten years. This time, however, there was to be no such happy ending. The Poles took an early lead when a free-kick deflected off Moore's outstretched leg and was turned past Shilton. In the second half, Moore received the ball square from McFarland with plenty of time to clear and casually made as if to turn and pass back to Shilton, but his first touch was uncharacteristically poor and the Polish striker Lubanski caught him, robbed him of the ball, ran on and drove it past Shilton to clinch a famous victory. Ball got himself sent off and relations between the England team and the English press hit an all-time low. Ramsey tried to take the blame for the defeat himself and that loyalty to the players that made him such a popular manager was repaid a few nights later in Moscow when the England party unanimously decided to ignore the performance of *The Sleeping Beauty* at the Bolshoi to which they had been invited. It was unfortunate that it was seen as a snub to their hosts but to the players it was a way of showing solidarity as a unit. Instead of a night at the ballet they opted to seclude themselves in the British Embassy and watch the 1969 feature film version of *Till Death Us Do Part*.

England's participation in the 1974 World Cup now depended entirely on defeating Poland at Wembley on 17 October 1973. It was the most important fixture since León, particularly since Netzer's match had already been erased from public memory. Bobby Moore was left out of the starting eleven, McFarland and Hunter forming the defensive pairing and the captain's armband being worn by Martin Peters. Moore sat on the substitute's bench, outwardly uncomplaining and dispassionate – but inside he must have been shrouded in misery. If Ramsey wouldn't pick him for a match of this importance, his time as captain of England must be over. England failed to win but that failure had little to do with the omission of Moore other than the fact that Poland's goal stemmed from a mistake by Hunter on the touchline that Moore in his prime would never have made. The problem was that Moore was no longer in his prime. Still, when the match started there would have been few among those present at Wembley or the millions watching on television who would not have been confident that England would eventually go through.

The conviction that the hapless Poles had arrived as sacrificial lambs had been confirmed by Brian Clough speaking on ITV on the Saturday before the match. The former Derby County manager, who had been sacked the previous day, had told the nation in no uncertain terms that the Polish goalkeeper Jan Tomaszewski was a clown. Besides, the England side was packed with goalscorers. In addition to the prolific midfield of Peters, Colin Bell and Tony Currie, Ramsey played three reliable strikers in Martin Chivers, Mick Channon and Allan Clarke, with Kevin Keegan and Derby's Kevin Hector on the bench.

Predictably therefore from the kick-off England poured forward, shots rained down on the Poland goal but the clown was equal to all demands. A goalless first half raised some anxieties but it was still believed that it was only a matter of time before the dam was breached. Unfortunately it was Clough not Tomaszewski who turned out to be the clown. One down after an hour to a goal by Domarski after a build-up that included bad mistakes by both Hunter and Shilton, England threw caution to the wind. Channon hit the post, Currie hit the bar, Bell and Clarke had efforts cleared off the line. Peters was obstructed on the edge of the area and in the only piece of luck that England had all night, the referee pointed to the penalty spot. Allan Clarke equalised with a calm that nobody else felt. With ninety seconds left, Kevin Hector came on and made a chance for Bell which Poland yet again scrambled off the line. The whistle went and England, who had never stopped attacking for the whole ninety minutes, were out. They must have created twenty decent chances. A reasonable score would have been 10–2. At the end Norman Hunter and Emlyn Hughes were in tears. Bobby Moore, who had watched helplessly from the bench, trudged sadly back to the dressing room. The next World Cup qualifying matches were three years away. He was thirty-two now and he couldn't even get into the team for a match of crucial importance. There was one more game for him, a friendly a month later against Italy which was lost to a goal scored by Fabio Capello, giving Italy her first ever win in England, and so Bobby Moore's international career ended.

The draw against Poland which meant England could not qualify for the finals in West Germany was, if possible, a greater blow to the national psyche than the defeat in León. When England flew back home in 1970 they could argue with some credibility that if Brazil were the best team in the world, they were not far behind. Nobody would have thought it odd if the World Cup final of 1970 had been contested by Brazil and England. In 1973, however, England's decline was only too plain to see, and for all the excitement generated by reaching the semi-final in 1990 it could be argued that England have only ever been quarter-final material ever since.

Moore himself was not only in decline as an ageing player in the early 1970s but the teams he played for were also on the way down. West Ham had never challenged seriously for honours since winning the European Cup Winners' Cup in 1965. They became a soft touch away from home and in 1970 they sold Martin Peters to Spurs in exchange for cash and a rapidly declining Jimmy Greaves. Just after New Year's Day 1971, the team travelled to Blackpool for what was a tricky FA Cup third-round tie at Bloomfield Road. The weather was dreadful and it seemed more than likely that the match would not go ahead on the Saturday afternoon so on the Friday night Moore, along with Greaves, Clyde Best and Brian Dear, slipped out of the Imperial Hotel and went to the boxer Brian London's nightclub called 007. They stayed for an hour and drank four bottles of lager, except Best who didn't drink alcohol at all.

There would have been no problem had the match been postponed, as they all believed it would be. Unexpectedly, however, it started on time but even so there would have been no problem if West Ham had won or just drawn and taken Blackpool down to London for a replay. The problem was the 4–0 defeat by a Second Division team on a frozen pitch. On learning of the players' breaking of their curfew via an outraged West Ham supporter who had seen the four players in 007 and who – having witnessed the disaster at Bloomfield Road – was still steaming on Monday morning, manager Ron Greenwood felt deeply hurt at being let down by the four. Their punishment could not be announced immediately because, by pure coincidence, this was the week that Moore featured on *This is Your Life*. Moore's response to his eventual suspension by the club was that the incident had been blown up out of all proportion:

'I know that when you are England captain, people are always looking for little chinks in your armour, little slip-ups that they can cash in on, so I tried not to give them the chance.'

The relationship between Greenwood and Moore, which had been in decline since the contractual standoff in 1966, now fractured. The manager was angry; the captain retreated into his shell to such a degree that he barely contributed anything at team meetings. His silence undermined Greenwood's authority and so it continued. His captaincy style had always been quiet, the players aware of who was captain because of Moore's aura and his remarkable sense of anticipation which enabled him, even when he had lost much of the small amount of speed he had once had, still to be in the right place at the right time to break up an attack and start one of his own. For England this lack of flamboyance did not matter because the national side had Alan Ball and others who could shout. One of the many qualities of the 1966 side was that there were almost eleven captains, such was the maturity of that team. Moore was the symbol of the side and the right man to be hoisted on to the shoulders of his team-mates but it was, as Ramsey always wanted, a team effort.

For West Ham it was different. In the late 1960s and early 1970s, they were a poor side and they looked to their captain, the captain of England, to provide visible leadership. This Moore failed to do, whether deliberately or not. He appeared an isolated figure. The word frequently used about him was that he was 'aloof' but, of course, that was intrinsic to Moore's character. The calm reassurance that he conveyed when he was at his best as a player was in part the result of that aloofness. Greenwood wanted to sack Moore in 1970, just after he had finished runner-up in the poll for the European Footballer of the Year. The worsening relationship was caused by more than the fracas after Blackpool. There was a slackness and lack of discipline throughout the playing squad which made West Ham an almost dysfunctional club. When Greaves moved from White Hart Lane to Upton Park even he was shocked by the lack of discipline and the amount of drinking that went on. It was tragic for the supremely gifted Greaves that he should have ended up there because he was well on the way to full-blown alcoholism. When Greenwood said Moore could go and play for Clough at Derby and then reneged on the agreement, it upset Moore but it wasn't entirely unexpected, such was the lack of trust between the two men.

Off the field, Moore decided that as his playing career wound down and he was no longer the captain of England, which had an intrinsic commercial value, he would seek to secure his financial future by investing in various businesses. His mock-Tudor residence in Chigwell which had cost him £11,500 was sold for £41,000. He commissioned an architect to build a new house which cost £80,000 to design and build and was called Morlands. When he spotted a charming manor house between Chigwell and Abridge in the Essex countryside he decided it would be the perfect setting for a country club. Woolston Hall would comprise a restaurant, discotheque, cocktail and lounge bars, a sauna, a golf driving range, a swimming pool and tennis courts. The operation was a fiasco. Debts mounted as the project suffered from a lack of fiscal management and it soared wildly over budget. For some reason Moore attracted the worst of luck and the worst of company. There were arson attempts, reports of gunshots in the vicinity and theft on a grand scale as he tried to bring his vision to life by demanding the best fixtures and fittings. Woolston Hall opened in August 1972 but was sold early in 1974 during the three-day week with trading losses of £242,000 and a total debt of more than £530,000. Moore was not the only investor but in the end he was left with all the bills. Moore was an honourable man but he was never the businessman he thought he could be. He never recovered his financial equilibrium.

Moore had shown an interest in money since those steely negotiations with West Ham in 1961 over the extra £2 a week to take his wages up to £30. The failure of Woolston Hall meant that Moore finished his football career worrying about how to make ends meet and pay the bills. Although the marriage to Tina was by now starting to show cracks he apologised to his wife for being unable to buy her the champagne dinners he thought she deserved. He had one last chance at financial restitution when he was approached by Mark McCormack who offered to do for him what he had done for Arnold Palmer, whom he had turned into Arnold Palmer Inc. McCormack's agency fee was 20 per cent rather than the 10 per cent that Moore had been used to giving to Jack Turner who had done so well to get him that column in *Tit-Bits*. Moore's mind was made up when he realised McCormack wanted 20 per cent of everything, including his football salary. Moore turned down the American and with him went any chance that he could enjoy a life after football commensurate with his achievements in it.

All he could do was to play on for as long as he could. He eventually moved to Fulham on a free transfer in 1974, joining up with Alan Mullery, and together they helped to take the Second Division club to the FA Cup final where they met, inevitably, a resurgent West Ham United. It was to be his last appearance at Wembley but it was not to be a successful one as his old club won 2–0. He went off to America to play in the NASL for San Antonio in Texas but he returned for a final season with Fulham in 1976–7 when he was joined by Rodney Marsh and George Best, possibly the two most ill-disciplined players in English football. In front of *The Big Match* Sunday-afternoon television audience, Marsh and Best tackled each other, causing guffaws in the commentary box and putting smiles on the faces of many, but for the man who had captained England it must have seemed like exhibition football or a charity match; in either case it was a long way from Wembley 1966 and Guadalajara 1970. It didn't help Fulham much either as they went from ninth in Moore's first season to twelfth in his next and seventeenth in his last. He was thirty-seven but he still refused to hang up his boots, travelling to Denmark to play for Herning Fremad, a club in their Third Division. The engagement lasted for just nine games. He expected an offer from a Football League club to become their manager but all that materialised was one from non-league Oxford City and then a brief, unsuccessful stay at Southend United in 1984.

His assistant during his time with Oxford in the Isthmian League was Harry Redknapp, who went on to far better things, but then Redknapp had what it took to be a manager and Moore, for all his ability as a player, did not. Moore was like Bobby Charlton and Gordon Banks who had similarly disastrous times in charge of Preston North End and Telford United respectively, yet, ironically, it was they who were the indisputably three world-class figures in the side of 1966. Jack Charlton, who did not possess anything like the talent of his younger brother, knew exactly what it took to be a manager. It is possible that the offers did not materialise because it became known in the boardrooms of Football League clubs that Moore simply lacked the ruthlessness necessary to be a successful manager.

The 1980s were not a particularly happy decade for Moore. He left Tina, who had been so conspicuously by his side during the triumphs of the late 1960s, because he had fallen in love with Stephanie, the woman who was to become his second wife. The newspapers treated him kindly. They owed him that much and Moore must have been grateful given his horror of exposing in public personal matters which he was desperate to keep private. He had a good time in Hungary on location in John Huston's *Escape to Victory*, which was the director's equivalent of playing out the dregs of a fine career with a Danish Third Division side. The footballers – Moore, Pelé, Summerbee, Ardiles, John Wark and most of the then Ipswich Town team – gave better performances than the actors. Michael Caine must have been grateful to have been given a double as good as Kevin Beattie.

Other gainful employment included stints as a pundit at matches broadcast by Capital Gold and as a journalist for the *Sunday Sport*. He never complained about this apparent fall from grace but it must have been depressing for all those fans who admired him so greatly to discover that he was working in a newspaper office above a dildo factory. Predictably, he told few people about his final illness, which he bore with all the fortitude and dignity he had displayed on the field in his years of glory. He remained heroic to the last.

In retrospect, it is possible to see that Moore's performance in the defeat to Brazil was the pinnacle of his career. It confirmed for the world the English belief that Bobby Moore was the greatest defender in world football. At the end of that game, Moore and Pelé exchanged shirts, their faces wreathed in smiles of warmth and friendship. The image of the bare-chested Moore and Pelé, their faces full of admiration for each other's ability and the manner in which they played the game, is one that elevates the very nature of sport and the sporting contest.

In one of the last scenes of Oliver Stone's biographical film *Nixon* (1995), the president wanders through the White House with Henry Kissinger. It is the night before Nixon is due to resign the office of president and the two men stop in front of the official portrait of Nixon's nemesis, John F. Kennedy, the painted face downcast and thoughtful. Nixon turns to Kissinger and says simply, 'When they look at him, they see who they want to be. When they look at me, they see who they are.' When we look at Bobby Moore on the shoulders of his team-mates in 1966, or in this unforced natural pose with Pelé, we see football as we want to see it, as Bobby More at his best portrayed it – committed, sporting, skilful and moving.

Moore, like Jack Kennedy, died young. He died before the negative aspects of twenty-four-hour rolling news channels made their intrusive presence felt. Moore came from an age when we knew little of the true nature of our sporting heroes, and his biographer Matt Dickinson believes that that is how Moore wanted it. It may well be that we do, too, that we prefer to revel in the golden myth of England's greatest captain – in the idyll that was 1966 – rather than engage with the more complicated truth. The image we hold of Bobby Moore up to and including the World Cup finals in Mexico in 1970 may not be the whole man but it is the best part of Man.

CHAPTER THREE

THE AGE OF GARY LINEKER

THE AGE OF GARY LINEKER

Gary Lineker's life before he was elevated by his goals and the fame that accompanied them was not unlike that of Bobby Moore or, for that matter, that of thousands of boys growing up obsessed with sport in the 1960s and 1970s. Lineker was born in Leicester and displayed his uncanny ability to score goals from an early age. His parents, Barry and Margaret, had so much faith in his potential that they undertook a troublesome inconvenient move of house to make sure their free-scoring son attended a football-playing school. When Gary was ten the family moved out of the city and bought a house at Kirby Muxloe, a village to the west of Leicester.

Between the time that I took the Eleven Plus and getting the result, we moved house. In the county there was only one grammar school that I could go to and it was a school that played rugby not football so I was sent off to live with my grandparents in the city for about six months whilst my parents looked for another house to move back into the city to enable me to go to a football school because the same thing had happened to my dad. He had passed the Eleven Plus and went to a rugby-playing school and regretted it for the rest of his life. He said, 'I'm not letting that happen to you.' I don't think anyone was particularly surprised I passed the Eleven Plus so there was no huge celebration or anything like that.

It is probably no coincidence that two of the four England captains whose lives form the centrepiece of this book passed the Eleven Plus, but Lineker understandably believes that academic attainment is no way to judge the intelligence of a footballer:

Footballers are a cross section of working-class society and generally they come out of tough areas, so I wouldn't have expected many of them to have passed the Eleven Plus. There would be the odd one but not many of them. Frank Lampard went to a private school and he's got A levels and I've certainly played with players who had university degrees. Some footballers are bright. To get to the top of the game you have to have a degree of intelligence even if it's just a sense of spatial awareness. Things that go through a footballer's brain when he's playing are phenomenal when you think about it.

Gary went to the City of Leicester Boys' Grammar School, where they played football. At weekends he was involved both in games for his school and club games for Aylestone Park. Prolific from an early age, he scored 200 goals in one season for his school team. Plenty of clubs scouted him but Gary's grandfather Harold knew Ray Shaw, who was the chief scout at Filbert Street, and Gary duly signed schoolboy forms there. Gary had the same placid temperament as his grandfather who had also been a promising schoolboy player but there was no money in football in those days and he had gone into the family business, G. A. Lineker & Son, a fruit and vegetable stall in the covered market in Leicester town centre. He was followed by his own son, Barry, Gary's father. The life of a market-stall holder clearly held no attraction for Gary: 'My dad sold the stall in the market for a few quid when he retired ten years ago. That was bloody hard work. It probably gave me the drive to succeed in football. Getting up at four in the morning and work all day till late in the evening like my dad did? No thanks.'

Barry Lineker had supported Leicester City all his life so Gary and his brother Wayne were given season tickets from the age of eight. There were thirteen apprentices taken on to Leicester City's books along with Gary Lineker, but he was the only one who made a successful transition to the life of a professional footballer. It helped that he continued to live at home as he didn't suffer the social upheaval that frequently derails young boys who have to leave home and live in a strange city once they have signed associate forms.

Lineker left school with four O levels, a number which he could have doubled had he bothered to apply himself, for his teachers quickly realised that he was a bright lad. His aptitude for languages became very clear when he was transferred to Barcelona in 1986 and then, in 1992 at the end of his career, to Nagoya Grampus Eight in Japan. His headmaster issued the traditional warning that he couldn't expect to make a living playing football, but he was never going to choose any career other than a sporting one. He was a fine free-scoring batsman as well and, if he did not make the grade at Filbert Street, he thought he would have a good chance of doing so at Grace Road because he also captained Leicestershire Schoolboys at cricket. In being talented at both sports he was by no means unique. Football was not a year-round sport before television told youngsters it was and all boys who loved sport played cricket in the summer. As late as the 1980s there were still footballing county cricketers like Phil Neale of Worcestershire who played for Scunthorpe United alongside Ian Botham. Leicestershire's Chris Balderstone, Worcestershire's Ted Hemsley and Warwickshire's Jim Cumbes had only just retired from professional football at the end of the previous decade.

When Gary Lineker emerged as a clean-cut English hero in the early 1980s, a new, television-age version of the sepia newspaper displaying the photographs of Billy Wright and the colour magazine promoting Bobby Moore, his arrival was welcomed with relieved gratitude by a nation that had had very little to celebrate since Martin Peters had scored the goal that had put England 2–0 up in the 1970 quarter-final that afternoon in León. The 1960s had seen some unpalatable moments. The League Cup final between Arsenal and Leeds United in 1968 had been a showpiece occasion at Wembley that displayed all the worst traits in English football. It ended in a miserable 1–0 win for Leeds courtesy of a goal by the left-back Terry Cooper, but with the acquisition of that first trophy Revie's Leeds were on their way. It would be grossly unfair to blame the rise of negative football on Revie's team. What we all knew was that in players like Bremner, Giles, Gray, Lorimer and Clarke, Leeds had footballers of undoubted talent. It was frustrating that they seemed to prefer to kick opponents instead of outplaying them, which they could do when they set their minds to it.

The 1960s had been a decade that had started with the delights of Tottenham Hotspur's Double-winning side and ended with Manchester United's European Cup-winning side boasting the talents of Best, Law and Charlton. Unlike today's utterly predictable Premier League in which Leicester City's unexpected success in 2015–16 was greeted with understandable hosannas by supporters all over the country, there were at least half a dozen teams every season who could have won the league. It was the time of Shankly's first great Liverpool side of Callaghan, Hunt and St John and of the Everton trio of midfield match-winners in the shape of Kendall, Ball and Harvey. Manchester City had their own holy trinity of Lee, Bell and Summerbee and Arsenal were building a side on its way to the Double of 1970–71 including Radford, Kennedy and George. Hugh McIlvanney later wrote: 'Much of what passed for glamour and creativity in the 60s was sham but the decade was a genuinely distinguished period for football in England with Moore, George Best and Bobby Charlton at the apex of a broadly based pyramid of exceptional talent.'

For all the strength and diversity of the English First Division, the players who were selected for the national team in the early 1970s made for an England side that, unlike their immediate predecessors, turned out to be less than the sum of their combined talents. Alf Ramsey, who had painstakingly assembled a World Cup-winning squad from the unprepossessing parts he had inherited from Walter Winterbottom, tinkered frantically with the engine but it never roared into life again as it had done in the 1960s.

It took the FA six months to sack Ramsey after the Poland game in 1973. By contrast, Steve McClaren went the morning after a defeat at Wembley by Croatia ensured that England would not qualify for the finals of the European Championships of 2008. It was not courtesy or pastoral counselling that accounted for the delay in 1973; that was simply the way things were done back then. It was certainly not because that failure to qualify for the 1974 World Cup was considered by anyone in English football – players, press, supporters or management – as anything other than disastrous and humiliating. It took weeks for England supporters to get over the shock and the wounds opened up again as soon as the tournament started. Poland did well, finishing third, which made some

England supporters think that, had their team qualified, they might have won it. This view rests on the rather large assumption that England would have been able to deal with the remarkable Holland team, who were clearly the best side in the tournament, with every outfield player comfortable on the ball and capable of playing in any position.

England had suffered footballing shocks before, but no previous setback had the impact of their failure to defeat Poland at Wembley in 1973, which effectively kept England out of world football for the next nine years. When they returned to the world stage in 1982 the team would exit from the competition undefeated but virtually goalless. In 1966, footballing triumph had led the country to believe that it was a world superpower again as it had not been since 1945, and that Harold Wilson's promises of a new Britain were being realised. What hurt so much in 1973 was that the England football team now seemed to symbolise nothing so much as national decline. For people uninterested in sport it can certainly appear as if linking football, the country's most popular sport, with the state of the nation is an entirely pointless exercise. Yet sport, as many emerging nations would be quick to point out, does more for national prestige than almost any other activity. A strong economy takes years to grow and in a global economy it is to a large extent dependent on forces outside the control of the people charged with reinvigorating it. Medals in the Olympic Games, a strong performance in the World Cup, England regaining the Ashes, the England rugby union team beating the All Blacks, a British tennis player or golfer at the top of the world rankings, an Englishman winning the F1 world championship, these successes resonate and they make their countrymen proud and happy.

In the mid-1970s, however, the performances of the England football team became a cause of national anguish, mostly because the Football Association, which had unceremoniously dispensed with the services of Alf Ramsey, chose the wrong man to take his place. At first glance the FA's choice was understandable. Don Revie had been the manager of a successful if much-disliked Leeds United for a dozen years, but during the 1973–4 season they underwent something of a change of style. Brian Clough, his nemesis, had called Revie's claim to have created a Leeds United 'family' one that 'had more in keeping with the Mafia than Mothercare'. Instead of kicking everything that moved, Leeds decided to play the opposition at football. They succeeded beyond their wildest dreams, going undefeated for the first twenty-nine games of the season (a record that stood until the Arsenal 'Invincibles' thirty years later) and winning the First Division by a distance. The FA tempted Revie to take the England job with the offer of a salary considerably higher than the one they had grudgingly paid Ramsey.

The country thought the England team was being reinvented in the image of the new decade after Ramsey's 1950s appearance and vowels as strangulated as those of Ted Heath, the prime minister who had emerged from a working-class home in Kent. Revie tried to turn England matches at Wembley into the football equivalent of the Last Night of the Proms by replacing the dirge of the national anthem with 'Land of Hope and Glory', just as, thirty years later, the England and Wales Cricket Board had the bright idea of disguising the vulnerability of England's top order to an early collapse by introducing community singing of 'Jerusalem'. Initially, it appeared to be successful as England comfortably scored three times without reply against Czechoslovakia in Revie's first game in charge.

Revie had negotiated for himself an annual salary of £20,000, nearly three times the miserly £7,200 the FA had been paying Ramsey at the start of 1974. The manager of England's only

World Cup-winning side retired on an occupational pension of £1,200 p.a. Revie extended the FA's largesse to the players, whose match fees were considerably increased. He also supervised a commercial deal with the sportswear company Admiral who made the shirts worn by Leeds United and who now became the official England kit supplier. Ramsey had not wanted money to sully the purity of the England shirt and would have regarded these innovations as anathema. He would also have denigrated Revie's initial attempts to woo the media. Ramsey, as we have seen, loathed the media and made no concessions towards them but, of course, when the time came when he could have used their support they were not to be seen. Ramsey felt there was no point begging the media to like him. If he won football matches he knew they would like him and if he lost them he knew the press would call for his head no matter how much they liked him so it was a waste of effort to seek their favours. Revie courted the media because he wanted to lose the unlovable tag which he felt the press had unfairly hung round his neck at Elland Road and which demeaned the great side he had built at Leeds. These were all admirable ambitions, but Ramsey was proved right in the end. As soon as England started to stumble on the field, the press launched a predictable onslaught on the new 'track-suit manager' whom they had previously hailed as the right man for a new era on his appointment.

At Leeds, one of Revie's strengths was the continuity of personnel in his first team, season after season. The side that made Leeds great was Sprake, Reaney, Cooper, Bremner, Charlton, Hunter, Lorimer, Clarke, Jones, Giles and Gray. The utility player Paul Madeley filled in wherever there was a vacancy. Eventually David Harvey replaced Gary Sprake, Gordon McQueen took over when Jack Charlton retired and Joe Jordan led the line in place of Mick Jones, but the core of that team remained unchanged for more than six years. When

Revie took over England he tried to re-create the concept of the family which Brian Clough had dismissed so witheringly. However, most of the Leeds players had been with Revie all their professional lives and had grown up with the carpet bowls and the bingo, had appreciated their wives' birthdays being remembered and the children's parties at Christmas. For Mick Channon or Ray Clemence or Alan Ball, however, these testimonies to Revie's caring nature were what happened at Leeds and made no impact on them. They were seasoned internationals and felt these attempts to foster unity to be rather beneath them. They certainly resented the 10 p.m. curfew which the Leeds players had always accepted without demur.

Revie also tried to introduce a sense of modern technocratic professionalism into the players' lives by presenting them with dossiers containing detailed information on each of the players they would be facing in the next international match. Brian Clough once more displayed his scorn for Revie's tactics. 'Dossiers!' he mocked. 'Footballers don't read dossiers! Footballers forget to bring their passports when they go on foreign trips. Footballers lose the keys to their hotel rooms!' He wasn't completely wrong. There is a difference between showing the players that the manager and coaching staff understand the nature of their opponents and have prepared training routines accordingly and overwhelming players with irrelevant information and making them so aware of their opponents' strengths that they forget their own.

In addition, the continuity which served Leeds United so well for so long disappeared when Revie took charge of the national side. Part of the problem was that instead of choosing eleven from a first team squad of fourteen or fifteen, Revie himself was overwhelmed by the vast resources now available to him. Unlike Ramsey, who experimented reluctantly and preferred to stay with a tried and tested group whom he liked and respected,

Revie could not make up his mind and stick to it. In his twenty-nine games in charge he picked fifty-two different players. His choices of captain reflected this state of uncertainty. Over the course of his three-year tenure Revie switched the armband around from Emlyn Hughes to Alan Ball to Gerry Francis, to Kevin Keegan and Mick Channon. Under Ramsey the captain was Bobby Moore and everyone knew it. When Revie left England nobody was quite sure who the official England captain was any more. It left everyone feeling somewhat unsettled.

Revie was certainly unlucky with injuries. Two of his key players, Roy McFarland at centre-back and Colin Bell, who was ready to assume the role played by Bobby Charlton under Ramsey, had their careers significantly interrupted by serious injury. It is doubtful though, even with those two constantly fit and available, that Revie's England would have approached the authority that Ramsey's team at its best conveyed. Admittedly, Ramsey did not have to qualify for the World Cup in 1966 when England were the hosts and in 1970 when they were the holders and when he did have to do so in 1973 he failed, but his successor seemed to be as out of his depth in the new Europe as Ramsey had been against West Germany in 1972 and Poland in 1973. Just as the United Kingdom was joining the Common Market and officially becoming part of the European Economic Community, England seemed to be increasingly puzzled by European football.

Tom Stoppard's memorable 1977 television play *Professional Foul* is centred on an international colloquium on philosophy being held in Prague to which a number of English academics have been invited, chief among whom is Professor Anderson (played by Peter Barkworth) who holds the Chair of Ethics at Cambridge University. Anderson is delighted to be there as the colloquium coincides with an England World Cup qualifying match against Czechoslovakia for which Anderson has acquired a ticket. The football is a subplot to Stoppard's main purpose, which is to dramatise Charter 77 and the iniquities imposed on academic freedom by petty Czech tyrannies. Anderson initially refuses to smuggle a controversial Ph.D. thesis out of the country because he feels it would be unethical and discourteous to his hosts, but he changes his mind when he is confronted by the reality of daily life in Prague under the Communist regime. He is staying in the same hotel as the England players and in the lift he warns two of them of a Czech move from a free-kick which, he has observed, has brought them many goals. The players laugh and ignore him. Later, after missing the game because of the main plot, he listens to a report of the action telephoned into the sports desk in London by a broadsheet journalist which, to his horror, contains a Czech goal scored from a free-kick given for a professional foul and scored in exactly the manner he had warned about. England have clearly lost badly. As Anderson quietly

leaves the room the journalist is enunciating slowly, 'Like...
tragic... opera, things... got... worse... after... the... interval.'
In this one speech Stoppard has precisely evoked the climate
surrounding the England football team under Revie.

Despite beating Czechoslovakia 3–0 at home in the first of
the qualifying games for the 1976 European Championships
England lost the return match 2–1 and finished second in a
group in which only the first-placed team advanced to the
knock-out stage. Until UEFA revised the format in 1980 this
was how the tournament was played so Revie didn't even
reach the quarter-final as Ramsey had done in 1972. Everything
now hinged on qualification for the World Cup finals due to
take place in Argentina in 1978. Whatever the tensions between
England and Argentina had been since 1966, Revie's job was
to focus on finishing ahead of Italy, Finland and Luxembourg.
In the event, qualification hinged on the game in Rome, which
Revie badly miscalculated. He made six changes from the previous match against Finland and included Brian Greenhoff
and Trevor Cherry, with a rare cap for Stan Bowles who had
been outstanding for Queens Park Rangers when they were
pipped at the post for the League Championship by Liverpool
at the end of the previous season. None of them were established internationals and, in a match of such importance, their
lack of experience cost England dear as Italy ran out comfortable 2–0 winners. Bowles, Keegan and Channon made no
impact on the impregnable Italian back three of Cuccureddu
and the formidable Facchetti and Gentile. Even though
England won the return match at Wembley twelve months
later by the identical 2–0 scoreline, Italy qualified for Argentina
on goal difference.

For the second World Cup in a row, England would not
even be one of the sixteen teams who competed in the finals,
and it certainly didn't help that Scotland reached the finals in

both 1974 and 1978. In the summer of 1973 the West Indies played three Test matches in England, winning two of them by overwhelming margins and drawing the other. The final Test at Lord's, interrupted for the first time by the need to clear a cricket ground following a bomb warning, was won by an innings and 225 runs as England capitulated before a triumphant crowd, seemingly composed entirely of West Indian immigrants or those of West Indian descent. It was a confirmation that the impact of immigration was starting to become widely visible. The following winter of 1974–5, England lost the Ashes in Australia as the fearsome fast-bowling combination of Dennis Lillee and Jeff Thomson battered England into submission. The press became increasingly vituperative about England's sporting failures as the old restraints that had moderated press reaction in previous years were discarded. England's increasingly desperate and ineffective performances on the sports field now seemed more and more symbolic of the successive crises gripping the country.

The quadrupling of oil prices from $3 to nearly $12 a barrel combined with an oil embargo in an immediate response to the West's perceived support for Israel in the Yom Kippur War of 1973 had an immediate impact on all Western economies causing both recession and inflation known by the composite term of 'stagflation'. The National Union of Mineworkers, who held a unique position in the British psyche, exploited the power given to them by OPEC by instituting a ban on overtime and so began the power cuts that caused the electorate to lose patience with the government. For Heath and his government this flexing of union muscles was simply too blatant to be ignored.

In early 1974 Edward Heath called a snap election as he tried to face down the unions who had destroyed his prices and incomes policy and forced a three-day week on a scandalised public. The guttering candles that burned in homes deprived of electricity in the winter of 1973–4 seemed like appropriate successors to the Union Jack as symbols of a nation in decline. Heath's election slogan asked the question 'Who governs Britain?' He was to receive a chastening answer. The result of the election held on 28 February was that the Tories acquired the largest share of the votes but Labour picked up twenty seats to finish at 301 while the Conservative party lost thirty-seven to finish at 297. Heath spent a frantic weekend trying unavailingly to persuade Liberal leader Jeremy Thorpe that the Liberals should join a Tory-led coalition, so on the Monday evening a surprised but delighted Harold Wilson returned to Downing Street at the head of a minority government. He was soon faced with runaway inflation as union disputes were resolved at the cost of high wage settlements with no consequent increase in productivity.

The composition of the new parliament made for an unstable government and within eight months the country was asked to go to the polls again. This time a slightly more convincing answer was given as a 2 per cent swing and a gain of a further eighteen seats gave Labour a tiny overall majority of three seats with which they were determined to govern. For the next five years they did, with the increasingly familiar sight of ill and incapacitated Labour MPs being pushed in wheelchairs, some of them attached to a hospital drip, through the lobby in order to vote as the Conservative Chief Whip refused to pair in accordance with long-standing tradition.

With the exception of their extremely vibrant and varied output of popular music, the 1970s have – not unfairly – had a bad press. The decade seems in retrospect to have been drab and depressing, one in which the colours brown and beige predominated in clothes and in interior design, symbolising the general atmosphere in the country. The almost even split in the House of Commons reflected a country that was similarly divided. The Thatcherites of the 1980s would deliberately distance themselves from the One Nation Tories of the 1970–4 government, while splits in the Labour party which started in the 1970s made the party unelectable for nearly twenty years. The humiliation of taking a begging bowl to the International Monetary Fund and the fear that the world order had been upended by Arabs in native dress shopping in Harrods should not disguise the fact that anyone who was in constant employment in the 1970s was likely to benefit from rising living standards. There was a constant fear about the fragility of the pound which had been devalued in November 1967 from $2.80 to $2.40 and continued to fall until, briefly, it almost reached parity with the dollar in the 1980s. Yet increasing numbers of British people continued to travel abroad: from 1 January each year ITV was filled with commercials extolling the virtues of package holidays in foreign resorts where you could be sure of sunshine – even if you couldn't be sure that your hotel had been built before you arrived there.

One of the problems with general history is that it suffers from the constant exposure of a small selection of events on television. Thus, the history of the 1970s is the story of the guttering candle in the three-day week and the rubbish piling up in the streets during the so-called 'winter of discontent', just as the story of the 1980s is the clash between striking miners and the police outside Orgreave Colliery and the sound of the bell on the floor of the Stock Exchange which ushered in the Big Bang of the de-regulated market, barrow-boy City traders and the culture of 'Greed is good'. E. H. Carr had written in *What is History?* about the limitations of what becomes an acceptable historical fact, but it has changed again with the ubiquitous and frequently iniquitous history documentary on television. Facts assume a greater significance when they are on television. The same shots are replayed time and again usually because a particular piece of film is free of charge, which is why it is so constantly broadcast. History therefore becomes the history of that which has been filmed, preferably in colour.

One of the images frequently used to portray life in England in the 1970s and 1980s is that of the football hooligan. Crowd disturbances at matches, youths fighting and racing from other gangs in the streets and the behaviour of Scottish fans on the pitch at Wembley following a home international against England in 1977 all have the same effect of indicating disgust at what seemed the inevitably violent corollary to a game of football. Scotland had beaten England 2–1 with goals from McQueen and Dalglish to the delight of the crowd of 98,000 of whom it was estimated that perhaps 70 per cent were Scottish. Certainly the match became notorious for what happened after the final whistle blew when visiting fans, many of them intoxicated (Gordon McQueen claimed he could smell the whisky walking up the tunnel) invaded the pitch, swung on the crossbar, broke it and then dug up sods of Wembley turf which they took triumphantly back to Scotland. It was perhaps delayed revenge for the theft of the Stone of Scone by Edward I. Scotland now had North Sea oil, a better football team and most of Wembley Stadium.

Revie had had enough. Fearing the sack from the autocratic Sir Harold Thompson at the FA, who treated him as contemptuously as he had treated Ramsey, Revie flew secretly to the United Arab Emirates and agreed to become that country's national coach on a four-year contract for a tax-free sum of £340,000. It would be impossible to imagine Ramsey (or indeed most English managers) behaving similarly. Ramsey might have loathed the English Football Association but he was a dyed-in-the-wool patriot. It was a sign of the times that

Revie was accompanied on his flight to the Middle East by a reporter from the *Daily Mail* which, of course, then ran the exclusive story (for the reported fee of £20,000, which was the same as Revie's annual salary from the FA). Ramsey's loathing of the press would have precluded such an eventuality. The photograph of Revie in a suit signing his lucrative contract surrounded by the sheikhs in native dress, combined with English resentment at the sudden increase in the cost of petrol, seemed to sum up in a single picture the way in which the world of Western hegemony and Middle Eastern subservience had been turned on its head. Then there was the small matter of the money.

There was money to be made in football in the 1970s, though nothing like the sums currently on offer in the Premier League, and football was full of managers who had been players in the days of the maximum wage and who were only too familiar with the financial insecurities of careers in management constantly at the mercy of incompetent players, hostile fans and the whims of dictatorial chairmen of weak boards of directors. Brian Clough, who had been born a few streets away from Revie in Middlesbrough eight years after him, was just as obsessed with money as Revie, and in both cases that obsession stemmed less from the greed that would have been recognised by Gordon Gekko than from the impoverished hard times of their early years that would have been recognised by Ena Sharples. The manner in which Revie had fashioned his escape from England had been less than admirable but the manner in which the FA behaved before and after was considerably worse. The outraged Thompson tried to ban him from English football for ten years. That decision was legally overturned but a combination of constant press hostility to Revie – who had been portrayed as betraying his country as surely as Benedict Arnold had betrayed his – and the later onset of motor neurone disease ensured that Revie's career in English football was effectively over.

It was predictable that the FA would replace Revie not with the People's Choice, Brian Clough, who would almost certainly take even less notice of Thompson than Revie and Ramsey had, but by the 'safe pair of hands' of Ron Greenwood. Under him, England football at least recovered its equilibrium and its sense of decorum. England did not go to Argentina in 1978 but qualified once again for football's premier tournament when it moved to Spain in 1982 and expanded from sixteen to twenty-four teams. Under Greenwood the England team found a new star in Bryan Robson and a regular captain in Kevin Keegan. After the dalliances with Alan Ball, Phil Thompson and Mick Mills among others, for the first time since Bobby Moore everyone knew who the England football captain was and everyone admired him for his whole-hearted commitment. He wasn't Bobby Moore, but he represented the tenor of his times just as Moore had done.

Keegan was one of a small number of English First Division footballers to make a success of playing for a continental side. The record of top-class English footballers in Europe was patchy at best. John Charles had left Leeds United to become a hero at Juventus in the 1950s but Denis Law and Jimmy Greaves had both failed in Italy at the start of the 1960s. Kevin Keegan, however, had won the European Cup with Liverpool in 1977 and then moved to SV Hamburg, dedicating himself to living in Germany and succeeding to the extent that he twice won the coveted European Footballer of the Year award (1978 and 1979) and was part of a team that won the Bundesliga title in 1978–9. Keegan had skilfully negotiated what is now called a buy-out clause facilitating his move abroad and another easing his way back to the English First Division with Southampton in the summer of 1980.

He handled his playing career and life as a manager after retirement with enormous adroitness, but you could always see the sweat pouring from the hard-working Keegan's brow. What endeared him to the country was his memorable appearance in 1976 on the BBC television series *Superstars*, one of the many programmes originated by Mark McCormack's television production arm. During one gruelling race Keegan fell off his bicycle at high speed. Despite suffering extensive cuts and painful abrasions, sufficient to make the viewing millions wince, Keegan climbed back on to his bike and cycled his way to eventual victory and into the affections of the nation. 'Mighty Mouse' wore his heart on his sleeve – most notoriously in the Liverpool v. Leeds FA Charity Shield at Wembley in 1974, when he was sent off for fighting with Billy Bremner and removed his shirt on the way to an early bath. He always gave his all for his country, though after winning the European Cup with Liverpool in 1977 he decided, like Edward Heath and Roy Jenkins, that the future lay in Europe.

Keegan left Liverpool just as Bob Paisley's side began its remarkable domination of the English Football League and the European Cup. He was replaced as Liverpool's main striker by the Celtic forward Kenny Dalglish who scored the winning goal against Bruges in the European Cup final of 1978 and in 1985 moved seamlessly from player to player-manager. His last season in charge, 1990–91, coincided with the start of Liverpool's quarter of a century of relative decline. With the help of an outstanding side, Dalglish carried Liverpool to three more European Cups in his first seven seasons with the club, their triumphs interspersed by two victories for Nottingham Forest and one for Aston Villa, giving English clubs a remarkable hold on Europe's premier trophy for seven years out of eight.

Even though English clubs, admittedly sprinkled with clever, skilful Scots, were able to impose their will on Europe

– thereby creating a renewed respect for English football – Greenwood's national side seemed unable to arrest the post-Moore and post-Ramsey decline. The latest nadir was a 2–1 defeat by Norway in September 1981 in a qualifying game for the 1982 World Cup in Spain. In truth, the result did not flatter the underrated Norwegians who were not intimidated by an early goal from Bryan Robson or by the presence in the England defence of Phil Neal and Phil Thompson, two regular members of the all-conquering Liverpool side. It wasn't the result of the match that imprinted itself on the minds of England supporters but the radio commentary of Bjørge Lillelien for the Norwegian Broadcasting Corporation who, at the moment of maximum excitement after the final whistle had blown, lapsed into a memorable rant:

> We are best in the world! We have beaten England! England, birthplace of giants. Lord Nelson, Lord Beaverbrook, Sir Winston Churchill, Sir Anthony Eden, Clement Attlee, Henry Cooper, Lady Diana, Maggie Thatcher we have beaten them all, we have beaten them all. Maggie Thatcher, can you hear me? Maggie Thatcher, your boys took a hell of a beating! Your boys took a hell of a beating!

In view of the Suez fiasco, Eden seems fortunate to be in such distinguished company and, of course, Beaverbrook was Canadian, though he would probably have delighted in plastering the commentary all over the *Daily Express*. Henry Cooper is oddly included in an otherwise predictable roll call of English public life, though it seems a shame that neither Shakespeare nor Dickens were name checked as Mr Lillelien concentrated largely on political giants, giving due respect to the prime minister of Britain's first post-war government who, by 1981, had largely been forgotten in his own country.

The rant was enjoyed enormously in the country that was supposedly the target of the Norwegian commentator's triumphalism. It has since been parodied frequently, which will ensure its durability, but the very fact that the English took what at first glance was a critical and humiliating diatribe to be a comedy routine that was endlessly enjoyable indicates that something fundamental had shifted about the country's response to its national football team. It could still be seen as idiotic foreigners behaving in a crass, stupid and ignorant manner but the durability of the rant suggests that is not the case. England were in the process of a long journey from the Land of Hope and Glory days of 1966 to the streets of Charleroi in 2000 and Wayne Rooney swearing at his own fans through the lens of a television camera after a disappointing goalless draw against Algeria in the 2010 World Cup in South Africa. There was an increasing acceptance that England was in decline and so was its football team. If you weren't inclined towards violence which, thankfully, most fans are not, the best possible alternative is comedy and Bjørge Lillelien's post-match summary never fails to raise a smile that accompanies a shrug of the shoulders.

Some decline was to be expected. Certainly Great Britain did not occupy the place in the post-war world that it had occupied in 1945. The British Empire was dissolving and so was England's sporting primacy. The fact that the British had exported the games of football and cricket as well as many other sports all over the world meant that they began international competition with a technical advantage, just as the Industrial Revolution of the late eighteenth century gave the country a head start in what is now known as the 'global race'. However, it was inevitable that at some point other nations would catch up.

In cricket, what the West Indies achieved at Lord's in 1950 and in many a subsequent Test match was what India, Pakistan and eventually Sri Lanka would do in their turn. In football, first Hungary and Germany, then Italy and Brazil and eventually the USA and Norway all humiliated England as coaching methods, new forms of nutrition and general fitness levels conspired to provide those countries with resources as good as or better than those to be found in England. The wonder is not that England eventually surrendered its supposed invincibility but that it had lasted as long as it did and that it had taken other countries so long to recognise England's vulnerability. Then it became a question of how the England football supporters would adapt to a role in the world among the also-rans which their parents and grandparents would have found intolerable.

On the one hand fans could simply accept that English players were no good at football, at least not when playing for the national team, and the best thing to do, as Lottie sings in *Mack and Mabel*, would be to 'tap your troubles away'. On the other hand, football hooligans could, at the slightest provocation, remind foreigners that England's footballers might not know how to defend, create or score but their 'supporters' were afraid of no one: by drinking industrial quantities of alcohol, causing significant damage to foreign property and – even more satisfying – damage to foreign people, they could show these upstarts that England was still a country to be feared. Of these two alternatives, the tap-dancing option was sadly less palpable than the head-smashing one, though the hooligans represented only a small if particularly visible percentage of England's supporters.

There has been a long-standing assumption that British economic problems and Britain's diminishing prestige in the new world order somehow manifest themselves in the performances of the England football team. There is more of a case to be made for this argument in the 1950s, when short-sightedness in the Conservative government was matched by a similarly blinkered view of the world of football as seen in FA headquarters in Lancaster Gate. When Harold Macmillan was invited to attend the negotiations being held by France, West Germany, Italy, Belgium, Holland and Luxembourg which were eventually enshrined in the Treaty of Rome in 1957 and the creation of the Common Market, his reply to his aide was, 'Tell them I'm far too busy dealing with Cyprus'. There certainly were problems dealing with Greek Cypriot terrorists of EOKA and the wily Archbishop Makarios, but Britain's initial scepticism of the European Economic Community was repaid by de Gaulle's seeming determination in the 1960s never to let Britain into it, despite Macmillan changing his mind after he became prime minister.

History does not obligingly offer us a defining moment at which we can state with confidence that Britain began its economic or political decline. Likewise, if one looks at the chronology of England's post-war football results, it becomes apparent that the graph does not point straight downwards from a high point in, say, 1947. The fact is that England never travelled particularly well and the defeat by Hungary in 1953 is invariably referred to simply because it was the first time England had lost at home to a team from outside Great Britain and Ireland. However, England had lost plenty of times abroad before 1953 but for some reasons to do with English insularity those defeats had been swept under the carpet, which is partly why the loss to the USA in Belo Horizonte wasn't the occasion for national soul-searching in 1950 that it would be today.

After all, it was very hot when England left the country to play their tour matches after the end of the Football League season so, for a start, the weather was against them. We have already seen how they had to tolerate eating the foreign muck that was served up abroad by people who seemed ignorant of a proper dinner which usually consisted of Brown Windsor soup, shepherd's pie and jam roly-poly. Then there were the foreign referees who didn't seem to understand that hard but perfectly fair tackling was allowed but spitting, shirt-pulling and diving were not. Defeats abroad therefore didn't quite count. Wembley 1966, of course, was a triumph but, as hosts, England did not have to qualify and their stuttering start in the group stages did not suggest that the ultimate triumph awaited them. If Rattín hadn't got himself sent off and the Argentina team had decided to play football rather than kick everything that moved on the Wembley turf, it would have been no surprise if England had gone out at the quarter-final stage in 1966. Against Portugal in the semi-final, England showed their class and in the final their entirely admirable spirit, stamina and skill earned them a justly famous victory, but it didn't last.

The graph of the England football team continues to show alternating peaks and troughs. It certainly seemed like a very low point in October 2000, when Germany beat England 1–0 in a World Cup qualifying game in the last match played at the old Wembley Stadium, and Kevin Keegan resigned as England's manager (rather appropriately) in the gents toilets immediately afterwards. Yet only four months previously the scoreline in the European Championships had been the reverse and, less than a year later, in the return match played in Munich, England achieved one of their most notable victories of recent years when they won 5–1. England, the country, hadn't changed much between the first of those three matches in June 2000 and the last one played in September 2001, yet results had shown a markedly different football team each time. Depending on the point of view you adopted, throughout those months England was basking in the Brown–Blair boom of the pre-Iraq War days or it was still suffering the terminal decline it had been experiencing since VE Day.

It's easy to see why the idea of decline might be exaggerated. The 1950s, that decade of blinkered conformism in which Britain's pre-eminent place in world affairs and at the top of sporting achievement was permanently surrendered, when as a nation we saw the world turn into a more dangerous place than ever before because of the real possibility, or so it was believed, of imminent nuclear annihilation, was also a time of almost unparalleled optimism. The war, with its attendant loss and bereavement, was a rapidly fading memory, the economy was producing almost full employment, rationing had been abandoned, there appeared to be an end in sight to polio, measles, rubella and diphtheria through simple inoculations, the birth rate was rising, and the world that was opening up for these baby boomers seemed to be one of peace, prosperity and endless opportunity. What sort of a decline was that?

In the days of Gladstone and Disraeli, Britain's acquisition of foreign lands and their economic resources helped to stimulate and service a growing domestic economy, but the vast majority of British people lived a life below stairs, physically or metaphorically, and the profits of the booming economy did not benefit them significantly. As late as the inter-war years, working and living conditions were so bad for the exploited mill workers in east Lancashire or unemployed coal miners in Jarrow that life was still as nasty, brutish and short for them as it had been when Thomas Hobbes had written *Leviathan* in the middle of the seventeenth century. In the era of Britain's irreversible decline over the past fifty years it seems that the suffering population can afford cars, foreign holidays, satellite television, central heating, smartphones and a range of food choices not available in the late nineteenth century to the richest of the minority who ruled the country and who lived in sybaritic comfort provided by the toil and drudgery of others.

The 1970s and 1980s were marked by industrial disruption and civil unrest, but there were also encouraging signs that some of the more unpleasant aspects of British society were slowly but surely starting to change. At the end of November 1978, Viv Anderson, the Nottingham Forest full-back, became the first black player to play for the full England team. It was a staging post on a journey that had led from the *Empire Windrush* through the Notting Hill race riots of 1958 to the disgraceful events in the Smethwick constituency at the general election of 1964 in which the Tory candidate Peter Griffith approved his campaign slogan 'If you want a nigger for a neighbour, vote Labour' and won the seat from the incumbent, the shadow foreign secretary Patrick Gordon Walker with a swing of 7.2 per cent to the Conservatives. Four years later, in April 1968, Enoch Powell spoke at a meeting of the West Midlands Area Conservative Political Centre and, as a true classicist, quoted Virgil as he spoke of his vision, 'As I look ahead, I am filled with foreboding; like the Roman, I seem to see "the River Tiber foaming with much blood".' As a provocative opposition to the Labour government's policy on Commonwealth immigration and its proposed anti-discrimination legislation, it could not have had a greater impact. It roused the London dockers and people all over the country who felt threatened by the rising tide of immigration from the former colonies. It raised the prospect of race riots, yet although there were outbreaks of violence and plenty of tensions for the next decade after Powell's speech, the fact remains that Britain did not sink beneath rising rivers of blood.

Football was a highly visible stage on which the themes of racial conflict were played out as black players started to make their first appearances as professional footballers in the 1960s. Few of them found it a comfortable experience. The South African Albert Johanneson, a fast and skilful left-winger for

Leeds United, was the first black man to appear in an FA Cup final when he played in the 2–1 defeat to Liverpool in 1965. He and Clyde Best, the Bermudian who played as a centre-forward for West Ham United from 1968, were treated to the full range of racist antagonism. The monkey chants from the terraces and the hurling of bananas deeply affected Best and almost destroyed Johanneson, who declined into alcoholism and died alone and almost forgotten in 1995. His cause as a regular player in the Leeds United first team was not helped by the emergence of Eddie Gray whom Revie clearly preferred, just as Best's appearances were probably boosted by the fact that nobody of Gray's talent emerged to take his place. Upton Park was always an odd place for Best to play, given that east London contained so many committed supporters of Enoch Powell and his racial theories, but Best's hard work and good humour eventually won the crowd over. In the end supporters, unless their racism is so deeply ingrained it simply cannot be argued against, will take to their hearts a player who commits himself to their cause and whose skill is such that he can make the team better.

It was not until the 1970s, however, that black players emerged in significant numbers, not just in football but throughout British sport. In 1972, Clive Sullivan, the Hull FC and Hull Kingston Rovers winger, captained the Great Britain rugby league side to a World Cup victory. John Conteh, the Liverpool boxer, became the WBC light heavyweight champion in 1974, a title he held for three years. Black cricketers like Gary Sobers, Clive Lloyd, Viv Richards, Joel Garner, Michael Holding, Gordon Greenidge, indeed most of that all-conquering West Indies team of the late 1970s, graced county cricket from the start of the decade. Warwickshire boasted four of them in the same team in 1972 – Rohan Kanhai, Alvin Kallicharran, Lance Gibbs and the wicketkeeper Deryck

Murray. Black faces were becoming an unremarkable sight on English sports fields and supporters mostly accepted their integration into what had previously been all-white teams relatively quickly.

Elsewhere in the west Midlands, Ron Atkinson, the manager of West Bromwich Albion, developed three young black players whom he jokingly referred to as the Three Degrees. Laurie Cunningham, Cyrille Regis (who were originally signed by John Giles) and Brendon Batson were part of an attractive side that finished third behind Liverpool and Nottingham Forest in the 1978–9 season. In April 1977, Cunningham, born in Archway in north London, was the first black player to be capped for England at any level above schoolboy international when he scored on his debut in 1977 for the Under-21 side against Scotland. He was later transferred to Real Madrid in the days when such transfers were virtually unheard of. Unfortunately, injuries restricted his appearances and he faded from the game in his late twenties after playing for other clubs in Spain as well as Marseilles. He died in a car crash in Madrid at the age of thirty-three but not before he had shown what was possible for young black men who wanted to play professional football. The year after Cunningham had first played for the England Under-21 side, Anderson, born in Nottingham, was selected by Ron Greenwood to make his debut for the full England side against Czechoslovakia at Wembley. That same year the BBC was finally embarrassed into cancelling *The Black and White Minstrel Show*. It had regularly claimed audiences of up to twelve million viewers, which was why the BBC was reluctant to abandon it, but the clamour from black activists and the liberal press never relented and in the end the BBC felt it had no choice. The death of *The Black and White Minstrel Show*, followed a few weeks later by the selection of England's first black full international, felt like a significant staging-post in post-war race relations.

The war wasn't yet won. Racial abuse would still be a feature of certain sections of certain grounds for many years to come. Well into the twenty-first century, black English players would be the target of racist taunts when playing in Spain and Eastern Europe. What made it so shocking was that for many of them it was the first time they had come across it, because by the end of the twentieth century English football had integrated its different ethnic minorities better than most countries. After Anderson and the three West Brom players came John Barnes, Des Walker, Rio Ferdinand and Ashley Cole among a host of others. The appearance of a black face in an England shirt no longer attracts any comment, which reflects the country's metamorphosis into a multi-cultural nation. It took some sports longer than others but that, too, reflected the society in which talented young sports people grew up.

Tennis and golf clubs did not boast many black members and the sad decline of cricket in state schools has meant that the England team in recent years has reverted largely to a mainly all-white one. In the 1980s and 1990s the emergence of Roland Butcher, Norman Cowans, Gladstone Small, Phil DeFreitas, Wilf Slack, Devon Malcolm, Dean Headley, Chris Lewis, Mark Butcher and Alex Tudor gave the England cricket team a truly representative look. Now only Chris Jordan, who was born in Barbados, is even close to appearing for England although Moeen Ali is a welcome addition to the Test and ODI side. Cricket is mostly played in independent schools because they have the money for the groundsman, the pitches and the equipment which state schools do not.

Black British teenagers do not identify with the West Indies cricket team the way their parents and grandparents did, so to that extent they have passed Norman Tebbit's test for what constitutes British identity. They do not turn The Oval or Lord's into the Kensington Oval in Barbados or Sabina Park in Kingston, Jamaica, the way their parents did during the West Indies tours of the 1960s and 1970s. If those West Indies teams were winning sides and since the retirement of Brian Lara, Curtly Ambrose and Courtney Walsh the West Indies have struggled, the key fact is that black British teenagers now consider themselves to be native black British not West Indian immigrants. Their allegiance is to Chelsea, Arsenal and Tottenham and their sport is football not cricket, because if they went to state schools and watched only terrestrial television they wouldn't have experienced much cricket. There is football to be played in the park and to be seen on television twelve months a year.

Until the emergence of BSkyB in 1990, football coverage on British television remained strictly a two-channel affair. As far as ITV was concerned, however, it was largely a *one*-channel affair. The commercial network remained perennially annoyed that the BBC could always claim smugly – when the two broadcasters went head-to-head with simultaneous televising of World Cup games or the FA Cup final – that audience figures confirmed viewers preferred the BBC coverage to that of ITV.

An indication of how nasty this rivalry could turn occurred during the 1969 FA Cup final between Manchester City and Leicester City. The Manchester City manager Joe Mercer had been a star of the BBC's 1966 World Cup coverage and Malcolm Allison, his coach and assistant manager, had been signed by ITV, for whom he was to make a big splash on its innovative panel for the 1970 World Cup in Mexico. Allison, who resented the fact that Joe Mercer was walking out at the head of the Manchester City team, had in any case been banned from even sitting next to Mercer because he was serving one of his many touchline bans for having verbally abused the match officials. Mercer was sitting on the team bench under the Royal Box and giving his comments into an official BBC microphone thrust under his chin during the course of the match, which were fed into the live transmission. Allison wanted those cameras on him. He felt he would be much more entertaining than Mercer, so much more insightful in his analysis. Instead he sat and suffered because, although his friend the journalist Paul Doherty was sitting next to him in the stand with an illicit microphone up his sleeve and asking the occasional question, his comments would be transmitted on ITV, and despite his future relationship with commercial television he knew perfectly well how few people watched ITV on Cup final day.

Not only were ITV resentful about their perceived inferiority on days of dual broadcasts but they resented equally the fact that *Match of the Day* had grabbed the prime football slot on Saturday nights. *The Big Match*, which London Weekend Television transmitted along with the regional variations in all other parts of the ITV network that showed matches local to their franchise area, was not transmitted until Sunday afternoons, by which time the Sunday newspapers had been read and it all felt a little second-hand. By 1978, the long-standing resentment had mixed with a more immediate commercial imperative for Michael Grade, who had recently been promoted from Head of Light Entertainment at LWT to Programme Controller, which meant he was responsible for all of the company's programmes and, in conjunction with the other Big Five Programme Controllers, their scheduling.

LWT's weekly franchise ran from seven o'clock on Friday evening until closedown on Sunday nights although LWT accused Thames Television of deliberately putting on unpopular programmes just before LWT took over. So heated were LWT's protestations that the IBA eventually allowed the company to begin broadcasting at 5.15 p.m. LWT nevertheless still only had three evenings a week to generate revenue where Thames had four, and Michael Grade was acutely conscious that the BBC consistently fired its biggest guns on Saturday nights. There was a strong belief among television schedulers, in the days when you had to get out of the armchair and press a button on the television set in order to change the channel, that people were actually too lazy to do so. Before the scheduler's nightmare – otherwise known as the remote control – became an everyday accessory, successful schedules were built on the 'inheritance factor'. A family that watched *Dr Who* and *The Generation Game* would stay with BBC1 for the rest of Saturday evening. Grade recalls:

> The battle for Saturday night was not really about sport. The BBC took the view that they had to win Saturday night. Anything that got good ratings in midweek like Dick Emery got moved into Saturday night. ITV's weekend schedule was masterminded by LWT but it didn't own the whole of the network for the weekend and you had to get the support of the other ITV companies. When Yorkshire came up with a big hit like *Rising Damp* they would never let us play it at the weekend. They kept it in a soft slot midweek against *Panorama* where the BBC weren't competing. It was a big struggle for ITV and particularly LWT and it took years to turn it round. The BBC had an unbeatable line-up – *Dr Who*, *Jim'll Fix It*, *All Creatures Great and Small*, *Kojak*, *The Generation Game*, *The Two Ronnies*, then *Match of the Day* and finally Parky. Little by little we turned it round starting with *Game for a Laugh*. That was the first big home-grown show ITV had

on Saturday night and then we started *The Professionals*
and it built from that.

Grade was particularly interested in sport himself because
he had grown up with his father, Leslie Grade, as a Charlton
Athletic supporter. When the time came for him to enter the
world of work it was Leslie who persuaded Hugh Cudlipp to
find young Michael a job on the sports desk at the *Daily
Mirror*. It was an awkward way in because nobody took
kindly to this son of a rich man being parachuted into the
sports department by the man who ran the paper. But for
Michael Grade, the football fanatic, it was an opportunity to
be grabbed with both hands:

My first assignment when I joined the *Daily Mirror* sports
desk in the summer of 1960 was to go and sit at the
Ministry of Labour to keep an eye on things as the footballers' strike over the maximum wage was being
hammered out. It was an object lesson for me because
Alan Hardaker, who ran the Football League, was dour
and taciturn and came out after each session and ignored
the press, but Jimmy Hill on behalf of the PFA came out,
sat down with the press, nattered away, gave us quotes and
a story and it was a good lesson to me in media management. In the days when there was just the BBC and ITV,
sport was a very competitive battleground. There was little
or no live football outside the FA Cup final. There was
only *Match of the Day* and *The Big Match* on ITV with
regional variations on Sunday afternoons. Boxing was also
very big in those days with huge tension between us and
the BBC to get the big fights with Barry McGuigan, Henry
Cooper, Sugar Ray Leonard and of course the heavyweight
title fights. There were always battles with Don King and

Harry Levine and Jack Solomons, who didn't speak to each other. There were also big arguments over duplication of coverage of the World Cups and the Olympics.

Grade wanted both to persuade the BBC to alternate instead of duplicate sports coverage because ITV was wasting money and resources on having to compete in a losing battle with the BBC, and at the same time make inroads into the BBC's seemingly impregnable line-up of popular programmes on Saturday night. The best way, he decided, was to make a frontal assault on *Match of the Day* which would be difficult because BBC and ITV operated an effective cartel in which they agreed on a joint approach to the Football League with a view to keeping down the cost of televised football. If he were prepared to break the cartel and alienate everyone at the BBC – and probably a lot of executives at ITV – it might be possible. Grade was always a man for decisive positive action.

In November 1978, Jim Callaghan's Labour government was about to enter the 'winter of discontent', but in ITV there was more than discontent: there was absolute panic. Grade had recently, after much effort, succeeded in seducing Bruce Forsyth from *The Generation Game* to LWT to front *Bruce Forsyth's Big Night*, which was to be the linchpin of the new Saturday-night ITV schedule. Forsyth received £15,000 a show and the programme was generously budgeted at £250,000 for each episode – astonishing sums for the time, and eloquent testimony to the importance of winning the Saturday-night ratings war. Unfortunately the new show, which began a run of twelve episodes in October 1978, did not appeal strongly to either audiences or critics and, even worse, *The Generation Game* – under a new host, Larry Grayson – recovered spectacularly from Forsyth's defection and continued to win the early-evening battle. Audiences for *Bruce's Big*

Night continued to spiral downwards. Grade had to find another way to dent the BBC's apparent impregnability.

On 9 November, as the House of Commons was debating the Queen's Speech, Grade went to meet Jack Dunnett, the MP for Nottingham East, a backbench Labour MP and former chairman of Brentford, now chairman of Notts County and a junior member of the management committee that ran league football. Grade and Dunnett knew and liked each other. Dunnett, like Grade, was Jewish; his family had fled to Scotland from Poland and Lithuania. He was also a man for the bold move. Before Robert Maxwell failed to merge Oxford United with Reading to form Thames Valley Royals, Jack Dunnett had suggested merging Brentford with Queens Park Rangers, which made financial sense but caused such outrage that he was forced to leave Brentford.

Dunnett met Grade in the Strangers' Bar, known as the Kremlin, and proposed that ITV should take exclusive charge of Saturday-night football. To an extent Dunnett could see that Grade was pushing at an open door. For years the Football League had resented the BBC/ITV cartel and felt strongly that television was getting football on the cheap. BBC and ITV together were paying around £500,000 a year, which meant, on the basis of equal shares for all ninety-two clubs, only about £5,000 per club. However, even as Grade and Dunnett discussed the possibility of what became known as 'Snatch of the Day', the BBC and ITV were jointly negotiating to renew the contract with the Football League under the terms of the old arrangement.

Dunnett was broadly in favour of the ITV bid and returned to talk to Hardaker and the Football League management committee. Meanwhile, Grade had the job – in an industry that traditionally can't keep anything secret for more than five minutes – of keeping any whisper of the new proposal away from anyone, particularly Jimmy Hill and the ITV negotiator Gerry Loftus. Grade returned to LWT and started to talk to John Bromley, his Head of Sport, who had been his boss when he had first started on the sports desk of the *Daily Mirror*. Bromley had enormous respect for Grade but even he was astounded at the risk his Programme Controller was prepared to run;

> I had to get the support of the ITV network and the IBA because we knew there would be a stink and we needed to keep them onside. Programme Controllers and Managing Directors decided we should keep it to ourselves and not tell the network Head of Sport who was Gerry Loftus at Granada because we didn't know whose loyalties were where and we didn't want it to leak. It was agreed that I was authorised to try and close the deal with the Football League. When the fertiliser hit the air conditioner, we agreed we would tell the BBC that we would have a conversation with them but only on the condition that we would look at alternating the Olympic Games because we were spending a fortune covering them head-to-head and they simply refused to discuss it with us. The IBA was very keen on alternation in the interests of the viewers and they were right. On that basis everyone at ITV agreed.

Paul Fox, who had left the BBC in 1973 after six years as Controller of BBC1 to take over as Director of Programmes at Yorkshire Television, was the first person Grade told. Fox, who understood very well the importance of the exclusive rights to football, agreed with the approach and backed Grade at the meeting of ITV Programme Controllers, which always took place on Monday mornings. On the Tuesday morning, Hardaker arrived at the Great Western Hotel in Paddington and over breakfast Grade explained to him and Dunnett what he had in mind. Giving ITV exclusive Saturday-night football would mean no Sunday-afternoon football on television and the halving of the amount of televised football might drive people back into the grounds again.

The result of the hard negotiations with Dunnett and Hardaker was that ITV would pay £5.5 million over three years for exclusive rights. The clubs would now get £17,000 a season, an increase of over 300 per cent. The BBC's *Match of the Day* would be starved to death. On the Thursday morning at the Wembley Conference Centre, the ten-man Football League management committee met and approved the new deal. At 2.30 p.m. that day, fifty-one men representing the entire Football League met and approved it by a vote of 50:1. The dissenter was the Coventry City managing director, Jimmy Hill. At 3.45 p.m. the nervous Grade and Brommers, as John Bromley was always called, were told the good news and at 7 p.m. LWT hosted

a press conference. By that time Jimmy Hill, now ensconced as the chief presenter of *Match of the Day*, had obviously told his employers why they were popping champagne corks at LWT. Hardaker then telephoned Alan Hart, the BBC Head of Sport, and gave him the bad news. By 7.30 p.m. the newspapers were hastily recomposing their front pages.

To the joy of the press, there was open warfare between ITV and the BBC. Jimmy Hill described Michael Grade and Brommers as hooligans. Alasdair Milne, the BBC Director of Programmes, went on *Nationwide* and called them 'Mafia with cheque books'. The bitterness caused the war to escalate. The BBC sued the Football League for breach of contract on the grounds that they couldn't negotiate with anyone else without informing the BBC first (which they hadn't) and sought an injunction to stop the deal with LWT. Gordon Borrie, head of the Office of Fair Trading, began an investigation to determine whether the new contract violated the Restrictive Practices Act – which it did. Both Labour and Tory MPs denounced this act of what they regarded as piracy. The European Commission said darkly they would see if it flouted the rule of competition as laid down in the Treaty of Rome.

The pressure that was brought to bear was eventually overwhelming. The deal was quashed and a compromise agreed so that the BBC and ITV would alternate Saturday-night football for the next four seasons. Michael Grade had taken on the establishment and lost heroically. Trevor East, who eventually became Head of Sport at ITV, believes that the spin ITV put on the compromise was a little disingenuous:

> The BBC overreacted to 'Snatch of the Day'. It was as if ITV had raped the BBC's mother-in-law. Michael Grade wanted to steal the football, all of it, from under the noses of the BBC. I remember he and Brommers punching the air

in delight thinking they'd nicked it. So all that stuff about all they wanted at the end of the day was alternation is just rubbish. The final deal meant that the Saturday-night football alternated from season to season for the duration of the contract, which I think was for four years between ITV and the BBC, but ITV's programme was still done regionally. We did the first year but now it meant a studio show. Gary [Newbon] did the presentation and in one of my most inspired moments I signed Jimmy Greaves to be our pundit. I think that was 1979 or 1980 and a few years later it became *Saint and Greavsie*.

Grade had always known that to pull off such an audacious move would be tough and he knew that the BBC wouldn't like it, but he thought it would be viewed as if ITV had poached Morecambe and Wise (formerly clients of Leslie Grade) – which they did as well. The world, never mind the world of television, now knew and rather admired Michael Grade so there was some compensation in his heroic defeat. He was no longer just the nephew of Lew Grade and Bernard Delfont. Bill Cotton, who had also moved from Head of Light Entertainment to running a channel as the Controller of BBC1, told Grade that he wouldn't get more than eight million viewers for an ITV Saturday-night football show and certainly not the fourteen million that ITV were hoping for. Cotton ensured that he was right by scheduling a big feature film against ITV's football show. After many more twists and turns, *Match of the Day* has remained a staple of the Saturday-night schedule on BBC1 for fifty years.

Everyone recovered from what had been a most unseemly spat. Grade, of course, went on to a stellar career which included returning to the BBC in 1984 as Controller of BBC1 with the connivance of Bill Cotton. The Football League was not unhappy. Their long-standing fears that television would destroy football were never borne out and, after the negotiations were completed in early 1979, its income from television increased fivefold to £10 million over the four years of the new contract. It was nothing compared to what was to come with the formation of the more acquisitive and avaricious Premier League but for the time being they were happy that football was no longer under threat from television.

The power of television in the national culture grew exponentially in the 1970s, its influence apparent in every aspect of life in the United Kingdom, from politics to the arts, and nowhere was that power more apparent than in sport. Michael Grade's uncle, Lew Grade, the irresistible force behind ATV Network, one of the Big Five of the ITV federation of companies, was the man who rescued Billy Wright. The former England captain might have failed as the manager of Arsenal but his was still a name to conjure with, a name that had a certain commercial worth. Even if Grade had simply wanted Wright for the commercial value of his name and personality it turned out to be an inspired appointment for both parties.

The initial assumption was that Billy Wright would become the face of ATV Sport, but it was quickly apparent that he was as comfortable in front of the camera as he had been as the manager of Arsenal who had just dropped a senior player with a short fuse. Trevor East, behind the camera, struggled to get the best out of his boss.

> Billy started on camera – he was hopeless – he couldn't even read the autocue. 'Here's Dennis Team with the Shaw changes' was one of his attempts. Once on a Friday night when he was winding up the programme, I told him to say goodbye and wish all the viewers a Merry Christmas and a Happy New Year – it took him sixteen takes before he

got it right. As a trainee assistant producer I could see what
was going on so I tried to persuade Billy and [ATV execu-
tive] Tony Flanagan to let Gary [Newbon] do the on-air
presenting and turn Billy into a pundit. I wanted Billy to
be the ATV equivalent of Malcolm Allison on the ITV
World Cup panel. I said to Billy that every week he could
choose a different subject, I would cut some pictures
together and then Billy would become the intelligent voice
of ATV Sport, analysing players, their strengths and weak-
nesses and so on.

Billy Wright's strongest point in television, as it had been in
football, was that everyone simply liked him – a lot. He was a
kind man who was interested in people – and that made him
a superb ambassador for ATV, as Gary Newbon remembers:

Lew Grade loved Billy and sent him to have lunch with
Guinness who ended up spending £5 million with ATV.
That made Billy very valuable to Lew. Billy had to get Lew
FA Cup final tickets for his American clients and Billy was
so nervous he would hand-deliver them. There must have
been a thousand people working for ATV and Billy knew
the names of every one of them. He was amazing the way
he retained that knowledge of people he had met for five
minutes; he could greet them by name two years later. He
never ever refused an autograph. He never refused a chat.
The difference between his generation and now was that
he came from ordinary people.

As Head of Outside Broadcasts at ATV, Billy found his
niche although he wasn't always the most conventional of
executives. He once asked the twenty-five-year-old Gary
Newbon to come up from Westward Television, which was

based in Plymouth, for an interview in Birmingham. When Newbon arrived he discovered that Wright hadn't told his secretary about the appointment and, instead of being behind his desk, had gone to see his dentist in London. As a fledgling drama producer at ATV in 1977, I discovered to my delight that Billy Wright was the man who was technically in charge of allocating the crew I needed for exterior filming. I spent a lot of time in Billy's office but very little was spent talking about film crews, although a lot was spent talking about Ferenc Puskás. If I needed two tickets to watch Manchester City at Aston Villa the ex-England captain was the man who provided them with a large smile and a warning of imminent defeat. Billy Wright, observed Gary Newbon, was a very famous man who never reminded you of the fact.

He had his demons, his convivial nature leading him into a dangerous addiction to alcohol. Just as he believed he had conquered those demons, in 1994 he succumbed to cancer at the age of seventy. Wright came from the era of the maximum wage, Moore from the era that followed its abolition, but both men won over a hundred international caps and led England on to the field on ninety occasions. Wright recovered from his mortifying departure from full-time occupation in football when he was dismissed by Arsenal in a way that Moore never really did. The FA had made an initial effort to look after Wright, but, for reasons that are still unfathomable, the FA never bothered to do the same with Moore. In view of what he and Ramsey had contributed to English football it remains astonishing that they were ignored during the 1980s in such a humiliating manner. Wright never lost his love of the game but there is no doubt that in middle age he felt much more secure being employed by a television company than he had been as the employed manager of a football club at the mercy of unpredictable results.

There was a considerable threat to football in the 1970s and 1980s but it didn't come from television. It came on the terraces of football grounds; it came from the streets surrounding football grounds; it came from the railway stations where rival gangs clashed and eventually it all spilled on to the pitch itself. Hooliganism had started in earnest in the late 1960s but it took nearly twenty years before the football authorities did anything about it. They insisted that it was a social problem, and that it was up to the government of the day to introduce legislation to solve it. The clubs did not see that they were in any way responsible and they remained intransigent until ninety-six people died in the Hillsborough disaster of 1989. The Labour government of Wilson and Callaghan that was in office when football-related violence started to make itself felt, just like the clubs where the trouble was occurring, effectively left the problem of football hooliganism to the police to sort out.

The author remembers only too well the moment in April 1974 when Manchester United fans invaded the pitch at Old Trafford after Denis Law, who had been transferred from United to Manchester City at the start of that 1973–4 season, had back-heeled a cross from Francis Lee past Alex Stepney. There was less than ten minutes to go and the defeat would send Manchester United down to the Second Division irrespective of other results. Law was immediately substituted but it was apparent to everyone in the ground that the hooligan element behind the goal at the scoreboard end were not going to watch their team being relegated without trying something to prevent it. Everyone in the ground could feel that a pitch invasion had been brewing for some time when fans with red scarves climbed out of the terraces and swarmed all over the pitch, causing the game to be abandoned. The Football League later confirmed that the result would stand as Manchester

United 0 Manchester City 1. On the train back to London
Euston gangs of hooligans roamed the corridors looking for
Manchester City fans on whom to vent their fury. The episode
was the nearest that the author, travelling in frustrated silence
with the future Director of the London School of Economics,
ever came to physical injury as a football supporter and – like
the result – it has never been forgotten.

These Manchester United 'supporters' formed themselves
into the 'Red Army', a hooligan 'firm' which caused mayhem
at grounds up and down the country the following season
when the club paid its brief visit to the Second Division. That
same year a Bolton Wanderers fan stabbed a young Blackpool
fan to death behind the Kop at Bloomfield Road during a
Second Division match. These two events led to the introduc-
tion of crowd segregation and the erection of fences at football
grounds in England, a move that was to have deadly consequences in 1989.

In the 1975 European Cup final in Paris, Leeds United were
beaten 2–0 by Bayern Munich after an appalling display from
the referee who disallowed a perfectly good goal by Peter
Lorimer and refused a clear penalty to Leeds. The referee originally gave the goal but was convinced by Franz Beckenbauer
to consult the linesman who had not raised his flag and who
had already run back to the halfway line. The goal was disallowed for offside against Billy Bremner, who had not been
interfering with play. The Leeds fans, who had seen enough
bad decisions go against them over the years and hadn't yet
forgiven Ray Tinkler for the goal he had permitted Jeff Astle
to score at Elland Road that robbed Leeds of the title in 1971,
could stand it no longer. They began to tear up the seats at the
Parc des Princes and hurl them on to the pitch. What ensued
was a riot in full view of the millions watching on television
throughout Europe. Leeds were banned from Europe for four

years (reduced on appeal to two) and the world became aware that there was a new 'English disease' to go with industrial strikes.

And it wasn't just Leeds or Manchester United or even Millwall fans – the usual suspects – who were turning nasty. In the late 1970s and early 1980s, the supporters of over twenty clubs formed some sort of gang to which they gave aggressive nicknames – West Ham United had the InterCity Firm, Chelsea had their Headhunters, Leeds United their Service Crew and Aston Villa the Villa Hardcore. When these clubs came to town, shopkeepers closed early and boarded up their premises. European cities reacted similarly when English clubs played in Europe or England played overseas. But neither the football authorities nor the government did anything about it until Margaret Thatcher got involved.

On 13 March 1985 violence erupted at Kenilworth Road during the Luton Town v. Millwall FA Cup sixth-round tie. Millwall were in the Third Division but under George Graham they were challenging for promotion to Division Two, while Luton were struggling at the foot of the First Division. Millwall already had a reputation for violence off the field but in 1985 such high-profile matches were not all-ticket and therefore open to anyone who paid at the turnstiles. For the relatively easy trip to Luton in a game of high importance to both clubs a large volume of away supporters gathered in pubs and in the centre of Luton three hours before kick-off. When violence inevitably broke out the police were ill-equipped to deal with it.

The battle moved on to Kenilworth Road. The turnstiles could not cope with the crush and became stuck. Inside the ground, the police were helpless as hundreds of the visitors scaled the fences in front of the stand to rush down the pitch towards Luton's supporters in the packed Oak Road End. A hail of bottles, cans, nails and coins saw the home supporters fleeing up the terraces, but their numbers, still growing as fans entered the stand, meant that there was little they could do to avoid the missiles. The players came out to warm up, and almost immediately vanished back up the tunnel as the rioters started ripping out seats and brandishing them as weapons. A message appeared on the stadium's electronic scoreboard, stating that the match would not start until they returned to their allocated area, but this was ignored; an appeal from the Millwall manager George Graham over the ground's loud-speaker also had no effect. It was only the arrival of police dogs that helped to clear the pitch. Unbelievably, the match began on time, with many peering down at the players after scaling the floodlight pylons. After fourteen minutes the referee took the players off but reappeared twenty-five minutes later and the match restarted.

Brian Stein scored the only goal of the game after half an hour, but the result was the last thing on anyone's mind. Luton's goalkeeper Les Sealey was hit by a missile hurled from the crowd and later a knife was found in the goalmouth where he had been standing. As in the Manchester derby of 1974, it was obvious that it was the Millwall hooligans' intention to invade the pitch in order to get the match abandoned and replayed starting again at 0–0. The extra police who had been summoned to deal with the extraordinary circumstances managed to keep the fans off the pitch, but as the final whistle blew they could restrain them no longer and were over-whelmed as fans ripped up seats and invaded the pitch. The players fled down the tunnel as a pitched battle raged. One policeman was hit with a slab of concrete and thirty others were also injured as the violence flowed out of Kenilworth Road and back into the town centre, leaving a trail of broken windows, damaged cars and wrecked property.

Luton lost 2–1 to Everton in the semi-final but recovered their league form to the extent that they finished in mid-table and Millwall won promotion six weeks after the chaos in Luton. But something had snapped: traditional football supporters, horrified by the scenes transmitted by television, started to dissociate themselves from the game. Many of the thirty-one men who were arrested appeared in the local magistrates' court the following morning and declared themselves fans of either Chelsea or West Ham United. Ken Bates, the chairman of Chelsea, not only vowed to erect fences at Stamford Bridge but threatened to electrify them. Luton banned visiting fans from Kenilworth Road for the next four seasons and introduced an ID card scheme for its own supporters.

The Luton Town chairman was David Evans, who in 1987 was elected Conservative Member of Parliament for the nearby constituency of Welwyn Hatfield. He was a classic Thatcherite, born into a working-class home in Edmonton, north London. At the age of twenty-five he borrowed £500 to start an industrial cleaning company which he sold in 1986 for £32 million. He served on the board of Luton Town from 1976 to 1990, becoming chairman in 1984. His positive response to the riots at his ground delighted the prime minister who could not understand why every other Football League club would not follow Luton's lead. What ensued was a culture clash between the football establishment and a prime minister who was determined to quell civil unrest wherever it broke out. Over the next few weeks Mrs Thatcher came into conflict with the FA who felt that the government had no understanding of the game. Cabinet papers released in 2015 indicate that she made her feelings abundantly clear.

Immediately after the riots in Luton she told her colleagues, 'It is not enough to condemn football hooliganism. More effective action must be taken to deal with it.' The sports minister Neil MacFarlane was instructed to write to Ted Croker at the FA but he was shown the full face of the maker's name on the bat as the FA played it carefully straight back down the wicket. The minister became peeved and wrote again, complaining, 'Your letter does not address my specific request about what action the FA intends to take.' Bernard Ingham, Margaret Thatcher's Chief Press Secretary, then offered blunt advice to the cabinet:

> The FA and the Football League should be roasted. They should be told in no uncertain terms that it is their game and that they must act to make it wholesome. The trouble at Luton Town is a watershed not necessarily because it is the worst incident but because it has engendered the thought after the miners' strike that this sort of behaviour simply cannot be allowed to go on.

The perceived connection between the miners' strike and football hooliganism bothered the government enormously and fuelled the passion with which they pursued the ID card scheme. As far as Thatcher and her cabinet were concerned there was no essential difference between striking miners and flying pickets fighting with the police outside Orgreave Colliery and football hooligans resisting arrest in the shopping centres of industrial towns. They were both evidence of an increase in civil disorder and they both had to be stopped, but the government found that the support and respect which the police had traditionally enjoyed from the British public started to diminish in the 1980s.

In 1981 riots broke out in Brixton as trust between black communities and the police evaporated. Four years later similar disturbances would break out on the Broadwater Farm estate in north London. When Lord Taylor conducted his investigation into the 1989 Hillsborough disaster he concluded that the higher up the police chain he went the less credible became the witnesses. Interminably delayed confessions from individual police officers after further investigations twenty-five years later proved he was right to be sceptical.

This breakdown in relations between the police and the people they were supposed to be protecting alarmed a Conservative government which had always championed the cause of the police. However, they saw no reason to change their minds throughout the period that Margaret Thatcher was prime minister. Michael Heseltine, a member of successive Thatcher cabinets during the 1980s, later remarked:

I remember very clearly the period of the 1979 election in which we had seen the Labour party destroyed by violence on the streets and this was symptomatic that the first solution to anything that happened was violence. It destroyed Labour, we came in and before we knew where we were there was a violent confrontation with the miners, we had

clashes at Greenham Common and with CND. There was
an atmosphere out there on the streets that was extremely
nasty and quite unlike anything we have got today.

Bernard Ingham certainly had a jaundiced view of the
people who ran the national game. He thought that boards of
directors were 'not generally very good or politically sensitive
or bright' and that football managers 'would be better off
looking after the players instead of giving press conferences in
which lots of trivia are given currency and provocative state-
ments are made'. As for the media, 'I have an extremely poor
view of football writers, generally a poor lot, failed in other
areas of journalism, with notable exceptions'.

In response, the FA was brusquely dismissive of Mrs
Thatcher's preferred initiative that club membership schemes
should be introduced that would require all fans to carry ID
cards. In a letter to the minister of sport it attempted to
acquaint an ignorant cabinet with the real facts of football life:
'There is a very real possibility that the need to check people
entering football grounds would cause irritation leading to
misbehaviour from a wider section of football supporters.'

It was true enough but it found no favour in Whitehall.
Indeed, the minister was incensed by what he saw as a lazy
response: 'It is not satisfactory. There is no analysis of the pros
and cons of a membership scheme, just an assertion that it
wouldn't work. I fear that their failure to adopt a sufficiently
analytical approach may be due to their approaching the task
with insufficiently open minds.'

The tone of the correspondence between government and
FA between mid-March 1985 and mid-May 1985 became
increasingly bitter. On the field of play the morale of English
football was enhanced by Liverpool reaching the final of the
European Cup for the fifth time in eight years. They appeared

to stand a good chance of retaining the trophy they had won in the previous year's final against Roma. But even this good news turned to tragedy. An hour before kick-off, trouble flared on the crumbling terraces of the dilapidated Heysel Stadium in Brussels. Violent clashes between Liverpool and Juventus fans led to the collapse of a wall and audiences around the world were greeted by the horrific sight of football supporters dying in front of the television cameras. By the following morning it was confirmed that thirty-nine supporters had died, thirty-two of them Italians. The international reputation of English football was in ruins. Mrs Thatcher was incensed not so much because of the problems it would cause English football clubs, but because it would make her relationship with European leaders much more difficult and not help Britain's cause in her negotiations with the European Economic Community. Her Private Secretary Charles Powell later said:

> Mrs Thatcher was indignant about Heysel, furious about the effect on Britain's reputation internationally. It was nothing to do with football. She hadn't got a clue about football. It was just this idea that British hooligans were ruining the country's good name on the Continent after they had been doing the same at home. She was determined to bring about change.

The morning after the Heysel Stadium disaster, Thatcher appeared on television to express her views very clearly. 'I watched last night and heard what people said and I felt exactly the same. I wish we could get those people responsible, get them before a court and [give them] stiff sentences so that they stop anyone else in their tracks from doing this.'

Instead, there were immediate calls for UEFA to impose a ban on English clubs participating in European competition.

When it came it would be a ban that would last for five years. However, if Mrs Thatcher thought that what happened at Heysel, taken together with the events at Kenilworth Road, would induce a change of attitude at Lancaster Gate she was greatly mistaken. The FA continued to pour cold water on her pet project. She called together a group of football officials and others closely associated with the game and asked what football was going to do about its hooligans. According to Ted Croker, she seemed ready to have professional football banned altogether. While others timidly kept their opinions to themselves, Croker allegedly remarked: 'We don't want this made public, but these people are society's problems and we don't want your hooligans in our sport, Prime Minister.' The prime minister was incensed. It was perhaps not a coincidence that Croker, unlike his predecessors as secretary of the FA, never received a knighthood.

If Thatcher thought she would receive a more sympathetic hearing for her ID scheme from the Football League she was to be disappointed. Graham Kelly, the lugubrious Football League secretary, wrote to her saying: 'a club membership card scheme could not be done. Football club chairmen feel very strongly that the idea is being put forward by people who do not go to football matches, have never been on a regular basis and do not have the inclination to attend at the present time.'

The BBC television commentator Barry Davies, who had had to spend an hour describing the distressing scenes at Heysel while UEFA debated whether or not the European Cup final could proceed, also questioned whether the measures advocated by the government were the right ones. He described the government's attitude as follows:

Football hooliganism was seen quite clearly as a football problem and that if the stringent plans that Margaret

Thatcher was putting forward actually took place they might solve the problem for football but they would push it somewhere else. In other words it's football's problem – you sort it out. I found that completely lacking in sensitivity as to where the hooligan problem came from. It became accepted that spectators turned up for a football match and were frogmarched to the ground. That attitude by the police led straight to the disaster at Hillsborough.

The Sheffield Wednesday-supporting Roy Hattersley, who in 1985 was shadow chancellor and deputy leader of the Labour party, also expressed doubts about the government's proposed course of action:

No one doubts the extent of the problem – it was the absurdity of the solution I objected to. The moral of this from a legal point of view was, as the FA said, it was people who had never been to a football match trying to impose a solution on football. Bernard Ingham came up with a marvellous idea, a campaign he called 'Goalies Against Hoodies or Goalies Against Wooftes', or something like that.

However, doing nothing was not an option that Mrs Thatcher was likely to endorse and as far as she could see the problem was that the football professionals had no idea how to solve the problem. They had absolutely no constructive proposals to make of any sort and Powell felt nobody could blame Margaret Thatcher for wanting to fill the vacuum. Hattersley disagreed but he accepted the fact that football hooliganism wasn't a problem for football alone. It was, as the football authorities had claimed from the beginning of this acrimonious debate, a problem for society:

I certainly don't want to support the football authorities.
No good supporter had a good word to say about them.
But Mrs Thatcher had a duty to come to a sensible conclusion and she came to an absurd conclusion very largely
because she relied on people who didn't know what they
were talking about.

Thatcher never pretended to know anything about football
but, to Hattersley's undisguised scorn, she relied on Bernard
Ingham for policy advice on football. That was because she
regarded him as the nearest thing she had to someone who
understood the sport, probably because Ingham came from
Hebden Bridge in west Yorkshire, which was certainly closer
to the northern heartlands of football than Grantham in
Lincolnshire. Conservative cabinet members might have been
sympathetic to the idea that it was a general social problem
rather than a specifically football one because it linked to
their conviction that it was further evidence of the worrying
breakdown in civil order. However, they felt, perhaps justifiably, that reform had to begin somewhere and if the problem
manifested itself in and around football grounds then the
response that this was a wider problem for society in general
was not an acceptable one in political terms. The prime minister had the press on her back demanding to know what she
was going to do about it. She reiterated strongly her belief
that the problem of football hooliganism had to be solved by
the football authorities.

The arguments on both sides had some justification.
Blaming society is the default excuse that is invariably
assumed by authorities who demonstrate an inability or an
unwillingness to take unpopular or difficult decisions. Yet
although Thatcher felt Europe looked on football hooliganism as the 'British disease', in fact there were similar outbreaks

of footballing violence all over Europe. Deliberate violence, the Conservative cabinet felt, was not caused by society. It was caused by people who wished to practise violence. The Ultras in Italy, Den Bosch in Holland and disruptive fans in Germany all had links to far-right groups who specialised in street brawls. To that extent England was simply part of a wider European problem, just as football claimed it was part of a wider social problem. This point of view didn't please Mrs Thatcher, who continued to berate the FA for its lack of action. It was only in the aftermath of the tragedy at Hillsborough in April 1989 that there was an acceptance that 'something had to be done'. Whether it was football's fault or society's fault no longer mattered. The fences had to come down, stadia needed to be redesigned and policing methods had to change.

Inadvertently, the arrival of the Premier League and the consequent rapid escalation of ticket prices and gentrification of crowds, though regretted by traditionalists, had the effect of pricing the underpaid hooligan element out of football. There were plenty of well-paid hooligans who still enjoyed a fight, but there is no doubt that, since the implementation of the Taylor Report at the start of the 1990s, evidence of hooliganism dropped significantly from what had been seen throughout the 1970s and 1980s. Most big matches no longer permitted entry through payment at the turnstile on the day, which meant that every match became effectively all-ticket. Eventually, alcohol sales were banned on grounds and football specials and fans were further contained and escorted. The courts issued more exclusion orders for problem fans and the widespread use of CCTV gave police and stewards better pictures of where the trouble was starting.

Football in the 1980s seemed to be caught in a downward spiral of hooliganism and declining attendances. Crowds which had totalled seventy-seven million in the late 1950s had fallen to around twenty million thirty years later. The English public fell out of love with football in the 1980s because of hooliganism, and half-empty grounds, even in the First Division, and a half-empty Wembley Stadium for England matches were visible evidence of this diminishing appeal. The grounds themselves fell into disrepair. The tax structure gave clubs tax relief on transfer fees but not on ground improvements, so there was no financial incentive to refurbish them. This sharp fall in public interest in the game gave television the whip hand in their negotiations with the beleaguered football authorities. At the same time, Jonathan Martin at the BBC and John Bromley at ITV had to justify their expenditure on football to their own bosses. In the mid-1980s Martin and Bromley offered the Football League only £1.86 million between them for the weekend highlights which formed *Match of the Day* and *The Big Match* and ITV regional variations, claiming that was all they were worth, that nobody was interested in them and they could take it or leave it. The old cartel, which had been disturbed by the so-called 'Snatch of the Day' seven years before, had been restored. The Football League bridled and turned the offer down, believing it to be far below its own valuation of what it thought football rights were worth. As a consequence, at the start of the 1985–6 season there was no football at all on television for the first six months. It did not return until January 1986. Astonishingly, the world continued to turn during this hiatus.

Once it was no longer seen on television, football's central place in the conversations of the nation disappeared with it. In certain circles it became a social embarrassment for supporters to admit their interest in the game. Patrick Barclay noted the change from the glory days of 1966 after which the culture surrounding football started to change:

Books started to appear that were not just slavish autobiographies or biographies – Arthur Hopcraft's *The Football Man* followed by Hunter Davies on Spurs in *The Glory Game* and you get Glanville referencing Italian football so football starts to creep into the colour supplements. Any hope that it would become fashionable in the 1970s and 1980s was then killed by the rise of hooliganism. Margaret Thatcher clearly had distaste for football and who can blame a prime minister who has to go into an EEC meeting in 1985 after thirty-two Italian fans have died at Heysel? Is she supposed to like it? I can remember distinctly going to parties in the mid-1980s as a football writer and desperately hoping people did not ask me what I did for a living. Whereas now when I go to parties I am equally afraid to say what I do for a living but now it's because I don't want to talk football all night.

The behaviour of the violent section of England supporters deteriorated still further as the national team failed to give it much to feel happy about. After an encouraging World Cup in 1986, the European Championship two years later was a catastrophe, Bobby Robson's England losing all three matches. The hooligans seemed determined to put in a performance to make the country even more ashamed as they rampaged their way through Düsseldorf, Stuttgart, Frankfurt and Cologne. Mrs Thatcher felt compelled to apologise to the German Chancellor, Helmut Kohl, a conversation she no doubt found extremely difficult.

There were few sporting heroes to be found in England in the 1980s. Ian Botham might have won the Ashes in 1981 and England regained the urn in 1985 with the aid of two of the country's finest batsmen in David Gower and Graham Gooch, but none of them had an answer to the overwhelming power

of West Indies during that decade. The England cricket team
suffered humiliating defeats at home in 1984 and 1988 and in
the Caribbean in 1985–6 (the first and last of these reverses
being 5–0 'blackwashes'). The British tennis team which had
performed so well in the Davis Cup at the end of the previous
decade now slipped back down the world rankings and a
British winner of Wimbledon seemed as far away as ever.
The British Ryder Cup side was beaten so comprehensively
and so regularly by the United States that, in the middle of the
decade, golfers from the rest of Europe had to be drafted in to
give the competition any meaning. England had won rugby
union's Five Nations Championship under the leadership of
Bill Beaumont in 1980 but made little impact thereafter until
the following decade when Will Carling's side emerged triumphant. There was certainly some comfort to be taken in the
Olympic victories of Coe, Ovett, Cram and Wells but perhaps
the most representative English sportsman of the 1980s was
Eddie the Eagle, who, at the 1988 Winter Olympics in Calgary,
finished eighty-sixth – and last – in the 70m and 90m ski
jumps. The worse he performed the greater became his popularity even if it originated in the British sense of humour. The
search for a genuine hero became increasingly desperate.

However, if there was one player in England who epitomised
the very best of football in the country during the 1980s it was
the man, who, at the end of it, became its captain. Gary Lineker
made his full debut for Leicester City as an eighteen-year-old
on New Year's Day in 1979. He wore Keith Weller's number
seven shirt but did not score in a 2–0 victory over Oldham
Athletic. His future agent, Jon Holmes, watching from the terraces, thought the debutant played appallingly and was
unimpressed. Leicester had been relegated from Division One
the previous season and were now sliding ignominiously

towards Division Three. Jock Wallace, the manager, must have shared Holmes's opinion because Lineker was dropped and did not play again until 24 April when he scored the winner in a 1–0 win at Notts County. Leicester barely escaped the drop, finishing seventeenth, and Lineker did not feature on the score sheet until the thirteenth game of the following season, 1979–80, when he scored both goals in a 2–0 win over Sunderland. Leicester were promoted, but Lineker found it hard to command a regular first-team place in the top division. The club also struggled and were relegated back to the Second Division. Life was not without incident at Filbert Street but it didn't lead to any kind of stability and suddenly the warning words of the headmaster of the City of Leicester Boys' Grammar School did not sound so clichéd.

It was 1982 before Gary established himself as a regular striker when Alan Young was injured at the start of the 1981–2 season and he was included from the opening day in a productive partnership with Jim Melrose. He finished that season as the club's leading scorer with seventeen league goals in thirty-nine appearances. Leicester reached an FA Cup semi-final before losing to Tottenham Hotspur, the holders and eventual winners, but Jock Wallace returned to Scotland to manage Motherwell and Gordon Milne took over at Filbert Street. Wallace's last act was to spend £15,000 on Alan Smith from Alvechurch and he and Lineker struck up an instantly successful partnership. In the 1982–3 season, they contributed thirty-nine league goals between them with Lineker claiming twenty-six of them in forty games as Leicester were again promoted to the First Division. The difference between the struggles of his first three seasons and the success of the fourth was mostly attributable to the quality that accounted for his success over the next decade – his speed. It was sheer pace that gave him the ability to leave defenders for dead as he demonstrated at Wembley in the 1986 FA Cup final when he embarrassed the slow-turning Alan Hansen to sprint away and put Everton into a lead they could not hold.

> The speed that I had was a gift from somewhere. I don't believe in God. You can't train for it. You can help a fraction by building up the strength to make you a little bit quicker but ultimately you are either quick or you're not. You've either got fast twitch muscles or slow twitch muscles. I had fast twitch muscles and I was seriously quick.

There was more to Lineker than just pace, though. Howard Kendall recognised the quality of his linking play and the intelligent awareness that was rapidly developing. Above all, what was impressive about Gary Lineker from an early stage was how he handled himself.

Lineker had quick feet and an agile brain but he was never cocky. He liked his family and he liked living at home, but to make progress he needed to leave Leicester who did not have the ambition or the resources to give him what he needed in 1985. When he scored he didn't go crazy and when he missed he never berated himself. His celebrations were more in keeping with Japanese Noh theatre than the climax of *A Chorus Line*. He could be infuriatingly casual in training, as he himself admitted, but there was always method in his madness.

It's a bit of a myth that I didn't like training. It's true that I got very bored with training that didn't really help me. It's progressed a lot since but in those days it was all very basic. I was talking about this to Ian Wright the other day and he said that most teams tended to work on defence and we used to be a part of helping the defence but that didn't help us much. That used to bore me senseless and five-a-sides never really interested me either. Even when we did finishing, which did interest me, everybody had to do it, so you had seventeen or eighteen players in the way and I had one shot every five minutes which I thought was completely pointless. Towards the end of my career, and I wish I'd done it all the way through, I used to say, 'Do you mind if I go and do some finishing on my own?' I would grab a goalkeeper and a coach and it was finish, finish, finish, finish because I knew I was getting something out of it.

Lineker's rapid improvement and goals were noticed by Bobby Robson who had taken over the England manager's job from Ron Greenwood after the 1982 World Cup in Spain. Lineker stepped on to the field as an England player for the first time in the match against Scotland at Hampden Park in

May 1984. His move to Everton came at the end of the 1984–5 season during which he was the First Division's highest scorer, and by which time he had become England's principal striker. It was his success with England that turned him into a household name. A successful club striker will be very popular with his own supporters but possibly not with the supporters of rival clubs. A successful England striker wins the respect and gratitude of most of the country and soon Lineker was exactly the player that Jon Holmes hoped he would become when he first took him on as a client.

Another of Holmes's clients, the striker Tony Woodcock, had already moved to Europe in a transfer from Nottingham Forest to FC Köln in 1979, thereby quadrupling his wages, but Holmes was never attracted by the prospect of easy money and thought carefully about his clients' long-term interests. In 1985, he thought it better that Lineker stay in England for another season to see what the 1986 World Cup would bring. Lineker was keen to go to Manchester United but United didn't have the money unless they sold Frank Stapleton, which they were unable to do. Liverpool made a bid, but there was always the chance that Liverpool would continue their tradition of playing their new signings in the reserves for a year and in a World Cup year this was not an attractive prospect. Besides, Dalglish and Rush were still the most feared striking partnership in English football and Lineker would by no means be certain of a place in the first eleven.

It was the six goals he scored in the World Cup in Mexico in 1986 that were the making of Gary Lineker. Until the group game against Poland, he was just one of a group of strikers – Woodcock, Francis, Mariner, Hateley, Allen, Withe, Dixon and Blissett – who had played for England over the past few years without establishing themselves as an automatic choice. His performance against the team that had been England's nemesis in 1973 turned Lineker into Roy of the Rovers at a time when English football was sadly lacking in heroes. The victory over Poland came after a disastrous start to the tournament in which a mistake by Kenny Sansom gave away the only goal of the first match against Portugal in Monterrey. In the second, Ray Wilkins was sent off and the inspirational captain Bryan Robson dislocated his shoulder. In the circumstances the goalless draw against Morocco was not a bad outcome, but it meant that England had to beat Poland or face an ignominious early exit.

The injury to Robson and the suspension of Wilkins meant that the instinctively conservative Bobby Robson had no choice but to make changes. The loss of Robson was keenly felt by Lineker:

> The best captain I ever played under was Bryan Robson. He led by example on the field. His work rate was unbelievable. He had that ability to get from box to box. He was a great defensive midfield player but he was also a great attacking midfield player. He was hugely respected both on and off the field by everyone. If you want your captain to grab a game by the scruff of the neck, he was the sort of bloke who could do that. It's just a shame he was injured so often. Someone else will step in. They might not be as good in that particular role as you but it happens frequently in football because players get injured quite a lot.

The goalkeeper Peter Shilton now took the armband, which – since he was inevitably far behind the play – seems to suggest that Bobby Robson did not believe that captaincy was so important. Steve Hodge and Peter Reid came into midfield, Trevor Steven replaced Chris Waddle as the wide man and – crucially – Peter Beardsley replaced Mark Hateley. It was only the second time he and Lineker had played together but it proved a hugely successful move and a watershed in Lineker's career as he scored twice in the first fourteen minutes and claimed another before half-time to win the game and take England through to the knock-out stages.

It seemed to most observers that the changes forced on Robson by injuries and suspensions were the key to England's change in fortune, but Lineker disagrees.

> We'd have probably done well in Mexico in 1986 if Bryan Robson and Ray Wilkins had stayed in the side so you can't attribute that success to their being out of the team. We didn't collapse and I suppose it proves my point in the end that the captain's role is not that significant on the pitch. Bryan was still our captain off the pitch. On the pitch he was a driving influence but the guy who came in to replace him was Peter Reid and he was a similar sort of player though not as good as Bryan Robson. He had the same kind of up and down the pitch ability and he was a natural leader himself and I'd just spent the past year with him when he was captain of Everton.

On the day of the Morocco game, Jon Holmes had received a telephone call from Joan Gaspart at Barcelona during which he agreed to fly to Barcelona the day after the Poland game to discuss a transfer from Everton. The thirty-eight goals Lineker had scored for the Merseyside club in the 1985–6 season was the reason for the call, but the hat-trick against Poland and the two further goals he scored in the 3–0 win against Paraguay must have helped to smooth negotiations even if the move was going to happen anyway. Many of those thirty-eight goals had come from Kevin Sheedy clipping the ball over the top of the defence for Lineker to run on to, but if he was going to improve he had to discover a more sophisticated way of playing. Holmes knew that he needed to play abroad. Barcelona under Terry Venables, they felt, was the right club at the right time. The former Queens Park Rangers manager had been appointed in the summer of 1984. He had won the title by ten points from Atlético Madrid to give Barcelona its first triumph in La Liga since Johan Cruyff's playing days. Venables now had a blank cheque. In his second season, Barcelona had finished a long way behind Real Madrid but they had won their way through to one of the most boring European Cup finals ever played, which they lost on penalties to Steaua Bucharest. Barcelona's Scottish striker Steve Archibald was now approaching thirty and Venables decided that it was time to replace one Briton with another.

Back in Mexico, Lineker scored again against Argentina in the quarter-final ten minutes from time, but it was not enough to wipe out the 2–0 lead given the South American side by one outstanding individual goal by Maradona and an earlier one which the same scorer attributed to divine intervention. If the defeat was frustrating for England and their supporters, it was the occasion for national rejoicing in Argentina. Maradona is alleged to have drawn a strong parallel between football and the Falklands War. It has to be said that, in translation, the language sounds very like an Argentinian journalist rewriting Maradona's words in the style of speech employed by footballers the world over.

> Before the match we said football had nothing to do with the Malvinas War but we knew a lot of Argentinian kids had died there, shot down like birds. This was revenge. Bollocks was it just another match... We blamed the English players for everything that had happened for all the suffering of the Argentinian people.

If English football supporters can still find parallels with the Second World War before every game against Germany, it was reasonable for Argentina supporters to believe that they could also use their superiority at football as a means of refighting a war that had caused such national humiliation.

Lineker returned home from Mexico a national hero. England's golden boy had planned a quiet summer wedding to his childhood sweetheart, Michelle Cockayne, but by now he was national property and the 300 uninvited guests who showed up at the Linekers' wedding in 1986 dwarfed the small group of well-wishers who had crowded round Billy Wright and Joy Beverley at the Register Office in Poole back in 1958. The media crush was so great that the official photographer could not get through, leaving the bride in tears. Life for the newly married couple in Barcelona was clearly going to be significantly different from life in Leicester and Liverpool. In the days of Filbert Street, the Baseball Ground and Burnden Park, a football ground like the Bernabéu or the Camp Nou was on a different planet. In the mid-1980s, Spain was the place for a fortnight's holiday of sangria, sunburn and – as Eric Idle would have added – 'last week's copy of the *Daily Express*'. It was not a place many English people saw as a place to live and work. Barcelona also offered a challenge that had no parallel in any English club – its football team represented the five million inhabitants of Catalonia in a political and not just a sporting sense.

The Linekers set up home in a four-bedroom villa on an exclusive estate in the town of Sant Just Desvern, a short drive from the Camp Nou. Jon Holmes had told them in no uncertain terms that they had to learn the language, having absorbed the lessons of Woodcock's and Keegan's time in Germany. There were also the salutary examples of the young Denis Law and Jimmy Greaves at the start of the 1960s who never really wanted to go and live in Italy but allowed themselves to be persuaded. When reality dawned they couldn't wait to come home. Lineker agreed with his agent's diagnosis.

> I looked at the players who had moved abroad and by and large it seemed to me that the ones who had immersed themselves in the culture and learned the language – people like Ray Wilkins and Liam Brady – did really well. The players who had had a go and learned the language rather than the ones who said, 'I'll go over there for a couple of years, get a few quid and get back', were the ones who were successful. I found learning Spanish to be reasonably easy especially if you did what we did and throw your-selves into Spanish society. I didn't exactly evade or shun expat society but I wanted the opportunity to learn Spanish quickly, added to the fact that I went to school three times a week – two-hour sessions at a time. After two or three months I could get by and then you keep learning as you go along. After a year I suppose I was pretty fluent.

Lineker's point about the importance of learning the lan-guage was reinforced when Mark Hughes arrived at Barcelona from Manchester United for a highly unsatisfactory spell before being loaned to Bayern Munich. Hughes was only twenty-two years old as opposed to Lineker's twenty-six, and the difference in maturity was stark. Lineker was effectively forced into translating for his compatriot, but it was not a long-term solution for the Welshman. Lineker's fluency with the language translated into a successful transition on the field where he adapted quickly to the Spanish style of play. In his first season with the club, 1986–7, he scored twenty-one goals in forty-one matches, including a hat-trick against Real Madrid, but Barcelona again finished second to Real.

The club made a bad start to the 1987–8 season and by the end of September Venables was gone, sent on his way by the traditional ceremonial fluttering of white handkerchiefs. Lineker continued to score goals under his replacement Luis Aragonés but his successor, Johan Cruyff, played Lineker as a winger rather than a central striker after his arrival at Barcelona in May 1988. The Dutchman, no great admirer of British football, believed, wrongly, that Lineker was an English player who could play only in traditional English formations. He played him out of position or substituted him so that he could never get into his rhythm which meant the goals dried up and he was eventually dropped.

Lineker's form with the national side initially remained strong after his move to Catalonia. In a friendly in Madrid in February 1987 he was given four chances, scored four goals and England ran out 4–2 winners. England qualified well for the European Championships of 1988 in West Germany but the tournament was a disaster with three defeats in three games, including one to Jack Charlton's newly emerging Republic of Ireland. In addition, Lineker was now struggling with club, country and health as he was stricken with hepatitis. It was his most difficult time since he had established himself in the Leicester City side. This was where his trust in his agent was repaid as Holmes skilfully played off one club against another until, in July 1989, he secured the transfer they wanted back to Tottenham Hotspur for an absurdly low fee of £1.1 million. Lineker repaid the transfer fee immediately, scoring twenty-four goals in his first season back in Division One. The scene was set for the triumphant climax to his career as a player on the world stage in Italy in 1990.

During the qualifying campaign at the start of the 1989–90 season, England secured a point in a goalless draw away to Sweden, a dull game best remembered for the image of Terry Butcher heading away crosses with a blood-stained bandage round his head. It made for a poignant image of England's heroic captain, but of course Butcher only had temporary loan of the armband as Bryan Robson was out injured yet again. Lineker scored only twice in the six qualifying games, almost as if he were saving himself for when it really mattered, for yet again, with the eyes of the country on him and in full view of the rest of the world, he distinguished himself bravely in the tournament in Italy.

Again England stuttered through the group stages, relaxing only after a Mark Wright goal against Egypt clinched qualification for the last sixteen. Belgium proved a tough nut to crack and it took a goal of sublime technical skill by David Platt in the last minute of extra-time to do it. The quarter-final against Cameroon was won through two well-taken penalties by Lineker, the first a vital equaliser eight minutes from the end of normal time. The other came in extra-time as England gained a somewhat fortunate victory and headed off to Turin for a semi-final against the newly reunified Germany which was to remain in the collective memory in the way 1966 did, but for different reasons. As in 1966, the Germans scored first, Andreas Brehme's shot deflecting unfortunately off the onrushing Paul Parker and looping over the despairing, desperately back-pedalling Shilton. For those who remembered León 1970 it was a chilling echo of Uwe Seeler's header looping over the despairing but static Bonetti. If England's progress during the five games played so far had been decidedly unconvincing, that sickening goal seemed to bring the best out of the team. Again it was Lineker who brought England back into the game with an equaliser, this time nine minutes from the end, but the penalty Lineker scored in the climactic shootout after a goalless extra-time proved valueless. Waddle and Pearce missed from the spot and the nation dissolved into tears matched only by those shed by Paul Gascoigne; after his booking it dawned on him – and everyone else – that even if England were to win the semi-final he would not be allowed to play in the final. His response touched the nation.

Gazza's tears symbolised the agonising defeat but also something much more profound as far as the relationship between the England football team and the British public was concerned. Women, who had not taken much notice of England's football players since Nobby Stiles danced his jig with the Jules Rimet trophy, were moved by the sight of the lachrymose Geordie. Getting nearer to the World Cup than at any time in the past twenty-four years had inevitably had the effect of drawing the nation closer together round the television set. The choice of Pavarotti singing 'Nessun Dorma' from the opera *Turandot* to accompany the opening and closing credits for the World Cup television programme was inspired. It certainly did more to promote 'The Three Tenors' than it did to increase audiences at the English National Opera but it gave football a 'sophisticated' veneer that took it ever further away from the nightmare of Heysel, Hillsborough and Kenilworth Road, Luton. Instead of the snarling face of the hooligan, football was able to present the tearful face of the clown, a much more engaging prospect.

The tears, the music, the agony of defeat combined with significantly larger television audiences to create a soap-opera effect which would be intensified by the unholy alliance of the Premier League and BSkyB. In fact, the audience that watched that match in Turin was far less than the thirty-two million that had watched the 1966 World Cup final and the twenty-eight million that had seen the outrageous violence exhibited by Leeds and Chelsea in their 1970 FA Cup final replay. It was actually smaller than the twenty-one million who had tuned in to episode 837 of *Neighbours* that January but nevertheless it did symbolise the start of a new era in televised football and a new more sanitised relationship between the game and its audience. Perhaps just as importantly, that match joined the pantheon of games that no England supporter who watched it live will ever forget.

The defeat in Turin hurt, as all such defeats do, but it didn't hurt the way it had in 1970. England had done well to reach this stage and we didn't think we owned the world the way we did in 1970. When Gascoigne disembarked from the plane at Luton Airport wearing a pair of comedy breasts it was regarded as admirably cheerful, typical of the 'daft as a brush' label which Bobby Robson had draped round his neck. In the unlikely event that Nobby Stiles had jigged round Wembley with the same accoutrements it seems unlikely it would have been greeted by anything other than total bewilderment and a feeling that some kind of moral line had been crossed. The country had changed and what it found funny and socially acceptable had changed with it.

When qualifying began for the 1992 European Championships, England had a new manager and a new captain. Graham Taylor had taken Watford from the lower reaches of the Fourth Division to Division One in five seasons, eventually finishing as FA Cup finalists and League runners-up. He then accepted a new challenge at Villa Park, winning promotion for Aston Villa back to the top flight at the first attempt and again finishing as runners-up to Liverpool. To that extent it was no surprise that he was offered the England job by the FA but what worked in English football in the late 1980s and early 1990s, still divorced from Europe after Heysel, was too unsophisticated to work against decent international teams.

Peter Shilton, who had captained his country on fifteen occasions, and Terry Butcher, who had performed that duty in seven matches (including the semi-final in Turin), taking over after Bryan Robson had dropped out through injury for the umpteenth time, had both been fairly anonymous captains. Far too much was made of Butcher's bloodied bandage as if that in itself conferred an immortal sense of heroism on him. Both men had played their last games for England in Turin so Taylor needed a new captain and Lineker was the obvious choice as long as Bryan Robson was still hampered by injury. One of the best-remembered images of the game came shortly after the booking of Gascoigne, when a concerned-looking Lineker – in an aside that was certainly not intended for the television cameras – mouthed 'Have a word with him' to his manager Bobby Robson, the sort of consideration that should really have been the province of Butcher. He may have been the fist-pumping captain which England supporters might have thought was to be desired but Lineker had brains. The advice to the manager came not from the nominal captain but from a man with an instinctive understanding of what was going through the mind of his Tottenham team-mate and indicated to the country that here was a captain-in-waiting. He didn't have very long to wait.

Both manager and captain seemed honest and approachable with good communication skills and consequent good relationships with the press. Lineker wanted the captaincy but he was not going to get carried away with the honour since he has a fairly cool and rational attitude towards the office and his own fitness for it.

I don't think I was a natural leader. I developed a certain amount of confidence over a certain period of time that perhaps turned me into one in the latter stages of my career. You automatically think that the more vociferous players are the natural leaders. That's not necessarily the case because vociferous people can spout a lot of nonsense. A good captain has an aura about him. It's hard for leaders to get respect from fellow players if they are not good players themselves. You need someone who is prepared to speak up and speak sense, but it's so different from cricket because once the game starts you have no influence whatsoever. People like to see the old fist pump but frankly anyone can do that. Generally it's a mixture of his quality as a footballer and his intelligence because to be a good captain you have to have a degree of intelligence above that of the average player and you have to have the respect of your team-mates and the respect of the management.

Taylor, who regarded Lineker with the respect that he inspired in most of his colleagues, sounded off confidently to Colin Malam, Lineker's first biographer.

He represented everything you wanted football to be represented by at that difficult time for the game. He had a

very good image and he handled the press very articulately
– something I considered important in an England captain.
He also had an opportunity to break Bobby Charlton's
scoring record, which I confidently expected him to do
over the next two years.

Unfortunately, the relationship was to prove extremely difficult for both parties. It wasn't helped by the fact that Lineker's
attention was diverted from football in late November 1991
when his son George, who was not yet eight weeks old, was
found to be suffering from acute myeloid leukaemia, his
chances of survival being rated at no more than 50 per cent.
Both parents showed immense courage in the face of every
parent's nightmare. Michelle effectively lived at Great Ormond
Street Hospital for six months. Stan Hey, the football journalist and television screenwriter, was working with Lineker
when George fell ill. He went to the hospital to leave a present
and offer his sympathies to the distressed parents and then
walked round the corner to the Russell Hotel to discuss the
television series Stan was to write which was to be set in Spain
with Gary as the adviser. As they were getting to their feet a
woman approached the footballer and thrust an autograph
book under his nose, rudely demanding a signature. Stan was
incensed by her insensitive behaviour at such a difficult time
but Lineker just smiled, signed the autograph and politely
wished *her* good luck. Good manners and that kind of for-
bearance cannot be taught by media managers.

Lineker predictably retains an admirably composed
memory of the trauma he and his wife experienced.

We all know that our family's health is so much more
important than a game of football but when what happened
to George started it brings it home to you with a vengeance.

The media presence was intrusive at first. George was rushed into hospital that night and we were told the bad news and then the very next morning there's a hundred journalists outside the door, but you know that if you're in the public eye that's what happens. Your focus is obviously the health of the child but on the plus side to get sacks and sacks of mail arriving from all over the country all through the day is overwhelming but it's incredibly supportive.

Even in the midst of this dark time, in an interview given to Rob Hughes in the *Sunday Times* Lineker managed a moment of calm detachment.

You would have to be an oddball not to realise there are wars and people dying of famine. It has taken this horrible disease happening to George to show us that the vast majority of people are kind caring people. [They] reaffirm your faith in human nature. I have always realised that football is not the most important thing in the world.

It was a sensible, mature, admirable sentiment, but for those people who failed to see the irony in Bill Shankly's much-repeated observation about football, life and death it suggested a semi-detached captain of the England football team.

Lineker's devotion to the cause remained as strong as ever, and he certainly appreciated the honour attached to the captain's armband. But he also appreciated the true nature of the captain's role and, in particular, its limitations as to what he can do in the course of a match.

You become a much more significant public figure when you become the captain of the England football team. You are now the spokesman for the team which I liked. I thought it was one of my strengths that I could articulate on behalf of the players. You become the key linkman between the players and the manager and the players and the press. That's much the more important role of being the captain because on the field nobody really behaves any differently when they get made the captain. You get to spin the coin but that's about it. You certainly can't change the tactics on the field. A football captain is hugely different from a cricket captain who can have a massive say on tactics. The tactical side of things in football all comes from the manager. Some people use captains more than others but by and large once you're on the pitch your job is to be the link between the manager and the players, the players and the press and the players and the general public. What you're trying to do is to create a better atmosphere for everybody. Frankly on the field, beyond tossing up and encouraging the other players, which everyone should do anyway, I've never seen a captain influence a substitution, or play this way or that way. You might go to the side of the pitch if things are going wrong and say, come on, we have to do something about this but that's as far you can go. The ultimate responsibility to change things is the manager's. The captain getting involved is just a no-no. I've never seen that happen anywhere.

George Lineker, thankfully for all concerned, survived his childhood leukaemia. His father, meanwhile, was increasingly aware of the march of time as he entered the evening of his playing career. Not that his predatory instincts showed any decline. In 1991–2, his last season at White Hart Lane, he scored twenty-four goals out of the total of fifty-eight scored by the entire Spurs team, which finished a disappointing fifteenth in the league. He was also given the Footballer of the Year award for the second time, having previously won it in 1986 at the end of his season at Everton. Lineker and Holmes discussed how he might best go out at the top and not slide down the divisions. He was mentally tired by 1992 and lacked the motivation to continue, but he was still captain of his country and determined not to let it down. He told Taylor he did not wish to continue beyond the 1992 European Championships and from that moment it appeared as though a fissure opened up in the relationship between manager and captain, which went into permanent decline. Jon Holmes observed the collapse as soon as Taylor started dropping hints to the press that he was thinking of replacing Lineker as captain. Holmes invited Taylor to lunch to discuss the problems but the England manager replied that the question of the captaincy was none of his business, suspecting Holmes of briefing against him to the press.

In the summer of 1991 there was an England tour to Australia, New Zealand and Malaysia. Many clubs withdrew players but Lineker wanted to go, though Spurs also had a summer tour and they didn't want him to go with England. A compromise was eventually reached in which Lineker pulled out of the tour to New Zealand and flew from Wellington to Tokyo for ten hours to help Spurs lose a meaningless game 4–0. Taylor had his suspicions that Lineker travelled to Japan to play in that game so that he and his agent could start negotiations with Nagoya Grampus Eight. Taylor complained to Malam:

> Here we have a man who is England captain, and when I made him captain he said he didn't want to look any further than the finals of the European Championship in Sweden. Yet a year later he is in Japan looking for his

future... I'm sure Lineker wanted to play for England all the time. The point I'm making is that he or his agent also saw a very good opportunity in terms of where there was some more money to be earned.

Holmes and Lineker responded by pointing out that a Japanese delegation came to Taylor and the FA and formally asked that Lineker be released from the England tour. Lineker seems to have done his best to accommodate everyone by playing for England and then flying halfway round the world to Japan but Taylor told Malam that he was not convinced of his captain's commitment to the cause and the relationship continued to disintegrate.

People look to the captain to see what the captain's doing. It's not so much the manager as the captain the other players are looking towards: seeing if he's out training, seeing if he's enthusiastic for training. As captain of England, he had a responsibility to come out onto the training pitch. I'm led to believe he didn't do it previously.

The sad end to Lineker's international career was like a motorway pile-up. Everyone could see it coming but nobody appeared able to do anything about it. Taylor dropped his captain for a game against France in February 1992, claiming he wanted to have a look at David Hirst and Alan Shearer together. The armband was given to Stuart Pearce as Lineker sat stoically on the bench until the second half began, at which point he came on and scored. It had been Lineker's goal against Poland in Poznań in November 1991 that had ensured England qualified for the 1992 European Championships. Taylor took a volley of criticism for his neglect of his captain but it was nothing worse than what previous England managers had suffered. What was obsessing the press and therefore the England football supporters was whether Lineker would be able to break Bobby Charlton's record of forty-nine goals. He scored his forty-eighth with a minimum of six matches – three friendlies and three group games in the European Championships – to go. Unfortunately, in a match against Brazil at Wembley, he missed a penalty and played poorly. Taylor implicitly criticised Lineker by praising David Platt's performance. After the twenty-man squad for Sweden was announced, Taylor gave interviews to two Sunday newspapers in which he said: 'When somebody is a national institution it's almost as if you can't touch them. I'm not into all that. Looking at it realistically, we could perhaps argue that we played Brazil with ten men.'

Taylor, according to Lineker, apologised to him in private, but when Lineker then effectively released the apology in public just by answering a journalist's question, Taylor then denied he had ever apologised. Then he apologised again. It was a shambles – much like the performance of the England team. In Sweden the first two games were goalless draws against Denmark and France. Lineker rarely looked like scoring; his touch seemed to have gone.

England and Taylor were not helped by the unavailability of Gascoigne who had tried hard to destroy his own career by his ludicrous performance in the 1991 FA Cup final. Taylor had already dropped him for a Euro qualifying match against Ireland at Lansdowne Road in November 1990, clearly regarding Gascoigne's unpredictable behaviour as not conducive to team morale and so might not have included him anyway. However, now that England had to beat the hosts in Stockholm to get out of the group, most of the country mourned the absence of one of the very few world-class players England possessed. Happily, they went in at half-time 1–0 up after an unexpectedly bright display. Lineker had created a goal for Platt after only three minutes. However, Ekstrom came on for Anders Limpar at the start of the second half and the pendulum swung decisively towards Sweden. Centre-half Eriksson headed in from a corner after fifty minutes and England found they could scarcely get out of their own half. Ten minutes later came the substitution that ended Gary Lineker's international career and defined Graham Taylor's international team management.

Although England were desperate for a goal, Taylor pulled off his main goalscorer and sent on Alan Smith who, he thought, would hold the ball up better and stop it coming straight back at the beleaguered English defence. It was no surprise when Tomas Brolin won the game for Sweden with eight minutes to go. Not even the combined efforts of Andy Sinton, Carlton Palmer and Tony Daley could rescue England. The game finished in the immortal *Sun* headline SWEDES 2 TURNIPS 1 alongside a picture of the manager's head skewered on a vegetable like the head of a traitor displayed on a spike on London Bridge. It was a national scandal. There were critical articles in the press from those well-known football experts John Junor and Bernard Ingham. It was all pointless. Gary Lineker was not on the pitch but it was all over.

Gary Lineker left English football just as the great revolution started. He has made a success of his second career as a broadcaster, so he can afford a certain detachment when it comes to comparing footballers' wages now with what they were when he was playing. However, having played most of his football when playing conditions were not significantly different from what they were when Clement Attlee was prime minister, Lineker looks with envy on the football pitches of the twenty-first century.

It's all relative to your era. Obviously the money and profile is different from Billy Wright's day and I earned in a year at my peak what a top player today can earn in a week. It doesn't particularly bother me. The only thing that I am envious about is the quality of the surfaces they get to play on. They are beautiful. We played on terrible pitches. Once you got past September it was a quagmire and the only grass was on the wing but I tried to avoid going on the wing. Then there were the frozen pitches and the snow and in spring the pitches would become unbelievably bumpy. The ball's better now also because it's lighter. When I started, we used training balls that collected water and it was like heading a cannon ball. I never headed the ball in training though. I only ever headed it if I thought I could score.

In 1992 Gary Lineker's playing future was to be in Japan but, before he left England, he made a start on what would be his new career in the media. During the gap between the end of the European Championships and his departure for Nagoya Grampus Eight seven months later, it seemed as if he was never off the airwaves. He went to the Barcelona Olympics with the BBC and then appeared on *Match of the Day* as a pundit and could be found hosting a weekly Radio 5 programme, *Gary Lineker's Football Night*. One measure of his spreading fame was the title of the 1991 West End stage play by Arthur Smith and Chris England called *An Evening with Gary Lineker*, set in front of a television on the night of the Turin semi-final. The man who was never booked or sent off was justifiably given the 1990 FIFA Fair Play award (though what FIFA knows about fair play is open to question). Along with the trophy came £25,000, half of which he gave to a Leicester charity treating children with cancer.

Gary Lineker has justifiably reached a place where he is known and liked by nearly the whole country. He reached the top of his career as a player through skill and hard work, acquiring respect with his goals, a respect he has retained through his second career in television. Brian Glanville, who is not given to extolling players without reason, admires Lineker greatly:

> I find Gary Lineker an extremely likeable man who showed you didn't have to be aggressive, you didn't have to be ruthless, you didn't have to be a thug to be an excellent player and succeed at the top of the game and Lineker was an excellent example in that respect. I remember when he was smashed in the mouth by a Paraguayan thug and went off the field with his mouth bleeding and he returned and scored. Afterwards he said of the incident, 'It was an accident. At least I hope it was.' He's an intelligent, shrewd man with a nice sense of humour.

Patrick Barclay, who has been covering football since the 1970s, feels similarly:

> I knew Lineker all the way through his career. He was the best example of the gentrification of footballers I can think of. He wasn't born in a stately home and he didn't have any social advantages. He had three things going for him which were: his skill, the nature of his character and Jon Holmes, his agent.

The difference between Kevin Keegan in the late 1970s and the early 1980s and Gary Lineker in the 1980s and early 1990s was that Lineker rarely appeared to break sweat on the field or off it. Keegan went on television in *Superstars* and worked his socks off before and after falling off his bike. Lineker went on television on the show *They Think It's All Over* which he partially owned. Keegan's agent negotiated a fee. Lineker's agent helped him to bank the profits. Keegan now appears on television occasionally as a pundit. Lineker is the face of BBC Television's football coverage and that of BT Sport and Al Jazeera. Keegan wanted to stay in the game as a manager with all the stress that entails because he needed the money and he needed to stay in touch with the game. Lineker stays in touch with the game from the comfort of a television studio. He doesn't need the money.

Keegan regarded life as a fight to be won. Lineker regarded life as a fight to be avoided but a battle to be won by cleverer means than mere pugilism. Keegan would cover every blade of grass in his unceasing efforts to carry his team to victory. Lineker knew there was absolutely no point in that. His job was to score goals and goals that were scored from six yards were just as valuable as goals scored after a mazy run half the length of the field. Keegan made a television commercial for

Brut aftershave 'slapping it on all over' with Henry Cooper after a strenuous workout. Lineker sat in the stands at Leicester City advertising Walkers Crisps, the local delicacy, by trapping Paul Gascoigne's fingers in the packet until the tears famously spurted from his eyes. Keegan was only one of the celebrities who endorsed the Brut brand. By appearing in a Brut commercial he was ranked with other top British sportsmen like the Olympic hurdler David Hemery, the motorcycle world champion Barry Sheene and the showjumper Harvey Smith. Perhaps more importantly, being selected by Brut demonstrated that Keegan was now considered visible enough to be seen on the same level as the American football star Joe Namath, the baseball batter Hank Aaron, the basketball player Wilt Chamberlain, the heavyweight boxer Muhammad Ali and the tennis player Vitas Gerulaitis. Keegan might have been endorsing Brut but the cosmetics company was just as firmly signalling its own powerful endorsement of a footballer who could sell its products.

Keegan knew the value of a good agent but he had the admirable Harry Swales not the innovative Jon Holmes. Holmes's original gamble that Lineker had the special qualities that he was looking for in a client seemed to have paid off as Lineker moved effortlessly from captain of the England football team to life as a professional broadcaster. Yet even as Lineker packed his case, ready for one last hurrah as a player in Japan, a young midfielder was making his debut for Manchester United in a League Cup match against Brighton and Hove Albion. David Beckham was destined to inherit Lineker's armband and demonstrate that whatever cultural significance Lineker had carefully acquired, it would be as nothing compared to the mania that would surround this young man. Lineker left for Japan in February 1993. That same month, Bobby Moore died.

CHAPTER FOUR

THE AGE OF DAVID BECKHAM

THE AGE OF DAVID BECKHAM

O n Monday 28 June 1993 a memorial service was held for Bobby Moore in Westminster Abbey, attended by the great and the good. It was a sober and dignified occasion in keeping with the character of the man whose memory was so widely cherished even if the country, and in particular the world of football, had shamefully neglected him for the last fifteen years of his life. A government which included such morally upright citizens as Neil Hamilton and Jonathan Aitken considered Bobby Moore unworthy of a knighthood. The Dean of Westminster in his address noted that Moore's achievements

stand as a symbol for all that is best in sport: the patient development of an innate ability, a thorough understanding of tactics and teamwork, and a relationship of mutual respect with those against whom he competed. We remember also the kindness and humour which marked his private life, and his loyalty and generosity to his family; the dignity which he maintained in public and in private, and the courage with which he faced death.

Bobby Charlton put on his glasses to read his tribute, Franz Beckenbauer read from Ecclesiastes. Jimmy Tarbuck chose a metaphor which struck a chord throughout the packed abbey. 'The Lord,' he said, 'has strengthened his team but weakened ours.' It wasn't just Bobby Moore who was being remembered that hot summer day by a generation whose time had come and gone. It was their whole way of life – English life as well as footballing life.

Moore seemed to be the demarcation line between one era and another; the last well-mannered footballer, the last true hero. In death he was no longer the failed businessman, the *Sunday Sport* reporter or the man who had been asked to leave the Directors' Box at Upton Park by the foreign owners embarrassed by his presence but for one last moment he was restored to his pinnacle as the golden boy of 1966. Had he lived a few more years he must surely have received that mysteriously delayed knighthood. Now the men of 1966 were raised to mythic status partly by football's specious heritage industry and partly by the inability of successive England teams to replicate what Moore's team had achieved. Charlton was knighted in 1994 and Geoff Hurst four years later. George Cohen, Ray Wilson, Nobby Stiles, Roger Hunt and Alan Ball were made MBEs in 2000 to join Banks, Jack Charlton and Peters who had already been officially acknowledged.

Moore's death inspired an outstanding piece by Hugh McIlvanney in the *Observer* which captured perfectly what it was about Bobby Moore that so engaged the country:

> Amid the coarsening of spirit that has been manifest in this country over the past couple of decades, there is a measure of reassurance in finding so much of the nation so deeply affected by the death of Bobby Moore... By being not only the captain but the unmistakable leader of the England team who in 1966 brought the World Cup to the islands that like to be considered the home of football,

the incomparable central defender made himself an abiding presence in countless lives... The impact of his death and the remarkably widespread ache of deprivation left by it cannot possibly be explained in terms of accumulated nostalgia... His bearing, the aura of imperious authority that almost defied any honest reporter to avoid the word majestic, grew directly out of his profound understanding of the job he had to do and an unshakable belief that no-one anywhere was better at it... Bobby Moore's life was tragically short but he learned quite a lot in the time he had, like how to be so much of a man that he turned into a hero.

In November 1995 Michael Parkinson interviewed the England midfielder David Platt, who told him that in his opinion it was more important to be judged as a person than as a player. Parkinson reflected further:

He says he came to that conclusion upon the death of Bobby Moore, when he saw how a nation responded to a man who was as modest on the street as he was commanding on the field of play. It is a sure sign of changing mores in our society that once upon a time – and not too long ago – anyone expressing the opinion that heroes on the pitch might also be decent members of society would be accused of stating the bleeding obvious.

In 2007, the FA unveiled a bronze sculpture of Moore outside the rebuilt Wembley Stadium which displayed an inscription that tried hard, possibly too hard, to capture everything about Bobby Moore that matched the memory of the man and the admirable artistic creation of the sculptor, Philip Jackson.

Immaculate footballer. Imperial defender. Immortal hero
of 1966. First Englishman to raise the World Cup aloft.
Favourite son of London's East End. Finest legend of West
Ham United. National Treasure. Master of Wembley. Lord
of the game. Captain extraordinary. Gentleman of all time.

It doesn't require a doctorate in English to suspect that the
English Football Association is not entirely conversant with the
subtleties of its own language. The word they were presumably
looking for was not 'imperial' but 'imperious', as McIlvanney so
elegantly conveys. On the other hand it is possible that the ghost
of the old FA chairman Mr Amos Brook Hirst descended to
invoke the spirit of England's football captain at the head of an
army of British redcoats planting the Union Jack to claim territory that would advance the cause of the British Empire. The
thesis of this book is that the England football captain reflects
the character of his age but, even half a century ago, Moore's
England was not the England of Palmerston and Disraeli.

Four years after Moore's memorial service, all eyes were again on Westminster Abbey as it hosted a service that this time attracted the mesmerised attention of the world rather than just the country. At the end of August 1997 Diana, Princess of Wales, died after a car crash in Paris. Her body was brought back to London for the funeral service in the Abbey before it was buried in the grounds of Althorp, the Spencer family estate in Northamptonshire. The death of Diana provoked an extraordinary public outpouring of grief. Mourners queued in their thousands to sign a book of condolence at St James's Palace and left flowers outside Kensington Gardens. Some three million people came into central London on the day of her funeral. Whether one views this reaction as mass hysteria or as evidence of the emergence of a new, emotionally unbuttoned form of Englishness, the contrast with the quiet dignity and sobriety of those who attended the funeral service for Bobby Moore is marked. If ever two events provided evidence of the changing nature of English society, it was these two services. It was reported that more than thirty million people watched the Abbey service on television, a figure that outstrips even the twenty-eight million who watched Barry Norman, Eddie Waring and Michael Aspel singing 'There is Nothin' Like a Dame' in *The Morecambe and Wise Christmas Special* of 1977.

It turned into a historic moment for the recently elected prime minister, Tony Blair. Even if the phrase was Alastair Campbell's, Blair's depiction of the dead woman as 'the People's Princess' was greeted joyfully. Armed with an overall majority in the House of Commons of 179 seats, his landslide victory in May 1997 combined with the virtual annihilation of the Conservative party gave him ten years of power. However, the events of 11 September 2001, which led to British forces fighting unpopular wars in Iraq and Afghanistan, would slowly diminish that initial burst of personal popularity.

Blair's Labour seemed in those early days a welcome contrast to the preceding sleaze-ridden Tory administration which
had proclaimed its faith in a 'Back to Basics' campaign.
Although Major himself emerged only as a slightly naïve lightweight it was clear that he was unable to control the
unpalatable mess that his government found itself in during
the mid-1990s. The Tory party was still the party of Margaret
Thatcher, whose attitude to sport in general and football in
particular had ranged from the casually indifferent to the
decidedly hostile. Blair's MPs found it politically advisable to
claim that they were football supporters whether they were or
not. Either way they were generally much more in touch with
the real concerns of the voters who had elected them than the
conservative MPs they had replaced. To the widespread embarrassment of football supporters throughout the land there had
even been an insert on the evening television news during the
1997 election campaign of Blair straining every muscle and a
certain amount of credulity as he exchanged headers with
Kevin Keegan, who during a previous election campaign had
been photographed kissing the cheek of Margaret Thatcher.
Football, it appeared, was to be an integral part of the new
Labour government's policy, which certainly separated it from
the government of Margaret Thatcher. It evoked in the minds
of many true supporters a sense of unease that the popularity
of the game was being cynically harnessed to provide a spuri-
ous 'street cred' for undeserving politicians.

In the wake of Diana's death it became clear that emotions
were to play a big part in Blair's Britain. The days following
the death of Diana were a time when the Queen was told how
to behave by tabloid newspapers and the Labour party's spin
doctor (who was at least a genuine supporter of Burnley).
Meekly, she broke with royal protocol by leaving her summer
residence at Balmoral and returning to London in order to be

seen to be grieving with her similarly afflicted subjects. Peter Hennessy observed the hysteria and the demands for the Queen to appear in public with some surprise.

It went on for several days and it fed on itself. It was a mind-changing moment for the royal family because the country believed that the Queen was hard-hearted, but people grieved differently in her generation. It was as if the British people who had always wanted to grieve in this way had never been allowed to. The stoical generation of which the Queen is the incarnation had a lot of loss in the war and they conducted themselves in the way that the Queen conducted herself. We were, or we used to be, a stoical, understated people. We now behave like whooping Americans on a game show.

Diana's death seemed to release the emotions of hundreds of thousands of people, many of whom must have watched the *Panorama* interview a gaunt-looking Diana gave Martin Bashir with their critical faculties in abeyance. After her divorce, Diana's increasingly desperate cries for attention had mostly been the butt of satirical humour and she suffered by being lumped together with her accident-prone sister-in-law, the Duchess of York, whose pantomime marital difficulties were chronicled with glee by the tabloid press. Weeks before Diana died, the author Leo McKinstry wrote in *Turning of the Tide*, a book analysing contemporary British society:

The House of Windsor has recently behaved like a dys-functional family with both the Princess of Wales and the Duchess of York displaying all the worst traits of our age of self-gratification. Even the most committed monarchists must have had their faith in the institution badly dented by the grisly pantomime cast of Major Ron, James Hewitt, Johnny Bryan, Steve Wyatt and Budgie the Helicopter. The mystique that is so essential to the monarchy has been exploded by the ill-advised parade of public confessionals from the younger members of the Royal Family. Walter Bagehot, in *The English Constitution*, wrote that 'we must not let in daylight upon magic'. With Dimbleby, *Panorama* and *Hello!*, we have had a blowtorch.

The crowds that gathered at a respectful distance outside Westminster Abbey in June 1993 were mostly men and roughly of an age close to that of England's fallen football hero. The crowds that hurled flowers at the hearse carrying Diana's coffin away from the Abbey and up the M1 were mostly female and roughly of an age close to the princess. Bobby Moore might have been a celebrity but people didn't load on to Bobby Moore the empathies that people thought Diana had for them. Without necessarily trying to do so, she convinced a lot of people that she was a warm-hearted, special woman who had suffered herself and that was why she understood their pain, wherever that pain had come from and whatever had generated it.

For those football supporters who had followed the game in the immediate post-war years, Bobby Moore's service was an elegy for their – swiftly passing – generation. They might have been loud, they might have been given to chanting at matches but they were not histrionic in the way that Diana's people were. The Queen's dignified retreat from the public gaze was not what her subjects appeared to want in 1997. The country had changed dramatically in the past few years and at the root of that change was television. It was television that began the elevation of David Beckham from footballer to cultural icon and it was television that dictated the second half of Gary Lineker's professional life.

The offer to Lineker to play in the J-League was part of a successful master plan to win selection as the co-host with South Korea of the 2002 FIFA World Cup. Nagoya Grampus Eight, sponsored by Toyota, was one of ten founder members of the J-League along with Nissan Marinos and Panasonic Gamba Osaka. There was very little attempt to disguise the essentially commercial nature of football in Japan. Lineker's first flying visit to Nagoya lasted four days and was conducted with his now customary charm, efficiency and flair for public relations. The brief visit comprised two press conferences, seven magazine interviews and three television appearances. The recent England football captain became the first British footballer to exploit his talent and celebrity status to an extent that is commonplace in sport on the other side of the Atlantic. As in Barcelona, the Linekers would attempt to immerse themselves in the language and culture of their new home:

> Japanese was different. It was ten times harder. I could survive in Japanese but I couldn't really have a conversation. I enjoyed my time at Grampus Eight, though. Everyone was very polite, it's a very safe society but a very alien form of thinking. The food was great. I wouldn't have wanted to have lived there for ever but for a couple of years it was an interesting experience. I could certainly have lived for ever in Barcelona.

It was while he was in Japan that Lineker's post-football career started to take more definite shape. He had been concerned for some time that he did not fall into the trap of failing to take due precautions against the day when his football skills were no longer in demand. He was also aware that the impact of unemployment after retirement after a life of constant, frantic action could have unfortunate social consequences.

It's not easy to find something else to do after football. There are only so many coaching and managerial jobs; there are only so many jobs in the media. The divorce rate of players between thirty-five and forty is astonishing – it's over 70 per cent. Players who have finished miss the adrenaline rush you get when you're playing, they no longer get the affection they used to get from people, they've become accustomed to a certain standard of living when they were earning well – and so have their wives. Several try a business and for one reason or another it goes wrong. Some turn to drink, then the divorce happens and another whole load of cash goes and suddenly they're in trouble. A lot of players now are earning so much they think it'll never happen to them and the sensible ones will put enough aside to be comfortable for a long time, but if you spend as much as you earn and then you stop earning at that level, life can get very difficult. Life after football is difficult. I was lucky enough to find something I could do and the industry is well paid. I'm one of the lucky ones. Obviously, others have gone into coaching or management and done really well but a lot of ex-players do really struggle. There's a lot of life after thirty. Nothing lasts for ever, especially in sport. It just goes on without you. Somebody takes your place in the team and you're dropped unless you choose to retire.

His agent, Jon Holmes, had been applying his mind to the problem for even longer:

The big leap forward for me was when we got *They Think It's All Over* on to television. A man called Richard Edis rang me up and said he was doing a new sports quiz for the radio but he knew nothing about sport. 'It's a satirical sports quiz and we're doing a pilot with Des Lynam, Rory McGrath and Rory Bremner. I'd like to get Gary Lineker involved.' I said to him, 'It's obvious you don't know anything about sport because if you did you'd know that he's currently in Japan. But I can get you Will Carling and David Gower.' He didn't know who they were either but he was happy with those two. We recorded it in the Paris Studio in Lower Regent Street. It was good and two days later I was meeting Brian Barwick, who was then Head of BBC Sport, and I told him about it and suggested he got it on to TV but he said he'd already talked to Des and Des didn't think it would work on television. I then met [Alan] Yentob and talked to him about it and in the end I was the one who brought Hat Trick and Talkback together. There was a big fall-out and Jimmy Mulville didn't like [the producer] Harry [Thompson]. McGrath had been involved with Hat Trick at the beginning and he'd gone over to Talkback so there was all that history as well. They made various pilots, none of them successful, but eventually Lineker came back and it started to work. The sportsmen needed to be credible stars otherwise the jokes wouldn't work. Being on that show taught Gary how to tell a joke and make people laugh. It was good preparation for his sign-off lines and his cheeky sense of humour.

Lineker is generous in acknowledging the significant influence Holmes has had on his career:

Jon doesn't suffer fools gladly. He's been a huge influence on my career, not on the football obviously, and not just negotiating contracts but on career moves and guiding me in the right direction. He was extremely helpful when I moved from one career in football to the next in television.

It was something I was always interested in, back to my mid-twenties. In the 1986 World Cup in Mexico, I spent a lot of time with the journos and I was always interested in how they wrote their copy. As with the radio and TV guys I was always happy to do interviews with them and I already knew I had no interest in becoming a manager or a coach. In 1990 during the World Cup, they named me 'Junior Des' and it wasn't because I was going prematurely grey. In my time as a player we stayed in the same hotels so you bumped into them all the time. It's all different today. Even then you knew who the one or two were who you couldn't trust but then you wouldn't sit with them. I talked to Jon and he was saying that I should do a bit of radio while I was still playing and write a few columns. I started writing for the *Observer* when I was in Japan. Before then I'd had a ghosted column in the *News of the World*. The *Observer* wanted something on the World Cup; I was a bit bored so I said I'd write it for them and they seemed to like it and I ended up doing a weekly column for them for a couple of years. I don't write much now because I am so busy with other stuff. I write all my own TV scripts but writing columns in newspapers is quite time-consuming.

Jon Holmes is as intrinsic to this book as our four England football captains. And that is not just because of his handling of Gary Lineker's career, masterful though that has been. It is because of his vision that took root in the 1970s that he could create a company in England like Mark McCormack's International Management Group in which the sportsmen he chose to represent were not only outstanding on the sports field but had the kind of character that he could finesse into an image that would attract commercial sponsors and broad-casters.

It was a conscious exercise in the global marketing of a squeaky-clean image. He knew that if he got that right, financial success was assured. Unlike so many agents obsessed by the short term, Holmes never became infatuated with money. He was so appalled by how little David Gower earned from playing cricket that he took no percentage at all from Gower's cricketing earnings. What interested Holmes was what he could do with Gower off the cricket field.

Holmes was public-school-educated but the experience appears to have inculcated in him a taste for rebellion.

I couldn't get into Repton which became trendy because [the Yorkshire cricketer] Richard Hutton went there and I developed a grudge against Repton, so I went to Oundle, which was a rugby-playing school, but I got everyone playing football against the local youth clubs. This was all part of my rebellion against the establishment because I wouldn't play organised rugby and I wouldn't play organised cricket for Oundle. Mostly it was an excuse for drinking and smoking. It was definitely not a rebellion against the family. There was a strong rebellious streak in the family – my uncle was quite radical and went on Ban the Bomb marches. Another uncle, Eric, was a conscientious objector to National Service, having been Head Boy at Wyggeston School. The sixties was about Tom Courtenay in *The Loneliness of the Long Distance Runner* and *Billy Liar*. I identified totally with everyone who was rebellious. I was always in trouble at school for all sorts of insurrections. I was a conscientious objector to doing Latin. I wanted to go to a dirty northern university where Finney and Sillitoe and Barstow went. Then I prospered academically in history and politics because I was motivated. I had a teacher who was a jazz musician but converted to teaching history and he inspired me. The housemaster wanted to get rid of me but the headmaster was quite an enlightened, liberal man who abolished fagging and he liked me despite the mayhem I caused. Once I stole the school bell, which seemed to me the very foundation of the school. One night I got up, stole it and threw it in the river, went back to bed and stayed awake for the rest of the night awaiting the mayhem the following morning. And then the bell rang. I couldn't believe it. They'd got a spare one and nobody batted an eyelid.

This instinctive rebelliousness served Holmes well in later life. He was never overawed by the biggest names in sport and he had an instinctive scepticism about the establishment. He was, in his own way, a maverick but one with a great sense of responsibility to his clients and a vision of where he could take them. Holmes emerged from Leeds University with a more than respectable second-class degree in politics, even though following Leicester City's cup run to Wembley in 1969 had caused him to miss vital tutorials. There followed a brief and unsatisfactory encounter with the *Leicester Mercury*: 'I soon realised that these provincial sportswriters were losers and some of them were quite unpleasant – they hated graduates. I quickly got quite disillusioned with that. They wouldn't let me write about sport. I was writing about dogs crapping on the pavement.'

When he was twenty-two, a year or so after graduation, a chance encounter at the golf club with a man who started talking to him about what Mark McCormack was doing with his sports management business led to Holmes joining Peter McGarvey at Benson McGarvey, which specialised in the growing field of financial services:

He had got connections at Leicester City who were a good side – Worthington, Weller, Birchenall, Shilton, then Gower came along. I am quite good at not being overawed. I just felt at home in that world. The players seemed to accept me quite quickly because they realised that I was street smart in the way they weren't and I'd been educated to a higher standard than they had been. I could talk their language, that was key. I never had a public school voice despite my mother's attempts to send me for elocution lessons. That was a complete failure. She blamed my father for taking me to football matches which was where I learned how to speak 'like that'.

Holmes believes that footballers are not as thick as they are usually portrayed, but that most of them are ill-educated and unsophisticated. He was aware from the start that the end of a footballer's career frequently meant the end of their significant earning power. He did not believe that this had to be the case:

Mind you, there are plenty of people you can't educate but the smart ones like Lineker respond. Footballers didn't have to open post offices, work in pubs or own news-agents. They were dreadfully exploited by the clubs. I saw lots of examples of managers saying, 'OK leave that to me, I'll make sure it's in the contract', and when we came to sign it wasn't there. There was no proper pension system, there was no proper injury insurance so as soon as you were injured and no use to the club you got booted out – just like what happened to Brian Clough at Sunderland.

Holmes was interested in those footballers who were likely to rise to the top of their profession and would respond to being managed. His first client was Peter Shilton, a man of enormous professional ambition, to which Holmes responded. Shilton was the obvious heir to Gordon Banks and he was on his way up as Holmes was starting in business.

I always thought that Brian Glanville was the top man in his profession so, at the start of my representation of Shilton, I rang him up and said I wanted to bring Shilton to have lunch with him. I thought that if Glanville came out and pushed Shilton to be the England no. 1 goalkeeper this will have an impact. I think it possibly did. Shilton was the best goalkeeper I've ever seen and most people who played in that era would agree. I can remember seeing him play for Leicester Boys and talking to him afterwards. I was trying to manipulate the press by getting the players and the media together. There was a producer called Jock Gallagher at BBC Pebble Mill and he agreed to put Shilts on one of Terry Wogan's very first shows for Radio 4, called *Wogan's World*. At that stage Shilton was more articulate than he later became and Gallagher said to me that he wasn't too bad. I said I'd like him to do more radio and get better at it because this was putting into practice what I had learned from studying McCormack. What made me think that McCormack was really clever were things like the Big Three, capturing the sport and turning it into a television programme. *Superstars* was a perfect example of what I called 'junk sport' – sport made specifically for television. And *Pro-Celebrity Golf*. You only became a big star by being on television and most footballers weren't on TV. I would ring up [DJ and radio presenter] Pete Murray's producer and offer to bring Shilton down to London to appear on *The Pete Murray Show*. At that time, I'm talking about the 1970s, they only

had showbiz people on programmes like that, they didn't
have sportsmen. I said to Shilts that when he finished he
could become someone like Jimmy Hill or Richie Benaud
or someone like that. Shilts was a star and there were few
of them around at the time. It didn't work and I suppose I
got fed up with him because he wasn't as professional off
the pitch as he was on it. Gary was. I remember looking at
Shilton's autobiography and he said something like 'Robert
Maxwell offered to pay off all my debts but I turned him
down and Jon finally got fed up with me and went off to
manage Gary Lineker whose personality was much more
suited.' There's no harm in Shilton at all but it didn't work
because he has his own well-documented personal demons.

Shilton turned into a trial run for the succession of high-
profile clients who adorned Holmes's short but select list.
Apart from Lineker, there was Tony Woodcock, David Gower,
Michael Atherton, Will Carling, Neil Webb, Lee Chapman,
Gary McAllister and John Barnes. Holmes was never the sort
of agent desperate to get himself on to *Sky Sports News*. He
was much more comfortable on BBC2 appearing on *The
Money Programme* when it produced a segment on the relationship between Gary Lineker and Walker's Crisps.

As Holmes's plans went into operation, Lineker is happy to
acknowledge that he enjoyed a fair amount of good fortune
along the way to becoming a television professional:

I was blessed with an ability to score goals and blessed
with an ability to be calm enough to do the job I do now.
Calmness probably links the two. I've got the ability to
cope with pressure and I got the breaks. I didn't get injured
until right near the end of my career, I scored goals at the
right time; when I went into TV, the training worked. I

got the opportunity because of what I'd done in football but then I really had to work hard. I had to work much harder then than I had done in football in many ways. I presented on radio and I was a pundit on television; then Bob Wilson left the BBC to go to ITV so I slotted into *Football Focus* and three years later Des Lynam leaves the BBC just as I felt I'd done enough to justify being given that role. So I've been lucky with timings and what other people have done to influence my career.

Jon Holmes was not the first agent to look for commercial opportunities for his clients away from the sport that had made them famous. That honour belonged to Bagenal Harvey and his representation of Denis Compton. After Harvey came agents like Harry Swales who represented Kevin Keegan and Ryan Giggs with some success, and Ken Stanley, who looked after George Best from a small office in Huddersfield. Best was the first player to be confronted with significant opportunities to build a career off the field, which turned the self-effacing Stanley into a figure of curiosity for Holmes.

I went to see Ken Stanley in Huddersfield, but in the end what he did for George failed because George went off the rails. The great thing that McCormack understood was that if you look after the sport, the sport will look after you. He told Palmer to come and play the Open here in 1960 because he knew that if the sport grew worldwide and Palmer was the top player in it, they would all benefit. That was always in my head. The problem was that this philosophy works better in an individual game like tennis or golf but in a team game the manager can frequently not want one superstar to stand out. Leicester, however, were happy for me to do things with Shilton because they thought if he earns money with me it will stop him wanting to move. If you did a ten-grand deal for a player with a club then that was enormous money. I didn't do Shilton's deal at Leicester; I did it when he went to Stoke. I'm not a bitter or a vengeful person in a negotiation. I just enjoyed winning against them and doing things that hadn't been done before. League contracts were still done with wages per week not annual salaries, and managers would tell players, 'You'll be earning eighty quid a week'. We had to get the contract signed and driven up to Football League HQ in Lytham St Annes so when I was doing Shilts's contract I made them buy his car. Alex Humphreys was a director at Stoke. He ran a company called C & C Supermarkets. And then when the annual salary I wanted came out at £363 a week or something like that I said we should round it up and he exploded his sandwich all over the table. 'How much is this car worth?' 'Three thousand,' I said quickly. 'Right,' he said, 'I'll buy it.' Then he came back and said the car was only worth a thousand but it was too late; he'd bought it. It was so unsophisticated. When Shilton went to Forest I negotiated with Clough by walking round and round the Forest car park at half past nine one Friday night. At that stage Clough was not a drunk. I knew he was desperate to sign Shilton because he'd wanted him at Leeds and Derby. He said he could sign another keeper but I knew perfectly well that Shilts was who he wanted and I also knew they had the money at Forest then. Clough could be physically intimidating though; he came in and kicked me.

The importance of the role of the agent inevitably increased as sport became more commercial and opportunities presented themselves to elite sportsmen. When David Beckham was agitating for representation in the Stalinist dictatorship of Alex Ferguson, his manager pointed him in the direction of Harry Swales who had done what Ferguson considered a good job for Giggs and for the notoriously publicity-shy Paul Scholes, both of whom he was still representing in 2011 when Swales was eighty-five years old. Beckham was prepared to listen to Ferguson on matters relating to football, but when it came to his off-field commercial activities he reckoned his wife had a better agent. In view of what has happened to Beckham since, it appears that he was right.

Beckham certainly couldn't have achieved his rise to world celebrity if he had not had talent as a footballer, but it was factors beyond his skills on the field of play that eased his entry into the ranks of pop-cultural aristocracy. He was fortunate in that the rise coincided with the early days of a Labour government that abandoned Clause Four and the traditional close if turbulent relationship with the trade union movement in favour of a new and even closer relationship with the world of spin and public relations. Labour now believed less in traditional Labour values of public service than in Thatcherite market-driven economics that fed the consumerist and celebrity-obsessed culture in which David Beckham and his 'advisers' flourished. Above all, the age of Blair was the age of spin and sophisticated public relations and it was that which turned a good-looking working-class footballer from east London into a global figure whose celebrity might have started with his football but ultimately owed relatively little to it.

Wright, Moore and Lineker were all celebrities in their own way, but they were known principally as famous footballers. Beckham is known because of things that are only tangentially related to football and that is because he began his career just as the media landscape was changing so profoundly. Beckham was the perfect man to be in the right place at the right time.

Lineker did well to emerge from the depressed decade in which he played. His goals for England, his captaincy of his country and his successful move to Barcelona and the exotic climate of the Catalonian coast, all marked him out as a shining light in an era too readily associated with Heysel, Hillsborough, Valley Parade and Kenilworth Road.

Television did not greatly care for its current relationship with football, which is why it could afford to be so blasé when the game disappeared from the nation's screens in 1985. It took a change in the media landscape for television to rethink that relationship. Recorded highlights, which had been the basis of televised football for twenty years, were no longer enough. A glance across the Atlantic quickly revealed that live sport would be the future. Trevor East was the Executive Producer for ITV Sport who, together with Greg Dyke and the ubiquitous Arsenal director David Dein, discussed a plan to form a breakaway league:

I reported back to Greg that we had an ally in Dein so what we needed to do was to get the top five clubs together which were then Arsenal, Spurs, Man United, Liverpool and Everton. What pushed us was that by late 1987 [the new satellite company] BSB had emerged and they were hatching their own plan with Ken Bates and Ron Noades and Trevor Phillips to nick the whole thing. I went along to a BSB presentation in my capacity as a director of Derby County FC. I came out of it and rang Greg and told him, 'I've just seen ninety-two Football League chairmen with pound signs revolving round their heads. We need to move quickly.' Amidst much acrimony and with the help of the big five clubs we managed to block the BSB deal. Then we did a deal for £44 million over four years for twenty-one live games per season – eighteen league matches, two League Cup semi-finals and the League Cup final. This was Greg and me dealing with the Football League directly and sidelining Brommers [John Bromley] who was not pleased about it but he was locked into the old duopoly. The same thing happened to him as had happened to Gerry Loftus at Granada during 'Snatch of the Day'. As part of the contract I got all ninety-two Football League clubs as they still were then to sign up to play in the League Cup in perpetuity which is why the Premier League clubs are still in it.

ITV had already started to make changes to the way football was presented on television even before the coming of the Premier League. Sky likes to proclaim that it changed the nature of football coverage on television, but in fact the landscape had been evolving in the late 1980s under the terrestrial broadcasters. East remembers:

We had eighteen to twenty-two cameras at the ITV live games in 1989, 1990 and 1991. We introduced hand-held touchline cameras, we introduced new graphics with players changing into team formations and things like that. What we didn't do at first was put the score onscreen all the time. Sky did start that but I nicked it off them very fast. When we lost the Premier League, we went out and bought the Champions League straight away and I put the score up there for the first time on ITV. I was sitting in the truck and I got phone calls from three or maybe even four MDs of the ITV companies, all saying, 'Get that bloody thing off the screen'. It looked awful, they thought. I said no. I'd been watching it on Sky and it worked. I told them they'd get used to it.

The first *Monday Night Football* match on Sky in August 1992 was an instantly forgettable 1–1 draw at Maine Road between Manchester City and Queens Park Rangers. The biggest talking point was the faintly incongruous appearance of the 'Sky Strikers', a troupe of dancing girls, equivalent to the cheerleaders who featured on US television during NFL games. It gave no sign of the impact Sky was to have on football and ITV executives who watched the unappealing display would have been forgiven for thinking that it was the ITV broadcast of the climactic end to the 1988–9 season which really marked the start of the new age of football on television. Going into the intimidating atmosphere of Anfield just a few weeks after the Hillsborough disaster, Arsenal had to beat the all-conquering home side by two clear goals to deprive them of another league and Cup Double to match the one they had claimed three years earlier. A goal by Smith early in the second half raised expectations but it was the second and decisive goal by Thomas in the dying moments that brought Arsenal the title for the first time since 1971 and encouraged the belief that television could deliver absorbing excitement in a perfectly contrived dramatic climax. From the start of the new decade football became a game watched live on television rather than a game for supporters to watch live in the ground.

Despite East's claims of technological innovation, the fact remains that when Sky Television absorbed BSB and then submitted a successful bid to the newly formed Premier League for the rights to televise its games, the media landscape changed significantly. Neither ITV nor the BBC had the air time on its channels to show so many matches whereas the creation of the Sky Sports channels meant that Sky had endless amounts of time to fill and live sport was its key component.

Test cricket, with its five days of play, suited the new channels very well, and the BBC started haemorrhaging the rights to a sport that it had covered for decades. By 1999 the broadcasting of England home Test matches was in the hands of Sky and Channel Four. From 2006 the rights were Sky's alone and Test cricket had apparently left terrestrial TV for ever apart from home Test highlights on Channel Five. Despite competition from BT Sport, Sky's current hegemony in sports broadcasting is a far cry from the dangers it faced when it began. Murdoch gambled his empire on the success of Sky Television and football was vital to his eventual triumph. While cricket's move away from terrestrial television to satellite broadcasting has been at best a mixed blessing for the growth of the sport, that hasn't been the case with football, despite East's early doubts:

> I thought when Sky started that it was a disaster for football, because it was lost to terrestrial television. ITV's bid was actually more attractive for the new Premier League both in financial terms and in terms of exposure, but they

went with Sky because Rick Parry fell under Sam Chisholm's spell and then there was the question of Alan Sugar. I was sitting in the hotel having delivered the ITV bid when Sugar was on the phone to Chisholm telling Sky to blow ITV out of the water. It wasn't at all transparently fair. Parry held up the proceedings in order to attract a revised bid. Sky didn't have any more cash. Instead they put a valuation in financial terms on all the promotion time and the sponsorship they thought they could attract over the season and they added that on to their cash bid. That's how they got to £304 million. In fact in cash terms it was high – £160 million – and ITV had bid higher. I think we offered early £170 million but for fewer matches. In those days it was still a hot topic as to how many matches you could televise before attendances would start to fall. Murdoch bet the whole of News Corp on that one deal. If it hadn't happened Murdoch would have gone bust and Sky would have been strangled at birth. It was heavy-duty stuff and Sugar saved them. Sugar, to save his own business [Amstrad], saved Murdoch but he got his payback. In 2007 Murdoch bought his company. That slipped right under the radar. It had taken fifteen years.

The marginalisation of BBC Sport and ITV Sport by the monolith that was Sky Sports, together with the ground improvements mandated by the Taylor Report under the aegis of the newly formed Premier League, created the new landscape in which football operated. It was much regretted by some traditional supporters as footballers became superstars in a ludicrous soap opera whose antics were lovingly detailed by the tabloid press.

The first player to 'benefit' from these changes was Paul Gascoigne whose antics appeared as often on the front pages of the tabloids as on the back. The public's fascination with him was a result of not just the goal for Spurs in the 1991 FA Cup semi-final against Arsenal or the brilliant solo effort for England in the match against Scotland during the European Championships in 1996, but also of the 'Dentist's Chair' drinking game in Hong Kong before that tournament began, the wrecking of his hotel room when Glenn Hoddle told him he was being left out of the 1998 World Cup squad and the tempestuous nature of his marriage which ended in claims of domestic violence.

Bobby Moore divorced Tina after he had fallen in love with his second wife, Stephanie, but although friends saw evidence of marital disharmony nothing ever appeared in the press. It would have mortified the eternally private Moore and the press knew it. Whatever rumours they heard they did not pursue. When Lineker divorced in 2006 and again in 2016 the events were treated with similar respect. The behaviour of the two players on the field and towards the press had earned them this kind of consideration. When Paul Gascoigne was interviewed on camera by a Norwegian journalist before an England game against Norway and was asked if he had a word for the people of Norway, he replied instantly, 'Yes. Fuck off, Norway.' Gascoigne's career ended sadly and his life subsequently has attracted press attention only in moments when he has allegedly been facing premature death.

Gascoigne was the embodiment of the old hard-drinking, hard-living, hell-raising working-class lad, all at sea in the rapidly changing cultural landscape of the 1990s and 2000s. Terry Collier of *The Likely Lads* would have adored Gazza and would have seen something of himself reflected in this Geordie hero. However, as *Whatever Happened to the Likely Lads?* demonstrated so well, all that remained open to a soldier on his return to civvy street was a succession of dead-end jobs and his old bedroom in his parents' house. Terry's traditional Newcastle working-class culture was already on the way out in 1973. The future belonged to Bob Ferris, newly married, wearing three-piece suits, his feet firmly planted on the management ladder with his wife's job as an assistant librarian doubling their disposable income and a new house with the other upwardly mobile couples on the Elm Lodge housing estate. Bob and Thelma would have felt at home at Beverley's soirée in Mike Leigh's classic 1970s suburban drama *Abigail's Party*.

In *The Likely Lads*, the original series transmitted in 1966, the two youths had both been apprentice electricians, but in 1973 changing circumstances took Bob out of the socio-economic group into which he had been born but left Terry stranded in it. The comedy stems from Terry's refusal to compromise his traditional working-class values and Bob being torn between his desire to subscribe to Thelma's bourgeois aspirations and his loyalty to Terry and his own roots. If Terry had been a footballer he would have been Paul Gascoigne. If Paul Gascoigne had watched the series his sympathies must have been with Terry. Perhaps a more accurate parallel would be Gascoigne as Bob and his late drinking companion Jimmy 'Five Bellies' Gardner as Terry, although Gascoigne's wealth and celebrity in the 1990s took him way beyond the Elm Lodge housing estate.

It seems reasonable to assume that David Beckham took a good look at the fates that befell both Gascoigne and Best and decided they were excellent models to avoid completely, for Beckham has managed to ride the waves of constant media exposure with extraordinary poise. Beckham was born in 1975 in Whipps Cross Hospital in east London, not far from Barking where Bobby Moore grew up. The parallels between the two men extend far beyond their birthplace and their captaincy of the England football team. There was a similarity of character between them in the way they conducted themselves. They were each dedicated to improving their skills in a way far beyond that of other professionals in their teams. They each suffered from obsessive compulsive disorder. It has already been noted how Bobby Moore's mother used to wash and iron the laces in his football boots before each game and how he liked his clothes ironed not folded and hung in the wardrobe in strict order, from the darkest colour to the lightest. When other players after training or a match would simply tear off their dirty strip and leave it on the dressing-room floor while they padded off to the showers, Moore would scrupulously fold his own filthy clothes and make a start on those of his team-mates. Ted Beckham was surprised to discover how neat and tidy his young son was. David, too, folded his dirty laundry and a parental suggestion to his teenage son that he might wear blue trousers and a clashing red shirt induced a toddler-like rage. His bedroom was kept constantly immaculate as if he was expecting a visit from Her Majesty the Queen or possibly Bobby Moore.

However, the political and social order in which Moore grew up was very different from that experienced by Beckham. Moore came from a solidly working-class Labour-voting family. Beckham's father was the son of a sweetmaker by trade and grew up in Sheerness where he scratched out a living making rock and sweets for holidaymakers. His own family started in a small flat in Walthamstow, then the sixth floor of a tower block in Chingford, then a three-bedroom house in Leytonstone, which is where he and his wife were living when David was born.

Ted Beckham had left school without any qualifications at a time when education was probably at its widest and most effective, between the impact of the Butler Act of 1944 and the growth of comprehensive schools in the late 1960s and early

1970s. He worked as a waiter at Brown's Hotel in Mayfair, then found a job with a small building firm doing re-pointing and roofing work. He walked out of that job in disgust when his boss refused to give him the afternoon off to celebrate the announcement of his engagement. Bobby Moore's father would probably have been disgusted at such dereliction and lack of working-class pride, but it is an interesting reflection of the way in which attitudes to work changed in the 1960s and 1970s. The thousands of hands that would go up at Longbridge or Dagenham in favour of strike action for any cause that union leaders cared to place in front of their supine members regularly demonstrated that the fear of unemployment which had been so all-pervasive in the years before 1939 no longer held the same power.

Unlike Moore and Lineker, David Beckham did not take the Eleven Plus. In the 1950s it would have offered his father a way out of the endless dead-end jobs he was forced to take, but by 1984 the system of comprehensive education made selection at the age of eleven an irrelevance to most state-school pupils. The ten-year-old David's football skills soon got him noticed by both Tottenham Hotspur and Manchester United after he had won a place at the Bobby Charlton Summer School in 1985. He trained with both clubs, both of which offered him terms. Mrs Beckham had problems with Alex Ferguson because she couldn't understand a word he said on the telephone, but in the end his and his father's long-standing support for United – which had begun, as it had for so many others, in the aftermath of the Munich air disaster in 1958 – proved the determining factor.

Spurs offered Beckham a six-year contract, all his training kit and boots and a signing-on fee at the age of seventeen, which he understood to be in the region of £70,000–£80,000. 'Cor, that's not bad, is it?' he is reported to have said to his father. 'When I'm eighteen I can get a Porsche!' Again, one can only note with some alarm the possibility of real psychological damage being done to youngsters who have such offers waved in front of them, only to have them removed when they fail to be offered professional terms and are thrown on the scrapheap at the age of seventeen. The same six-year contract – two years on schoolboy forms, two years as a YTS apprentice and two years as a full-time professional – was offered at United but with a signing-on fee of a mere £30,000 and £300 a week in wages after the mandatory £29.50 a week as a YTS apprentice. Times had changed since the days when the signing-on fee was a crisp ten-pound note and Jimmy Greaves had been sent into the secretary's office at Chelsea to steal luncheon vouchers worth half a crown. Beckham chose to sign with United.

Beckham was to enjoy good fortune in many respects, not least in being part of an exceptional Manchester United youth side at a time when Liverpool were losing the great players who had won them so many trophies in the 1970s and 1980s and were failing to find adequate replacements. However, while footballing ability, and, indeed, footballing success, comes to many young men, nobody in the English game has had a professional career quite like that of David Beckham. In his case, it was the media, and particularly television, that defined the nature of that success. It was David Beckham's fortune that his rise to fame coincided with an exponential increase in the reach of television. It was his goal from the halfway line at Wimbledon in August 1996 which distinguished him from the rest of the Class of '92 and captured the attention of the nation, not just football followers. Yet there have been plenty of such goals since 1996 that do not get endlessly repeated. Xabi Alonso did it for Liverpool against Newcastle in 2006, Rivaldo did it for Barcelona against Atlético Madrid in 1998 and Charlie Adam did it for Stoke City at

Chelsea in 2015 but none of them remain in the English consciousness like Beckham's on the opening day of the 1996–7 season.

By then he had signed with the agent Tony Stephens who was already representing, among others, David Platt, Alan Shearer and Dwight Yorke. It was through Stephens that Beckham was offered the chance of a free Jaguar which he rejected, much to the amazement of his father, in favour of buying his own Porsche. However, Beckham would prove to be something rather more than just another high-profile footballer with a taste for conspicuous consumption. What would make Beckham genuinely famous and an object of adoration for millions who could not name three players from any of the sides Beckham played for, was the soap-opera nature of the life he was to live.

That life really began when Beckham was introduced to Victoria Adams – aka 'Posh Spice' of the pop group the Spice Girls – by her agent Simon Fuller in the Players' Lounge after a 1–1 draw against Chelsea in 1997. Initially at least it bore a marked resemblance to that of Vicki Lester (née Esther Blodgett) and Norman Maine in *A Star is Born*. At first, the established star (Adams) illuminates the newcomer before the lesser figure at the start becomes the established favourite and the fading star is obscured by the shadow cast by the new sun. Adams may have found success in the fashion industry but it is her husband's image which continues to blaze the brighter. The relationship which caught the public imagination very quickly was to become an unfortunate source of trouble for Beckham during the early games of the 1998–9 season as his new girlfriend became the target of vitriolic, abusive chanting from the terraces.

Beckham's time of trouble began when he was sent off in England's round of sixteen match against Argentina in

Saint-Etienne in the 1998 World Cup. The England manager
Glenn Hoddle had warned Beckham that he needed to curb
his impetuosity, which is why he was so incensed when
Beckham contrived to get himself sent off just after half-time
for a sly kick at Diego Simeone in retaliation for a foul by the
Argentinian midfielder. Simeone needed no further prompting
to roll around on the floor like Laurence Olivier in his death
throes at the end of *Richard III*. On another day, another
referee might well have pulled out a yellow card instead of a
red. Even then it perhaps wouldn't have assumed the propor-
tions of a national tragedy if David Batty and Paul Ince had
not missed their kicks in the inevitable penalty shootout to
send England out of the tournament after a heroic display
with ten men. The cheating Argie, such a beloved national
stereotype, interestingly attracted less condemnation than
the inept Cockney lad. After the match the England manager
simply said, 'He cost us the match.'

It wasn't just Glenn Hoddle who excoriated Beckham. The *Daily Mirror*'s headline the following morning was TEN HEROIC LIONS AND ONE STUPID BOY. He was vilified in a way that Lord Haw-Haw might have recognised. Back in east London, reporters were banging on the door of his parents' home at 7.30 the following morning. When the Beckhams looked outside there were thirty photographers and three television camera crews in a road that was barely wide enough for two cars to pass. Nobody could leave the house. The Beckhams discovered that their phones had been tapped and their friends and relatives had been contacted by the ravening hordes of press desperate for their reaction to the disaster in Saint-Etienne. The reporters stayed there for a week. Beckham himself was hung in effigy outside the Pleasant Pheasant pub in South Norwood. It might have been a joke but it wasn't a particularly funny one.

The phone-ins hummed with discussions of what could be considered a suitable punishment for such treason now that public disembowelling was sadly frowned upon. A poster outside the Mansfield Road Baptist Church in Nottingham proclaimed that 'God Forgives Even David Beckham' but it only emphasised how out of touch the Anglican church was with its potential congregation. In one phone-in a West Ham supporter suggested that everyone in the crowd, wherever Beckham played, be issued with a red card to wave at him when he ran on to the pitch. 'He lost us that game, there's no doubt about it,' the fan complained bitterly. 'That's what ordinary football supporters think, and they are entitled to show how they feel about it.' The female presenter demurred. What if, she asked with some horror, such antics ultimately forced David Beckham to leave the country? 'If only we could get rid of him that easily,' the man replied. So it was in July 1998.

The tabloid press and the phone-ins were by no means the only places where Beckham was condemned. At Leeds, where Manchester United and their supporters had never been very popular, he needed a police escort just to get *into* the ground. At every away ground where Manchester United played at the start of the 1998–9 season, the abusive chants could be heard but Beckham did not crumble and, indeed, responded outstandingly well. In the first game against Leicester City he equalised direct from a free-kick in the ninety-fourth minute. Although it would be a few months before the boos died down, what was remarkable was not just the quality of Beckham's football but his refusal to complain. He kept his head down and became an integral part of the team that won a famous Treble for Manchester United. Beckham had his limitations as a player, but the dignity and composure he displayed in the 1998–9 season meant that nobody could doubt his temperament thereafter. Whether he was acting on instructions from his manager or his agent, or whether his good behaviour simply had its roots in the instinctive good manners that are so characteristic of Beckham's personality, it was a signally successful tactic. Soon the boos turned to cheers. It helped that he was associated with a winning team and that 1998–9 turned out to be Manchester United's *annus mirabilis*. Again he had displayed immaculate timing. The rise of Beckham was coincidental with the long-delayed return to prosperity of his club and the ever-widening appeal of football as a game to be consumed rather than one to be played. Every strand of the media was hungry for football and for footballers. By the start of the new millennium the search was on for an iconic national footballing figure to replace the now forlorn Paul Gascoigne. Beckham and the new age were made for each other.

He was helped coincidentally by the dawn of the new culture that followed the start of the Blair government and its obsession with spin and public relations. Cool Britannia, the Brit Art and Brit Pop movements were tailor-made for new media stars like Beckham. He made an impact on the art world when he featured in Sam Taylor Wood's twenty-four-hour-long video stark naked and asleep in a glass box. It is hard to imagine any other footballer who might have been asked to feature in similar fashion – except possibly Emmanuel Adebayor who can manage to give the impression of being fast asleep on the field of play in the middle of a Premier League match. Or any player in a side managed by Louis van Gaal.

If Beckham had played for Southampton would he have become the David Beckham the world knows? Matt Le Tissier was just as talented a player, arguably more so, but Le Tissier never played for United and Southampton were never in danger of winning anything. In addition, he never possessed Beckham's good looks, which were such a significant element in his rise through the ranks of celebrity, but even mention of Beckham's attractiveness came at a price. The comedian Jo Brand memorably said that he had the body of Hercules, the face of Adonis and the voice of Tinky Winky.

Beckham was clearly a fine footballer if not a great one, though opinion is divided. George Best, who might have been less than objective as Beckham threatened to take his place in the hearts of United fans, was clearly unimpressed. One Saturday afternoon on Sky Sports he unburdened himself of the opinion that Beckham had no pace, no left foot, he couldn't beat people, he couldn't head the ball and he didn't score enough. 'Apart from that he's not bad, I suppose,' concluded Best with a wry smile. The Northern Irishman left out the fact that Beckham was a superb passer of the ball over forty yards. He also ignored Beckham's outstanding ability to cross the ball into the danger areas and to find the net from free-kicks. If Gary Lineker gave his name to a West End play Beckham raised the stakes when in 2002 the feature film *Bend It Like Beckham* was released.

Gary Lineker, more secure in the respect of his peers, takes the opposite point of view from Best:

> Beckham was a great footballer, and possibly underestimated. He had different abilities from, say, someone like Best. He had a great work ethic, wonderful technique and he was the sort of player I would have dreamed of playing with because of his crossing and the vision and awareness of his passing. He was almost unique in his ability to cross a ball. He's also a very likeable person. I've met him many, many times. He's nice to everyone. He's transcended football in many ways. He's now an international celebrity superstar, a global superstar not just because of his football but because he's this fashion icon and the good-looking face of many products. It's a great brand that works. Good luck to him. He's doing something different. He's not gone into management and he's not gone into the media. He's found a different vehicle and he's done it very well. He's always presentable, he always looks smart. He says the right thing and he doesn't make mistakes.

Beckham did once refer to the now disgraced FIFA vice-president Jack Warner as the uncle he never had, but at the time he said it he was presumably acting under instructions from the fawning FA who were desperate to acquire Warner's vote for England's ultimately doomed 2018 World Cup bid.

Lineker is not alone in his admiration for Beckham as a professional on and off the field. Trevor East thinks similarly:

> I don't know Beckham but on the few occasions I've met him he's been nothing but charming. I'm pretty good at

spotting fakes but I think he's genuine. I've seen him morose but we all get like that at times. Maybe at a party he is looking over your shoulder to see if there's anyone more interesting in the room but that's how he's been coached and trained since he was nineteen. He gets away with it well. He's got some good advisers round him.

Many of these advisers came into Beckham's life via the woman who became his wife. No such PR retinue had accompanied the childhood sweethearts whom Bobby Moore and Gary Lineker had married. Billy Wright may have married a well-known popular singer, but when he did so he was already the most famous footballer in the land, and, anyway, the concomitant media interest in his marriage was limited by the social niceties of the late 1950s. By 1999 there were no significant social niceties and when David Beckham married Victoria Adams the media interest was global. Unlike Billy and Joy, who were flattered but slightly disconcerted by the interest shown outside Poole Register Office, and Michelle Lineker who was positively upset by the arrival of unannounced members of the general public at her wedding, the Beckhams actively encouraged the attention and effectively invited the rest of the world to share in it. They staged their wedding, at Luttrellstown Castle in Ireland on 4 July 1999, as if it were a royal occasion and in a manner calculated to ensure maximum exposure for the Beckham brand. It appeared immaterial to them that the tackiness of the whole thing – with its golden thrones, diamond coronet for Victoria, an alleged cost of £500,000 and a reputed seven-figure exclusive deal with *OK!* magazine for the photographic rights – became a predictable and widespread object of scorn.

Beckham's fame and the attention it attracted was starting to unbalance the teams he played for. His manager at Manchester United clearly resented it. When, in February 2000, Beckham telephoned to inform the club he couldn't make it to training because his baby wasn't well and he had to stay home and look after him, the news was not received well by a manager with more old-fashioned values who clearly believed that if a child was poorly it was the duty of the mother to give up her work in order to look after it. Ferguson, however, not for the first time misjudged the mood of the country. It is arguable that he was expressing views that were thirty years out of date.

To the surprise no doubt of traditional footballers, Beckham by now was attracting a coterie of gay fans who liked the idea of a handsome footballer wearing a sarong and – according to unsubstantiated legend – his wife's underwear. There wouldn't be too many footballers who would welcome support from such a quarter but Beckham's metrosexual image was all-inclusive. His apparent softness, tolerance and vulnerability were entirely at odds with the traditional image of the macho, heterosexual footballer, but Beckham's celebrity value continued to increase nonetheless.

When Peter Taylor took over as caretaker manager of England in November 2000 for the game against Italy in Turin, his first announcement was to appoint David Beckham as captain. It was to be no repeat showing of *The Italian Job*, however, as Italy won 1–0. Beckham had made it to the top of his profession and, with his gentle charm and warm smile, was regarded as a worthy successor to Moore and Wright. He certainly wasn't naturally articulate like Lineker but, like the latter, he made sure he had the benefit of good media training and he could follow a script when one was presented to him. Inevitably, though, he was more comfortable letting his feet do the talking and they were never more eloquent than in England's vital World Cup qualifying game against Greece on 6 October 2001.

It was somehow appropriate that the game should have been played at Old Trafford in front of his adoring home supporters. As he was to do a few months later at the start of the Commonwealth Games in Manchester, Beckham walked out at the head of his national side, holding the hand of Kirsty Howard, a very sick little girl from the Francis House Children's Hospice. She had to have her oxygen bottle wheeled out alongside her, and Beckham made sure that all the England players walked at a pace that was comfortable for her. The game should have been a relatively straightforward one for England who needed either to win or at least get the same result as Germany to qualify for the finals and avoid a tricky-looking play-off match against Ukraine.

In the unexpectedly warm October sunshine, the crowd had been in carnival mood before the kick-off, but good humour gave way to anxiety as Greece scored first. Sheringham equalised in the second half, but Greece retook the lead a few minutes later. The news that Germany were drawing against Finland clearly affected the nervous crowd and the players became increasingly anxious. In the ninety-fourth minute England were awarded a free-kick just outside the Greek penalty area. Sheringham wanted to take it but Beckham over-ruled him. It was his team, it was his game, it was his time and it was his free-kick. He curled the ball superbly into the net to finish what had been for him the most outstanding game he was ever to play for his country. This was Beckham as Roy of the Rovers, seemingly one of the two prerequisites for a successful captain of England, the other being the less interesting and infinitely more predictable clenched-fist hero as exemplified by Butcher, Robson, Adams and Terry.

The soap opera that is Beckham's primary appeal to those of his followers who do not care greatly about his football had many more twists still to come. Having dragged England to the World Cup finals in Japan and South Korea apparently single-handed, he proceeded to break a metatarsal bone in his foot during a Champions League quarter-final two months before the tournament started. One tabloid newspaper printed a photograph of a foot on its front page and asked the nation to pray for its recovery. In a nation that palpably preferred to read that newspaper rather than the Book of Common Prayer it seemed an odd thing to do and the result, which owed little to prayer and more to medical science, was that Beckham went into the World Cup finals only half fit. It was to have unfortunate consequences as he pulled out of a tackle in the quarter-final against Brazil which led directly to Rivaldo's equaliser. A mistake by Seaman in goal, lobbed by a speculative Ronaldinho free-kick, finally crushed Beckham's dreams for 2002.

By the time the 2006 World Cup came around Beckham was no longer a Manchester United player. In his 2013 autobiography Ferguson revealed that he sold Beckham to Real Madrid in 2003 because the player thought he was bigger than both the club and the manager, although the manager's attitude to Mrs Beckham made it clear where he thought the blame really lay. It was the Beckhams' celebrity lifestyle that made him incompatible with the ethic Ferguson promoted at Old Trafford. Relations between the two men, which had been deteriorating since Beckham's marriage in 1999, reached their low point after a 2–0 home defeat to Arsenal in the FA Cup in February 2003. In the dressing room during the post-match recriminations, Ferguson lashed out at a boot which hit Beckham in the face and left a gash above the player's eye. Beckham never said anything but he ensured that the wound was exhibited for all the world to see.

There had been plenty of flashpoints prior to the incident following the Arsenal game. Beckham once arrived at training wearing a beanie hat with twenty photographers in tow. Ferguson had discovered Beckham was planning to unveil his latest haircut in front of the cameras and ordered him to remove the hat at a pre-match meal, but the player refused. Ferguson threatened to drop him, ruining the midfielder's plan to reveal his freshly shaven head moments before kick-off. Ferguson wrote that Beckham had gone 'berserk' at the instruction. There was only going to be one winner in the war between Ferguson and a player, no matter who his wife was. Shortly afterwards Beckham was on his way to the Bernabéu.

The transfer didn't hurt the brand that Beckham was seeking to manufacture. Real Madrid was a bigger club than Manchester United in terms of its global reach and he was still

the captain of England. Quite what kind of a captain he was
and the vital importance to him of the 'Beckham brand' was
seen in stark contrast in October 2003, just before a qualifying
match in Turkey for the European Championship finals to be
held the following summer in Portugal. Rio Ferdinand had
recently missed a drugs test at the Manchester United training
ground in favour of driving into Manchester to go shopping.
His stupidity earned him widespread condemnation and the
FA responded by dropping him for the match in Istanbul,
although the FA disciplinary hearing, which eventually ended
with Ferdinand receiving an eight-month ban, had not yet
taken place. On this point of 'principle' Gary Neville led an
insurrection, threatening that the England players would not
even get on the plane if Ferdinand were not reinstated. To the
men who had played for England under Sir Alf Ramsey the
idea of a strike must have seemed farcical. They could not even
persuade their manager to let them take their heavy winter
suits off in hot weather; they could not persuade him to choose
a film other than a western when they all trooped off to the
cinema together.

Interestingly, the battle turned into one between Mark
Palios for the FA and Gary Neville for the outraged proletar-
iat. The two men who should have been most visible in this
storm, Sven-Göran Eriksson and David Beckham, were notable
for their absence. It would be impossible to imagine earlier
England players adopting this attitude of defiance but if they
had, there is no doubt that Billy Wright and Bobby Moore
would have been leading the charge up the ladders and out of
the trenches. Gary Lineker is explicit in defining the England
captain's job as acting as a bridge between the players and the
management. Beckham, no doubt strongly advised by those
whom he paid to do it, decided that in such a toxic atmosphere
discretion was the better part of valour. Whatever the

temptation might have been to wave a flag in defence of a man subjected to a perceived injustice, it was Neville (unwittingly recalling the antics of Fred Kite, the ludicrous shop steward in *I'm All Right, Jack* memorably played by Peter Sellers) who therefore took the brunt of the negative comment in the press and on the airwaves. Eriksson, too, had no taste for confrontation and both men were no doubt much relieved when what had threatened to be the storming of the Bastille turned into a slightly awkward coach ride from Sopwell House hotel in St Albans to Heathrow Airport.

The match in Turkey ended in a hard-fought goalless draw which would have been easier for England had not Beckham blazed a penalty over the bar. Nevertheless, the vital point meant England would go to the European Championships with no little expectation of success and Beckham, at twenty-nine and fully fit, would be able to demonstrate to a wide audience his skills as a player and as the captain of a feared international side. In the event, the 2004 European Championship finals brought little joy for Beckham and his quest to promote himself as a footballer on the world stage, being chiefly notable for the emergence of the Everton teenager Wayne Rooney and the surprising triumph of Greece. Beckham had an almost entirely anonymous tournament until, in the crucial quarter-final against Portugal in Lisbon, which ended 2–2 after extra-time, he seemed to lose his footing on the sandy surface and sent the first penalty, yet again, high over the bar. England lost the shootout 6–5.

It was at the 2006 World Cup in Germany that Adam Crozier, briefly the FA chief executive, had predicted that the 'golden generation' of Beckham, Steven Gerrard, Frank Lampard, Ashley Cole, Gary Neville, Michael Owen and Paul Scholes would reach their peak. This time the tournament was to be played in Europe as opposed to somewhere very hot and indubitably foreign on the other side of the world. England went into it as one of the favourites. In 2003, Beckham must have witnessed the ecstatic reception given to the England rugby team that won its World Cup final against Australia with a dramatic drop-kick by Jonny Wilkinson in the dying seconds of the game. He might have been surprised by the similar response – including an open-top bus tour and a Downing Street reception – given to the England cricket team after it regained the Ashes in 2005. He would certainly have understood the deep ache in England football supporters to show just as much adoration for its World Cup-winning footballers. Bobby Moore's image was established for all time when he held aloft the Jules Rimet trophy. Beckham must have believed that he and Moore, so alike in so many ways, were destined to be the two England captains to stand proudly on top of the football world.

However, Deutschland 2006 turned out to be just the latest in a series of English disappointments, more famous for the shopping activities of the wives and girlfriends of the players than for footballing success. BBC Radio 4's *PM* programme covered the arrival of the WAGs at the team's hotel with a live broadcast that gave them the sort of prominence previously accorded to American presidents or popes on their first visit to the United Kingdom. It was a symbolic sanctification of the contemporary status of football but it gave a somewhat skewed perspective on the game's priorities or possibly just the dearth of intelligence within the BBC.

By 2006 Beckham had become a problem for the England team which his greatest supporter, the England manager Sven-Göran Eriksson, refused to acknowledge. Beckham's move to Real Madrid had been a great success from a commercial standpoint but his performances on his return to England had become increasingly ineffective. Brian Glanville thought that

Eriksson reorganised the pattern of England's play to accommodate Beckham to the detriment of the team when he employed him in what Glanville termed 'a quarterback role'. Eriksson himself attracted almost as much press attention, and of a similar nature, as his captain. On his appointment in 2001, the *Daily Mail* had welcomed him with the sorrowful recognition that 'We have sold our birthright down the fjord to a nation of seven million skiers and hammer throwers who spend half their lives in darkness!' The almost immediate satisfaction engendered by the 5–1 victory in Munich temporarily quietened this sort of xenophobic reaction but, bespectacled, with silver hair and a receding hairline, Eriksson looked less like the natural successor to Winston Churchill and more like the Derbyshire batsman David Steele emerging from the Lord's pavilion to face the terrifying prospect of fast bowlers Dennis Lillee and Jeff Thomson and memorably dubbed 'the bank clerk who went to war'.

The unprepossessing figure of Eriksson nevertheless managed to have his surprisingly colourful sex life displayed for public consumption as he passed from his glamorous

Italian lawyer girlfriend Nancy Dell'Olio to the TV presenter
Ulrika Jonsson and a secretary at the FA called Faria Alam,
who revealed rather winningly that the England manager
always carefully stacked and turned on the dishwasher before
commencing anything more romantic. If it wasn't Sven's sex
life that caused a stir it was his almost insatiable greed. He was
revealed to be talking to Chelsea about abandoning the very
well-paid England ship for the even better-paid shore of
Stamford Bridge, or possibly Old Trafford, and finally he was
set up by the undercover tabloid reporter Mazher Mahmood,
the so-called 'fake sheikh', in Dubai, and exposed in the *News
of the World*. The *Sun*'s farewell was 'Goodbye Tosser' as it
called him 'a passionless bungler'. Eriksson was clearly excellent at calming the hysteria of the Kevin Keegan regime but
never managed to inspire his troops. Gareth Southgate
remarked about Eriksson's performance at half-time in the
World Cup quarter-final defeat against Brazil in Japan in
2002: 'We were expecting Winston Churchill and instead we
got Iain Duncan-Smith.'

Whatever the doubts of some players, there was a strength
in the relationship of Eriksson and Beckham, not dissimilar to
that between Winterbottom and Wright and between Ramsey
and Moore. They each seemed to embrace the celebrity lifestyle as warmly as Ramsey would have contemptuously
dismissed it. Certainly, as long as Eriksson remained the
manager, Beckham's place in the England team appeared sacrosanct even if his Spanish club side did not share that opinion.
He had another poor World Cup in Germany, outpaced and
laborious throughout, and was eventually substituted by
Aaron Lennon in the quarter-final against Portugal, which
England contrived to lose yet again on penalties. Shortly afterwards, Beckham resigned the England captaincy in an
emotional press conference that appealed greatly to devotees

of daytime tabloid television. He would never now hold the World Cup aloft: he would never be another Bobby Moore.

Brian Glanville was never a fan of Beckham's captaincy, claiming that he barely realised that Beckham *was* the captain, so insignificant was the impact he made, despite the fact that he captained his country on 59 of his 115 appearances. His summary of Beckham's contribution to the game overall is withering in its contempt and uncannily reminiscent of the judgement pronounced by George Best:

> Beckham was a complete fraud. He had a great right foot, but as an outside-right he couldn't run, he couldn't beat a man, he couldn't get to the bye-line and pull the ball back. What he did was to lob in shells like Big Bertha. He was excellent on free-kicks, had a very dangerous shot with his right foot. To give him all those caps was insane – all those silly little five-minute appearances as a sub. He reminds me of what F. R. Leavis wrote of the Sitwells – that they belonged to the history of publicity rather than the history of poetry.

Gary Lineker, however, holds an entirely contrary opinion:

> He was a good captain of England, players liked him. He did the job as well as you could do it in that he was a good spokesman off the pitch and that's what a good captain has to be. In football that's really all you can be. Unless you played with him you don't know how he handled things in the dressing room as the representative to the management. Only people who played with him know that. I've not spoken to any players who speak negatively of him and that says a lot. Beckham is unbelievably loved. My son George adores everything that Beckham does. All of us will get people who don't like us – whether it's because he played

for Manchester United, whether for football reasons or out of pure envy of his success. They might say he's not the brightest, he's not a great speaker, he has this high-pitched voice, but I think you could tell from the way he played his football how bright he was. He makes the right decisions all the time on the pitch – when to cross it, when not to cross, when to cut inside, when to drop into a deeper position. People take these things for granted but you can't teach it. It's instinctive. It's spatial awareness, a kind of intelligence of awareness of everything that's going on around you. You cannot do that if you're thick.

David Bernstein became the chairman of the FA in January 2011, shortly after the embarrassing failure of the 2018 World Cup bid in which Beckham had been involved. The cult of Beckham remains a puzzle to him:

Beckham is a phenomenon I simply don't understand. He is a marketing man's dream of course – a decent footballer but certainly not a great one – a great crosser and a deadball specialist but not a great player. Of course he is managed by a marketing genius... Beckham represents the celebrity culture that I am not very keen on. It's just so superficial. It's a triumph of image over substance. I'm not a Beckham fan but you have to admire what he has achieved. Andy Murray won Wimbledon and that victory will always be associated with him. I'm not sure that Beckham has done something specific as a player that will always be associated with him in the same way.

Beckham divides the nation. Very roughly, people who are Beckham's age or younger tend to be much more admiring and understanding of him than those who are older, who are much less sympathetic to the lifestyle image he conveys. His tattoos, to those who abhor tattoos, are unsightly and revolting. To those to whom tattoos represent desirable body art they are something to be admired and copied. Age is not the only determining factor since there must be plenty of ageing Hell's Angels and sailors with anchors tattooed on their arms still around but for most people in late middle age and beyond tattoos had traditionally been the preserve of Hell's Angels and sailors and possibly criminals. That is clearly no longer the case, but Beckham's visible tattoos mean he has aligned himself firmly on one side of the fence. Those on the other side of the fence are unlikely ever to cross it.

Whatever else Wright, Moore and Lineker did in their lives *off* the field, their fame was almost entirely related to what they did *on* it, although none of them, while captain of

England, was presented with the commercial and promotional opportunities offered to Beckham. The images of Beckham off the field have such a ubiquitous presence that they tend to overwhelm what he achieved on it. Certainly, Wright, Moore and Lineker had their detractors, as anyone in public life has, but Beckham was always the butt of jokes in a way that none of the other three were.

Older people who are not particularly comfortable with contemporary music or contemporary television will also (although by no means in all cases) tend to be uncomfortable with Beckham because Beckham symbolises the age of boy bands and reality television. In a way Beckham, aided by Simon Fuller, turned himself into a one-boy boy band, and if Beckham would have been unlikely to have appeared on television in the age of Wright or the age of Moore because of his background and the way he spoke, it didn't matter at all in an age in which reality television shows grabbed the ratings and the air time. Television, always on the lookout for cheap, endlessly repeatable shows for which the public revealed an instant liking, fell upon *Big Brother*, *The X Factor*, *The Apprentice* and the rest of the new genre with cries of ecstasy. Beckham didn't need to appear on these shows. He was far too important for that, but his appeal reached out to viewers of these shows and beyond. He could appear in his underpants on television or on giant posters without a shred of embarrassment (or, some thought, a shred of modesty) and he would be widely admired. Most men in their underpants are looking for their trousers; Beckham was looking for public adoration.

Simon Oliveira, Beckham's publicist since 2004, is the managing director and co-founder of Doyen Global, the company which helps to expand his activities outside the United Kingdom. A bright, intelligent man, Oliveira emerged from a background not dissimilar from that of his client.

I come from a council estate in north London so all those jokes about Beckham being stupid I thought were motivated by snobbery. They listen to him and they look at him and they say anyone who looks like that and speaks like that, what can he possibly know? He's been involved with a football club since the age of fourteen and his focus was entirely on becoming a footballer, but though he was never immersed in schooling, it doesn't mean you're less intelligent but simply that you haven't gone through the educational process in the way others have. If you're three moves ahead of the opposition on the football field that means you are innately intelligent, sharp and astute. He wouldn't have been in the position he is now in, to have made the decisions he has from a management perspective, or to have achieved what he has on the football pitch, or to have made the money he has throughout his career, or to have chosen the people he has surrounded himself with, if he wasn't intelligent.

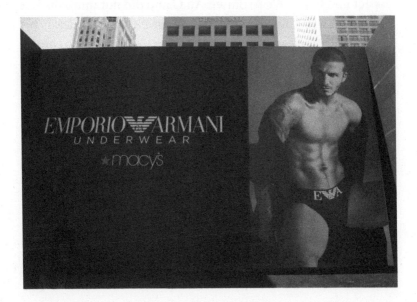

It is odd, then, that the jokes about Beckham, even when he was the captain of his national team, were always that he was as thick as two short planks. In 2001 he and Victoria gave hostages to fortune when they were interviewed for Comic Relief by Sacha Baron Cohen as Ali G. Victoria put up a decent battle as she fought him off for as long as she could, while her husband laughed nervously alongside. Ali G's opening comment to Beckham was a pointer to what was to come. 'Now, just because it's Comic Relief don't mean you can speak in a silly voice.' The Beckhams sportingly put up with a series of uncomfortable questions about their private life and the state of their marriage. Referring to the Beckhams' taste in decor and clothes, Ali G asked: 'So, they is some people who suddenly get loads of money who become very tasteless. How has you two managed to avoid that?' Beckham giggled. Victoria admitted that some people might think that what they bought and displayed was indeed tasteless.

The point about Beckham is that his audience did not expect him to be able to outwit Ali G and did not think the less of him for being unable to do so. What they admired was his smiling tolerance and his sportsmanship for agreeing to subject himself to exposure and ridicule. It is a smart person who knows his limitations and clearly Beckham is very self-aware. Whether or not it was a policy worked out by his 'advisers' or an instinctive feel for what the public demanded from him, he made no attempt to fight back when he was mercilessly ridiculed by Ali G, when abused by the press and the fans after Saint-Etienne, when Ferguson went on the attack, when he was dropped by Fabio Capello at Real Madrid or, just as hurtful and perhaps more surprising, when Steve McClaren, on taking over from Eriksson, told him his England career was over. In the latter two cases he made no complaint but simply worked harder. Eventually he was restored both to the Real

Madrid and the England starting line-ups. It betokened an admirable determination and it gave the soap-opera story of his life in football a happy ending. Beckham would go on to extend his England career into the Capello era, eventually breaking Bobby Moore's record for the most caps for England for an outfield player, although of course, as Glanville pointed out, Moore didn't win caps for short-lived appearances from the subs' bench as Beckham did.

Beckham has long since abandoned his position as a mere footballer, albeit a decent one and captain of his country. His rise to fame was propelled by football but his ability to remain there, indeed positively to increase that already highly visible profile, stems from the self-propelling nature of celebrity. His intrinsic worth should really amount to nothing more than the sum of his many achievements, but the fact remains that that worth is due to the value that his many adoring fans place on it. Lineker is associated with Walkers Crisps as Denis Compton was associated with Brylcreem, but Beckham endorses so many products it would be impossible to associate him instantly with any one of them. Despite this commercial promiscuity, sponsors come back for more because association with Beckham means global, not just national, sales.

The essence of advertising is to convince people to buy things they don't need but that they might desire. They don't need convincing to buy milk or bread but they do need to be persuaded to buy a particular brand – Police sunglasses or Armani underpants, to name two of Beckham's chosen targets. However, it could be argued that anything can be made into a brand. The England cricket team spent the summer of 2015 desperately trying to convince the public that they were playing a new brand of cricket. Whatever this amorphous use of the word 'brand' might mean, it certainly lacked conviction when they were beaten by over 400 runs at Lord's and by an innings at The Oval, but that didn't stop the indefatigable image makers and media managers. Almost anything can be made into a brand to be sold and consumed and it is frequently argued that Beckham himself is a brand, which his commercial advisers are only too anxious to encourage and manage. Oliveira reveals that:

> When he was still playing we would never have done an advert for alcohol and we made a decision not to go with fast food or gambling. Once he had finished playing, we looked at the Haig idea because we thought it was interesting. It had been famous but it was rather lying dormant when they came to us and we had the chance to help to revive it. It needed refreshing and transforming and it gave us the opportunity to work with a classic historic British brand. He really enjoyed the creative planning of the campaign, how to build this new strategy. The UNICEF relationship he's had now for over ten years dates back to his days at Manchester United. It's the first time in the history of the UN organisation that they've created a separate fund because he has seven different projects around the world like changing one country's water supply; in El Salvador we're trying to stop violence against children committed by armed gangs; we're trying to reduce infant mortality and stunting in Papua New Guinea. It's an incredibly ambitious series of projects into which he has thrown his whole being and heart. We want to work on a few things but do things that are truly original and transformational. He's always been keen to use his power as a force for good.

All four of the captains whose lives form the kernel of this book became famous because of their talent as players, but what separates them from the other captains of England is that their lives offer particular insights into the changing nature of the society in which they lived. In many ways, Beckham is the most extraordinary of these four men simply because his career coincided with a technological revolution that offered opportunities for a previously undreamt-of level of global commercial exploitation of his looks, celebrity and lifestyle. Billy Wright became a much-liked television executive; Bobby Moore's attempts to succeed in business failed disastrously, but he bore the sufferings imposed on him by the studied ignorance of the FA and the tragedy of his final illness with all the grace and dignity he had displayed on the field. Over ninety matches, Moore and Wright set the benchmark for what a captain of England should be. Lineker was a smart and clever footballer who captained England in only fifteen games and who rarely had the support of an increasingly paranoid manager. The mistrust that developed between them and the brevity of his time as England skipper militated against his becoming a captain on the level of his two predecessors, particularly since he was surrounded by players who would never have been considered good enough to have played for England in the era of Wright or Moore.

Beckham played more times for his country than any of the other three and stands fourth in the list of long-serving England captains but, despite having better facilities and better support at his disposal than Wright and Moore, and far better players than those whom Lineker led out, he could not be called a successful captain of England. Given the heightened expectation created by the false concept of the 'golden generation', the side he captained underperformed badly. The nation was disappointed but not always surprised at successive tournament disappearances at the quarter-final stage. The football world had changed and only perhaps the readers of the red-top tabloids who dressed up as Spitfire pilots or Crusader knights expected England to be at the top of it. Maybe that was why tabloid editors seemed surprisingly reluctant to let go of the jingoistic prejudices of the age of Billy Wright.

Before the semi-final of the European Championships of 1996 the *Daily Mirror* sent an armoured car to the hotel where the German footballers were staying and printed on its front page a photograph of Stuart Pearce and Paul Gascoigne in Second World War helmets underneath the headline ACHTUNG SURRENDER! If they can't let go of the Second World War, why should other countries not continue to assume that England is still obsessed with it and that the country's football administrators have not adjusted to the fact that, in the twenty-first century, football does not belong to England and the British Empire?

In fact, England's football administrators understand very well that the power in world football has devolved and that it won't be too long before a country from Africa or Asia wins the World Cup, but still it is forced to confront the consequences of national stereotyping. David Bernstein, a successful and principled chairman of the FA, notes:

The reaction of foreigners to England and its football team is schizophrenic. When they come to matches at Wembley they love it. They are in awe of Wembley; they are very respectful of England's football history and so on. The president of the foreign FA always speaks with great respect of England when he is at Wembley. All that history and so on, it's certainly genuine. However... when you meet them again at a FIFA Congress or whatever it's an entirely different story. When they're in that situation there are definitely many countries who regard us as arrogant; certainly the prejudice against England is deep-seated and it's still there. I am very conscious that the situation requires great diplomacy, you have to be very careful about what you say; you can't afford to seem pushy or sound in the slightest way arrogant. It's partly about how the FA was perceived to have behaved in the past but it's also about England's status as a former colonial power. The old African colonies are very sensitive and you have to be aware of that. Malaysia and Sri Lanka are now all part of the new world family of football and they used to be ruled from London but they aren't now and though the people you meet weren't necessarily alive then, we are all conscious of that unspoken history. If you speak out in the way I spoke out about Blatter's unopposed re-election [in 2011] there will be some fairly Anglophobic forces ranged against you. Some people were aghast that anyone could criticise Sepp Blatter. I felt that FIFA was like the old-time Soviet Praesidium. It was all orchestrated on a big scale and beautifully stage-managed. When I stood up and said something unexpected and not particularly welcome it was a big shock to many of those countries.

Victory over England still appears to give some countries more satisfaction than victory over other countries who do not share England's imperial history. It is clearly unfair to expect England players in the twenty-first century to be representatives of an imperial policy which started in the seventeenth century, particularly as some of them will undoubtedly have been born into families who emigrated from countries that had once been British colonies. This is just one of the factors that make the relationship between the country and its football team so much more complicated now than it was fifty or sixty years ago, as David Bernstein acknowledges:

Then the FA looked after the England football team and
the FA Cup. Now it's quite different because of the advent
and the strength of the Premier League and its all-powerful
domination of English football and, of course, the
Champions League. The FA Cup has lost a lot of its
attraction. It was inevitable; it would have been almost
impossible for it not to have done so with the growth of the
other competitions. On the other hand I think there is still
a huge desire to support England in the country. I think
people are desperate for the England football team to have
success, which is why there is so much despair around
when it all goes wrong.

In fact, football was now being regulated not by the FA but
by legal bodies such as the Monopolies and Mergers
Commission that blocked the BSkyB takeover of Manchester
United in 1999. The Office of Fair Trading ruled against price
fixing in replica shirts and it was the European Court that
decided that the Sky/BBC monopoly over football rights was
illegal.

The hold terrestrial television used to have on the British
population has been eradicated by the growth of satellite and
cable and the profusion of channels to appeal to every taste.
One of the consequences of the diminution of 'water cooler'
television is that England's matches in the big tournaments
have now become one of the few occasions on which the
nation gathers together to watch television at the same time,
which is why its response to victory or defeat appears to be
unjustifiably magnified in its importance. Football before
1992 appeared on television at strictly controlled and not very
frequent intervals. As a consequence a great deal of football
history vanished because it was only seen by crowds who went
to a particular match on a particular day. By contrast, today

some part of every Premier League game appears on television and most of the Football League matches can be found somewhere. Almost any game today can be summoned on to a screen at will. If it can't be then it's not history, a view that logically E. H. Carr, who professed no spoken allegiance to any football club, would nevertheless have to agree with.

Football is part of the national debate. To be ignorant of football is to be ignorant full stop. Everybody has to have an opinion about José Mourinho, everybody has to support a club because it is socially de rigueur to do so. Football-crazy children who could once recite the names of every league ground in England can now, thanks to the constant exposure of the game on Sky Sports, on ESPN, BT Sport or through football computer games, reel off the starting eleven of Valencia or Feyenoord. It is the same mania expressed in a different context. Perhaps more concerning is the fact that no politician can assume a place on the national stage without a ready-made opinion on football prepared by his spin doctor. John Major gave the appearance of a genuine passion for Chelsea, formed in the days of Roy Bentley and Jimmy Greaves. His successor as prime minister, Tony Blair, made an entirely specious claim to have supported Newcastle United and stood on the terraces at St James' Park to cheer his hero Jackie Milburn – who left the club before little Tony was four years old. Gordon Brown was excused because his support for Raith Rovers aroused bewilderment in England in people who couldn't find Raith on a map, but David Cameron attracted predictable scorn for temporarily forgetting he was a fervent Aston Villa supporter and announcing he supported West Ham United – until he was publicly reminded of his previous life-long commitment. He was no doubt confused by the similarity of their home strips. Burnley supporters beware.

Football, or at least the Premier League version of it, is now regarded by politicians as one of Britain's great industrial success stories, like Lancashire cotton and shipbuilding on the Clyde had been in the nineteenth century. As New Labour rode a wave of unsustainable growth in banking, as house prices escalated to a level far beyond the actual worth of the house, so football became 'a great product'. It wasn't a great game with its cheating, spitting, feigning injury, diving in the penalty area and a variety of other disreputable patterns of behaviour which would have surprised and disgusted Billy Wright, but it was, so it was claimed, a great 'product'. When David Cameron flew to China to persuade the world's perceived strongest growing economy that Britain was also booming, he took with him, among others, Richard Scudamore of the Premier League as evidence of his country's new-found ability to produce what the world wished to consume. It was perhaps an unfortunate choice of companion as a few months later the exposure of Scudamore's emails revealed to public view opinions of a decidedly old-fashioned sexist nature.

The negative impact of the Premier League on England's recent performances is too obvious to warrant any questioning of it except by the Premier League itself, which blusters constantly that it does not recognise any causal connection between the national side's decline and the fact that only 30 per cent of players who start their matches are even eligible to play for England. Most of the owners and most of the managers are no longer English so it is hardly surprising that Premier League clubs have little interest in the health of the England team. They loathe it when their players are called up to play for England because they might return injured and because their energies are expended in the national cause and not in the cause of making foreign-owned clubs, with eyes constantly on the global market, even richer. The success of Manchester

City, owned by the private equity company Abu Dhabi United Group for Development and Investment, certainly has an impact on the world standing of Abu Dhabi. The success of the England side has none. Before the recent purchases of Raheem Sterling and Fabian Delph, only one regular member of the Manchester City starting eleven, Joe Hart, was English. The same argument can be applied to most of the top sides in the Premier League with the possible current exception of Tottenham Hotspur.

There is no doubt that the England football captains have all wished to have been in charge of a successful team but it would be impossible to be unaware of the countervailing pressures on them of the need to perform and succeed at club level. Thirty-eight Premier League matches take up most of every season. England matches are essentially interruptions to the football calendar. Since the reality is that England are unlikely to win either the World Cup or the European Championships in the near future, it is quite understandable that the commitment to the national cause of John Terry, Steven Gerrard and currently Wayne Rooney has been less than total, no matter what words they may deliver for public consumption. Does that make them less patriotic? Has the transition from Wright to Beckham, through Moore and Lineker, been a straightforward diagonal line down the graph of patriotism?

Fortunately for Beckham and his retinue of advisers he had things to offer his country beyond success on the football field. That makes his story different and it is not yet finished. His publicist Simon Oliveira speculates on what he might achieve in the next ten years:

> He'd love to inspire the current generation of England players to be more patriotic – that's a huge passion of his. UNICEF and other charity work will still be a huge part

of his world. But then there's the magic stuff – the stuff you don't expect. Will he get the offer from the FA to manage England? Or Manchester United? Or will he have a successful movie career? He'll be fifty years old in 2025. I wouldn't be surprised to find he's navigating a successful test mission to Outer Space. Nothing should ever be ruled out. Nothing is impossible for David Beckham.

Bobby Moore might have climbed out of the team hotel window to run off to NASA. He would certainly have found it more fun than another screening of *El Dorado* in the company of Alf Ramsey. Billy Wright would have shaken his head at the prospect and smiled. He would have been much happier eating fish and chips and talking about football than flying into Outer Space. Gary Lineker would have anchored the studio broadcast of the space flight but he is far too sensible to want to be sitting in a small capsule being propelled into the stratosphere. On the other hand, if they do play football on the moon or on Mars or Jupiter or Saturn, David Beckham will own all the teams and all the broadcasting rights before the next space mission leaves Cape Canaveral. The England football captains have certainly travelled a long way since Billy Wright first read that stop press on the bus journey from the Wolverhampton Wanderers training ground to his digs in Tettenhall.

LIST OF ILLUSTRATIONS

p. 1 Billy Wright leads out England against Hungary at Wembley, 25 November 1953 (Popperfoto / Getty Images).

pp. 26–27 Billy Wright celebrates his 100th cap for England after victory against Scotland at Wembley, 11 April 1959 (Keystone / Getty Images).

p. 44 Billy Wright at home with his landlady, Mrs Colley, 1950 (Popperfoto / Getty Images).

p. 49 England football manager Walter Winterbottom, November 1954 (Popperfoto / Getty Images).

p. 50 Stanley Rous, Secretary of the Football Assocation, 1948 (Topham Picturepoint).

p. 77 Joe Gaetjens scores the only goal of the game during the USA's World Cup group match vs England, Belo Horizonte, Brazil, 29 June 1950. The unhappy goalkeeper is England's Bert Williams (Popperfoto / Getty Images).

p. 85 The Dome of Discovery and Skylon at the Festival of Britain, June 1951 (The National Archives / Getty Images).

p. 91 Billy Wright exchanges pennants with Hungary's Ferenc Puskás at the start of England's traumatic game against Hungary, 25 November 1953 (Popperfoto / Getty Images).

p. 98 Chris Chataway beats his Russian rival Vladimir Kuts to break the 5,000- metres world record at White City, London, 13 October 1954 (Keystone / Getty Images).

p. 116 Peter Dimmock, Head of BBC TV Outside Broadcasts, January 1960 (Topfoto).

p. 120 Billy Wright poses with his wife Joy Beverley and her sisters Teddie and Babs at his wedding, 27 July 1958 (PA Photos / Topfoto).

pp. 126–7 Bobby Moore holds the Jules Rimet Trophy aloft after England beat West Germany 4–2 in the World Cup final at Wembley, 30 July 1966. (Popperfoto / Getty Images).

p. 134 Jimmy Hill, President of the Professional Footballers' Association, talks to members of the press at St Pancras Town Hall, London, 10 January 1961.

p. 139 The eighteen-year-old Bobby Moore of West Ham United, September 1959 (William Vanderson / Getty Images).

p. 156 Jimmy Armfield leads out the England team as captain against the Rest of the World, 23 October 1963, with Bobby Moore behind him (A. Jones / Getty Images).

p. 181 Prime Minister Harold Wilson chats with Bobby Moore at the Annual Sports Writers Association Dinner, 9 December 1965 (Topfoto).

p. 191 Argentina's captain Antonio Rattín is sent off during an acrimonious World Cup quarter-final against England, 23 July 1966 (Bentley Archive / Popperfoto / Getty Images).

p. 205 Bobby Moore and his wife Tina, who is wearing an England football shirt, on a photo shoot in 1972 (Terry O'Neill / Getty Images).

p. 213 Bobby Moore with team manager Alf Ramsey at the 1970 World Cup finals in Mexico (Popperfoto / Getty Images).

p. 222 Bobby Moore swaps shirts with Pelé after Brazil beat England 1–0 in a group game at the World Cup in Mexico, 1970 (Mirrorpix).

p. 227 Bobby Moore leaves the field, followed by Alf Ramsey, after England lost 3–2 to West Germany in the World Cup quarter-final, Mexico, 14 June 1970 (Popperfoto / Getty Images).

p. 241 Michael Caine and Bobby Moore pose before the charity premiere of *Escape to Victory*, September 1981 (Ray Moreton / Getty Images).

pp. 244–5 Gary Lineker celebrates after scoring for England against West Germany during the World Cup semi-final in Turin, 4 July 1990 (Chris Smith / Popperfoto / Getty Images).

p. 256 Kevin Keegan is watched by manager Don Revie during an England training session, 7 February 1977 (Popperfoto / Getty Images).

INDEX